At the Drop of a Veil

At the Drop of a Veil

Marianne Alireza

Blind Owl Press
An imprint of
Mazda Publishers

Blind Owl Press
An Imprint of
Mazda Publishers, Inc.
P.O. Box 2603
Costa Mesa, California 92628 U.S.A.
www.mazdapub.com

Library of Congress Cataloging-in-Publication Data

Alireza, Marianne.
At the Drop of a Veil/ Marianne Alireza.
p.cm.
ISBN: 1-56859-102-0 (alk. paper)

1. Saudi Arabia—Social life and customs. 2. Alireza, Marianne—
Journeys—Saudi Arabia. I. Title.
DS215.A43 2002
953.805'3'092—dc21
2002033792

Those of us who lived in the Arabia of the 1940s and 1950s can hardly believe the Saudi Arabia of today. No one from that period could have dreamed that this land, which through the first half of the twentieth century was more or less closed to the rest of the world, and whose people had little reason to live any differently than they had in any century before, would change so drastically.

Over sandy wastes and coastal regions and inland plateaus modern cities have arisen. Where for millennia the vast land was stitched together by nothing but camel caravan tracks, there are now great highways linking all the major cities. People who not too long ago were hardly aware of the world beyond now fly their national airline to worldwide destinations and board in-kingdom airplanes operating like shuttle buses, which have opened up their own country to themselves. In my time we had little idea of what the rest of the kingdom was like because we couldn't get there. Our identity was regional, whereas the Saudis of today have a true sense of being a nation.

Change was jump-started by the revenues from oil discovered in commercial amounts under Arabia's sands in the late 1930s. At that time the economy was one of bare subsistence, based on the sale of dates and animal hides and the collection of head taxes from pilgrims going to Mecca and Medina — the Arabian cities which, with Jerusalem, are the three holiest places in Islam.

The oil monies started filling the royal coffers in the 1950s and grew thereafter to such staggering amounts that Saudi Arabia became unique among countries embarking on all-out development; it had no need to borrow funds, no need to tax its subjects. It did, however, need workers, sophisticated and otherwise; in the early years of change, illiteracy was still high, a large proportion of the population was nomadic, and there were not enough trained Saudis. Labor had to be imported. Foreigners poured into the kingdom in numbers that peaked at two million or so in the great development, modernization, and industrialization boom of the 1970s and 1980s.

Thus did a truly incredible transformation take place in just a few decades — a time frame surely unparalleled in history. Even more remarkably, Saudi Arabia weathered the upheaval while simultaneously educating its people. There are now one or two generations of a new breed of Saudis — men and women who are "Saudi-izing" their nation, capably assuming roles and tasks previously taken on by people from other countries. For some, of course, the degree of change has been small. Certain elements of village life, of Bedouin life, and that of other segments of society have been either untouched — or unmoved — by today's dynamics.

Sociocultural changes have happened too, but more gradually. In this ongoing process, new ways are accepted only as they fit within the framework of Islam. Saudi Arabia has no separation of state and religion, and the Koran contains not just God's word but moral and civil codes that are part and parcel of a Muslim's daily life. No "Friday-go-to-mosque" religion this! True, the last word on any alteration of the role and status of women still lies with the men of society and the men of the family. But anyone who judges from afar should understand the difference between what is clearly written as allowed or forbidden to women and what is but tradition or the imposed wishes of men, handed down through centuries of male domination and masquerading as religious dictate. One added note: Islam in the seventh century A.D. gave its women followers status and rights that were relatively fair and equitable (long before any other culture did). And today literate Muslim girls and women can read their Korans themselves.

When I was in Arabia we had none of the seesawing causes that people have today. Our direction was static, our customs set, and traditions followed without question. We had no inkling of the opened-up life or different roles for women that were in the offing. We did what had always been done, even our speech regulated by unvarying formulas of greeting and response and social behavior. These patterns were essentially niceties, to be observed and perpetuated, but my grandchildren today know nothing of them.

With outlets limited, we didn't go places and we didn't do much in any sense familiar to Americans. When people ask me about this, I say that in the first place there was nowhere to go and, in the second, we *did* do something very important: we lived together. This was what the Arabians knew so well how to do and what I had to learn.

In the monotony of that life I used to marvel at the serenity, equanimity, and rich gifts of personality of the women I knew, and I would ask myself, "If they can be like this without education, what could they be with it?" Well, now I know, and I still marvel. The upheavals in their lives have been great, but the women's special qualities are still there, sustained by faith, perhaps, or by centuries of acceptance and survival.

It pleases me enormously that although I was one of the youngest in the household so many years ago, I am now a respected elder of a noble Arabian family that has stood by me through the years and has continued to consider me one of them, never breaking the connection in spite of everything that has happened. I spend two to three months a year in the kingdom; my townhouse in Jeddah was a gift from my children, all of whom live and work in Saudi Arabia except my youngest son and his family, who live in California.

To date I have fifteen grandchildren and two great-grandchildren. When I think of the good blood I contributed to this tribe, my rather undisciplined sense of humor gets the better of me. My grandparents on one side were English-Irish-Scottish and on the other side Polish and full-blooded American Indian. If that isn't funny enough, I succeeded in registering my children — Hamida, Faisal, Tarik, Nadia, and Ghassan — on the tribal rolls of the Creek nation in Oklahoma. The wonderful thing is that they are all as proud of that as of anything else in their rich heritage. I am told they love to flash their Bureau of Indian Affairs cards and watch the reactions — they are probably the only Saudi American Indians in the world.

That I had the experience of living as I did when I did it — someone going to Saudi Arabia now would not find what I lived — and that I then was able to watch the kingdom build to its present important position in the world community are realities I cherish. People say it's remarkable that I made my peace with life in old Arabia, but I say no. What is truly remarkable is that those around me helped me make my peace. I was the only different one in that homogeneous society of yesteryear — a western Christian member of an extended family that was really extended. At first it was all so old, so new, so strange that if people had acted otherwise toward me, I might not have made it. It was in my worst moments that they helped me the most, and then we laughed together.

So this is a story of people who proved that even though we came from worlds apart, we could give respect, tolerance, understanding, sensitivity, and love to one another and make a human bond. If I had it all to do over again, would I? You bet! I wouldn't have missed it for anything!

Pasadena, California
March 1991

Glossary

alhamdulilah Thanks be to the Almighty

arusa bride

ashkourik I thank you (when addressing a woman)

Bedouin (pl. *Bedou*) An Arab of any of the nomadic tribes of the deserts of North Africa, Arabia, and Syria

buksha an embroidered square of material in which presents are wrapped and on which clothes are stored or carried

carawita an Arabian divan

dafur stove

Dhul-Hijja the month when Moslems perform the prescribed pilgrim rites

djinn devils or evil spirits

effrengi foreign, foreigners

Eid-al-Kabir the great feast which follows Ramadan

eustaz teacher

galabeeya the long dress of Sudanese men, especially the colorful rich brocades of Sudanese servants in Egypt *gaysa* special Bedouin theater, now a thing of the past

ghutra checkered headdress favored by the Bedouin

gishta the creamy, crusty product which forms on the top of boiled milk cooling in a kettle; *also* segmented fruit of big black seeds covered with sweet, white flesh

Hadj Pilgrimage to Mecca; eighth, ninth, and tenth days of Dhul-Hijja

harem (pronounced "hareem") the respectful name given to all the ladies in a household

igal the black wool or gold-wrapped top on the headdress

inshaalah If God wills it

jaria slave girl

kohl the black eyeliner used in eastern countries

konafa name of a Lebanese pastry

mother literally, *marat-ammi*, "wife of my uncle," when expressed by a daughter-in-law, reflecting the common practice of first-cousin marriages

muezzin the crier who calls the faithful to prayer five times a day, usually from a minaret

mutawuddi the state of purity reached by washing before prayer

mutfarrajeen the onlookers, heavily veiled and cloaked women, who are present at all weddings and big receptions; they are allowed to attend without invitation if they remain disguised

Qamar-ad-din the traditional apricot drink to break the fast during Ramadan; literally, "moon of the religion"

Ramadan the fasting month; in Moslem countries a cannon's boom announces the exact break of day when fasting must begin and the precise moment it ends when the sun sets

sahoor the before-dawn meal eaten before a day's fast

Shaikh a man versed in the Koran and its laws; *also* the polite form of addressing a man

shershif filmy cotton sheet specially made for use in prayer

shisha water pipe

shokran thanks

shoogdoor a conveyance carried on camels' backs—a gaily decorated enclosed frame with tasseled curtains all around and fancy carpets and pillows inside

sitt lady

sitti milady; also, grandmother

steta an older sister

suk marketplace

sumada the white headcloth favored by city Arabs

surwal men's pants

tisbahi-ala-khair may you awaken in goodness; good-night

tobe men's dress

toombac tobacco or smoking mixture smoked in a *shisha;* if it is good it contains dried apples or other fruit

zeffa name of the first part of a Moslem wedding; shrill trilling by women who escort the *arusa* to her bridal chair accompanied by drumming

Chapter 1

IN THE MOUNTAINOUS ARABIAN DESERT above Mecca, at a place called Hawīyah, the favorite wife of the king sat on a low couch and greeted the seven cloaked and veiled women who entered her tent. Um Talal was the favorite wife's name, and her visitors lifted the black coverings from their faces, kissed her hand, and went to sit on the carpet in front of her. The traditional exchange of welcome and greeting then began.

"God welcome you," said Um Talal, and the ladies responded,

"May God give you long life."

"God save Your Majesty, very well, thanks be to the Almighty."

"And your husband and the children, are they well?"

"Thanks be to God, they are well and kiss your hand." While the ladies talked a slave girl came in to serve tiny cupfuls of coffee from a special brass pot, and maidservants in colorful dress were summoned and dispatched with whispered orders. The contrast of Oriental splendor within the tent and the bleak windblown desert without was typically Arabian, and in this special tent of a special wife, sequins and jewels shone and everyday belongings were of fabled quality. The carpet on which the ladies sat was beautiful and symbolized the best of eastern luxury, but under its intricately woven design one could discern the contour of the desert sand on which it lay. In other tents dwelled the king and his court and other wives and other women, and the many children, but Um Talal held court like a true queen and merited the respect her visitors came to pay. On this particular day the usual pattern was followed until suddenly the queen scanned the faces of the women before her and asked the unlikely question: "Which of you is the American?" From the huddle of black-cloaked figures several voices answered at once, pointing out to her the figure on the end as the person she sought.

I was that American. The year was 1945, the month was September and Saudi Arabia's King Ibn Saud was camped with his courtiers and family as he was every year before the start of the pilgrimage season. If Um Talal's question seemed strange in that high desert outpost, it was not more strange than the feelings I was experiencing. I had been in Arabia but a short month with my husband, Ali, and I did not yet know the language, but this country was to be my home for the next twelve years and the group of Arab ladies who had answered for me were, respectively, my mother-in-law Lady Asma Alireza, my sister-in-law Zainab, and my brother-in-law's wife Hayat. With us were a Syrian lady named Sitt Gemila Pharaon whose husband was private physician to the king, her sister Inaam, and a young Lebanese named Almas who spent some of her time being midwife to the ladies of the royal family and the rest of her time as head nurse at the Government Hospital in Mecca.

Fresh from America, I was far from adjusted to the different world I found in Arabia, and my Arabic vocabulary had not grown much beyond the common expressions of *alhamdulilah*, *inshaalah*, and *shokran*.* But if the unfamiliar land and

* See the Glossary for these and other common Arabic expressions.

tongue, the bewildering customs, and living with kind but nonetheless unfamiliar people in unfamiliar lodgings left me groping in unreality, the visit to the king's camp in Hawīyah transported me to pure fantasy in a storybook setting. I would catch myself smiling in wonderment that it was really I sitting crosslegged on an Oriental carpet in the middle of the desert, veiled and cloaked like a figure from the Bible, and feeling so far away from home I knew it must be at least a couple of centuries away.

I laughed at the lone lightbulb dangling from the center post of our tent, for it was as out of place as I. It should have been instead a magic oil lamp whose genie could perhaps explain my presence there. I wasn't a tourist passing through or an alien with a limited visa — I was a member of a prominent Arabian family and, more surprising, bound to the customs and ways of Arabia as surely as if I had been born there. My body had gone through the motions expected of me the past few weeks, but my mind had trouble assimilating the change, and on the day of our visit I had been in Arabia far too short a time to be accustomed to the differences in daily living, let alone face with any degree of normalcy a visit to the queen. If I could sit there wondering why the scene wasn't complete with ostrich-feather fans wielded over us, or at least over the queen on her couch, I was really drifting because I knew better. My brain was numb with the effort of meeting situations entirely beyond my ken, and when I tried to move I realized I was numb from the waist down, too. Sitting crosslegged on a rug was a new posture for me and both legs had gone to sleep while my mind flitted in fancy. Neither could I stretch them, because one of the lessons I had learned was never to turn the soles of my feet toward an Arab lest he be insulted. I could only hope that my relatives, whom I always watched closely for signs of what to do next, would not suddenly stand up to leave and force me to totter after them.

My mother-in-law was now talking about me to Um Talal, whose questions centered around the fact that my trip to Arabia had been made in the company of five princes, the youngest of whom was Um Talal's son, His Royal Highness Prince Nawaf. He had evidently told her of my presence in their group and spoken of my small attentions to him during the trip. My friend Almas, who had learned English at the American University of Beirut, translated Um Talal's expression of gratitude to me for my kindness to her son, and I was pleased that the boy had mentioned me to his mother, and touched by her desire to thank me. I was floundering in an attempt to answer her when a slave girl came in with the message that the king was on his way to see Um Talal and so would we please move to an adjacent tent where refreshments had been prepared for us?

We were taken to a kind of corridor between tents where bowls of grapes and glasses of "sherbet," a heavily sugared drink made from crushed pomegranates, had been placed on a cloth in the sand. Plates of date pastries and almond cakes also dotted the "table" but they in turn were so heavily dotted with flies that my desire for any refreshment was gone. I stayed close to Zainab, and as we sat down I had a good look at the grapes in front of me. They were covered with dust and flies and I threw a desperate glance at Zainab with the message that I just couldn't touch them. She understood, and in her quiet, ever-thoughtful way, asked a servant for a glass of water in which she washed my grapes and saved me and my hostesses the embarrassment my refusal to partake would have caused.

After refreshments we were taken to another area in the camp where a large two-room tent was furnished with ornate gilt armchairs and many carpets. Ladies of the royal family joined us and for the first time I saw in its full glory the dress of the Nejdi royal women. Their billowy robes had gold embroidery and multicolored sequins which made every inch of the garments glitter under lacy black outer coverings. The sleeves were so tightly fitted from elbow to the wrist that I wondered how they got them on, until I was told that the sleeves are sewn onto the arm at each wearing and ripped each night when undressing. There must have been fifteen yards of material in each heavily embroidered dress, not counting the voluminous sheer lace which cloaked the whole. The women's faces were tightly framed in a wraparound band and the sequined border of the headdress held its place above the forehead by sheer weight. I was surprised and impressed by the physical height of these princesses. The women I had seen in the Hejaz area, where we lived, had generally been short and slight, but these Nejdi women were exceptionally tall and inclined to be heavy. We met daughters, wives, in-laws, cousins of the king, and one very old woman who sat quietly and alone in a corner, who reputedly was Prince Faisal Al-Saud's grandmother. They all moved with such grace that I, who was forever tripping over my one-layer cloak, wondered how they managed to move in such a stately manner wearing so many folds of material.

One of the most congenial of the young princesses was Prince Abdullah Al-Faisal's wife, who was of particular interest to me because I had met her husband in California and became well acquainted with him on our trip to Arabia together. She had a wonderful face, with clear skin and lovely eyes beautifully set off by the encircling band of her headdress. It was difficult to guess ages, but although she appeared to be very young, I knew she was already the mother of two sons.

The others talked and I watched and from time to time when one of the many scenes before me seemed to float off in a mist, I'd have to refocus my eyes to make contact with reality again. I could not shake my wonder that I was a part of it all. It was as if one self was watching a fancy stage performance through the small end of a pair of binoculars suddenly to find another self sitting among the players. I knew I didn't know the lines — I had never even heard of the play — but there I was, costumed and made up, taking part and moving along with the others, but dumb to the dialogue and unaware of my cues.

Conversation stopped when slaves brought in a meal of whole roast lamb, mounds of white rice, and various vegetable dishes in sauces. The huge trays were put on the floor and two black slave girls set about serving the meat. Practically straddling the steaming roasted animal, they thrust their hands in and tore and ripped off the flesh in great hunks, tossing the pieces unceremoniously onto the plates. My eyes popped at the spectacle and I reacted without thinking by turning in shocked disbelief to Zainab and putting out my hand to imitate the meat-yanking process I had just seen. Zainab's eyes narrowed and flashed warning, her hand shot out and pinioned mine to the rug, and only then did I come to my senses and realize I was ridiculing my royal hostesses, mocking their manners. To this day, my only excuse is that seeing wasn't believing, and while I prayed none of the princesses had noticed my breach of conduct, I found out later that Zainab had not been altogether successful in preventing my gesture from being seen.

The meal continued and I drew back to my silent role of watching and waiting. When everyone had had her fill, a large brass bowl of water was brought in. It looked like something gleaned from the Crusades and I wondered if it had a symbolic meaning. Well, it wasn't symbolic or anything of the sort. It was for the very practical purpose of giving drink to the ladies now finishing their rice and meat, and I watched with growing misgiving as it passed from hand to hand and mouth to mouth. A good deal of lamb fat had accumulated on it by the time it got around to me, but I had already done my silent check with Zainab, who had answered my beseeching look with a slight nod, and I knew I must take my sips with the best of them. It was torture waiting for the bowl to reach me, but when it did I drank. That is, I drank in a fashion, cheating more than a little by putting the rim of the bowl almost down to my chin instead of my lips and then tipping a bit of water over my mouth without really drinking. No one but Zainab, I think, knew the difference.

When I could bring myself down to earth that day I delighted in speculating what the folk at home would say "if they could only see me now." Somehow, far away as they were, I clung to them mentally for lack of anything familiar in my immediate surroundings. I couldn't understand the language where I was, and I couldn't draw upon previous experience for support because there was none. All was new — all! I tagged behind the smocked capes of my in-laws in situation after situation and copied them as nearly as I was able. They were marvelous in their help, but in our last hour at Hawīyah even they were to experience something new.

His Majesty the King had heard our family was in his camp and commanded our presence in private audience. For women, this was a favor seldom accorded and it caused great excitement, but in the midst of the ensuing commotion an astonishing thing happened. Zainab, my solid guide and mentor in Arabian customs and social obligations, dumbfounded us all by flatly stating that she would not go to the audience. She thus became the problem, not I. We argued with her to make her see that a royal request is a royal command, and we even pleaded with her. We went so far as to try to push her into the king's tent when the time came, but she stubbornly wrapped her hands around a tent post and refused to budge. The cause of her action is not clear. Perhaps it lay in vivid memories of her father's surrendering to Ibn Saud the city of Jeddah of which he was governor, or of events leading up to it, or perhaps she was just shy. Whatever it was that made her so dead-set against meeting the king, the rest of us went without her.

They had told me I must bow and kiss the king's hand, and I had worried myself into a great state by the time we filed in. I had a hard enough time keeping my veil in place while standing erect and was sure I would not only stumble over my cloak but lose the cursed veil as well in the performance of my duty. My mind drew scary mental pictures of my veil plopping down over the royal hand I bent to kiss, and then what? Was I to be tumbled off and have my passage revoked on this magic carpet I had been on all day?

Our nervous waiting came to an end when the word was passed from aide to servant to mistress to guest that His Majesty was waiting, and we were led to the proper tent. We removed and left our shoes at the tent's door flap and entered in single file. His Majesty was seated in a large throne chair on the left as we went in, but it was difficult to see — partly because we had entered from bright sunshine to the relative darkness of the tent's interior. As I groped behind I kept telling myself, watch the others, watch the others, for this usually was my only hope, I thought, of getting through things successfully. We filed in in order of seniority, so my mother-in-law was first and I was last because I was youngest, or at least newest. I strained to see and moved up as the others one by one did their obeisance and went to form a seated line on the rug before the throne. Then it was my turn, and it was almost a letdown to know when I collapsed trembling in my place at the end of the line that I had not faltered once but had paid my homage as nicely as you please.

Even under my veil's two thicknesses of black georgette I got a good look at the king and was properly impressed. His six-foot-four-inch frame seemed even larger than that in his robes, and I thought he had the biggest hands I had ever seen. His face was still strong despite his years and despite the old battle wounds which scarred his face and one eye. Over his head was the red-and-white checkered cloth topped by the square gold headdress of royalty, and the robes drawn around him were heavily bordered in gold. He gestured continually with his right hand as he spoke, first to this one and then to that one. In his talk with Lady Asma he praised her sons, Ali and Mohamed, and told her how well thought of and what a fine and worthy man her husband, Shaikh Abdullah, had been. He also told her of the respect his family had for her and added that they all liked to think of her as *Ummuna*, which means "our mother" — a name which made her none too happy since the king was a good many years her senior. She spent the next few days loudly disclaiming her eligibility for the title thus bestowed on her.

I was not following the conversation, of course, but heard about it later. At the time my overwhelming concern was what I would do when my turn came and His Majesty gestured at me with that big hand of his. As he went down the line I tried dry-mouthed to remember my two best words of Arabic, *alhamdulilah,* and *inshaalah,* which were, after all, two of the most important words in daily use. It was a toss-up, since I would not really know what was being said to me, and it was certain in either case that their use would be limited in any sustained conversation. At one point I forgot these troubles momentarily when it struck me as funny that the King of Arabia could sit there with a straight face and talk to those faceless mounds of black cloth before him. It was even funnier that I was one of them, but my giggle was suppressed when I remembered he was used to it and that it would be some time before I was. So I concentrated on how the veils sort of puffed out in little pulses when the lips behind engaged in conversation, and then my hands began to sweat as closer, closer, my turn came and I heard that word *Americania* again. That meant me, and I heard the great voice boom something at me. "Er — ahh — alhamdulilah," I said, and the kind face beamed and nodded, my mother-in-law said a few words on my behalf,

and suddenly it was over. We rose to go and I prayed my tin-
gling asleep-again legs would hold me until I got out. His Majesty extended his hand to be kissed again as we exited one
by one in the same order in which we had entered. Since I was
the last person in line I was left alone with him the final few
instants, and to my horror I heard him addressing me again.
He had not said anything other than "Good-bye, God go with
you" to the others and I had no idea what he said to me or
why. Utterly confused, and alone because by then the others
were already outside, I stammered and wondered what I could
say when my tongue finally grabbed and uttered one of the
words racing around in my mind, so that I did answer His Majesty and tripped out into the sunshine.

Please, dear God, I wished for no more surprises. I wanted
by now only to leave. Mercifully, I found the others thanking
everyone for the nice day, our driver was called, and we left
for home. Home, I thought, but this time my mind refused to
rise to challenge the tide of crushing unfamiliarity which had
characterized that day and which even the word *home* conveyed.
Yes, even home was strange, but still it was an anchor that I
wished desperately to reach.

Alas, though, all was not yet over for me that day. When my
husband came home that night he was in a roaring good humor, and could hardly stand he was laughing so hard. He
barely managed between guffaws to ask the question, "What did
you say to the king this afternoon?"

"What did I say? How do I know what I said? Why?"

"Ho-ho!" he said. "It's all over town what Alireza's American wife told the king. And His Majesty thought it so funny
he told the story himself during his evening audience."

"Well, out with it! What *did* I say?" I shrieked. "Stop
laughing, and *tell* me!"

"Okay! You've heard of the king's sense of humor — he
knows full well you are Christian, and he knows equally well
that you do not understand Arabic, but he could not resist

telling you in parting, 'We hope you become a Moslem.' You delighted him by coming back with the one and only really perfect answer. You told him, 'If God wills it.' "

I never did become a Moslem, but there was another aftermath of our visit. When we arrived home that night an invitation to tea the following day was received from Princess Abdullah Al-Faisal. We went at the designated time, servants took our cloaks and veils, and we were ushered into a room where Her Highness greeted us warmly and bade us be seated. I looked around the room in which she had chosen to entertain us and found it beautifully appointed in the best of western taste with the very finest French furnishings. We took our tea from a gleaming silver tea service on spotless white linen, and the china cups and plates would have done the Queen of England proud. Delicious tea cakes and Oriental specialties were placed on our plates by impeccable servants who wielded the serving tongs as if they were born to them. No lesson was more beautifully taught and in learning it my respect and liking for the princess was firmly and permanently established. It was quite clear that she had seen my derogatory gesture the day before and this was her way of showing me that while they were offering no excuses for their way they were also quite capable of outdoing us in ours.

The challenge she put to me was beautiful by its silence and as noble in purpose as the tall gracious princess was noble in bearing. I do not deny that it took me a long while to meet the challenge, but whenever I caught myself judging from a western perch, I tried to remember that it was no contest. Their way was good for them and I must balance what I was accustomed to with what I must learn, and realize that both sides had much to give. My friend the princess understood this and had thought enough of both herself and the newcomer American to make the point that each can travel the other's road.

Chapter 2

Ours was a college romance. People always asked where we met, and Ali loved to say he found me among the fossils. He was right, too — he picked me up when I slipped on wet rocks during a fossil-gathering paleontology field trip. In his smooth British accent he said, "May I help you?" He could, and did, and soon I had a date with the tall, dark, and handsome Arab.

At the university Ali was studying petroleum engineering because oil resources were just beginning to be developed in Arabia and business administration because his family were prominent merchants, bankers, and commission agents. My courses were in Spanish and French, and my thought was to combine my stenographic, secretarial, and language talents and go into business in South America. My plan faded after a year and a half when Ali and I began to talk of marriage and discuss my going to Arabia with him. The problem was that no Saudi subject had ever married a western girl before, and we had wild thoughts wondering if he might be exiled if he married me. That was not so, of course, but some "breaking of ground" was necessary to get the approval of his king and the blessings of his family. That task fell to Ali's brother, Mohamed, eight years his senior. It was he who, years before, had sat patiently hearing the family object to sending Ali abroad to study and then send him anyway. It was feared the boy would lose his religion, forget Arabic, and alienate himself from his country and its customs by favoring western ways. Bringing home an American wife now would appear to give credence to some of their fears, but Mohamed did what had to be done and secured the necessary blessings. As for my family, they knew and liked Ali but questioned the advisability of marriage because our backgrounds were so different. Among other things, they were worried about Moslems being allowed four wives, and Ali carefully explained that the *harem* (pronounced "hareem") was not what they thought but the respectful word for all the ladies in a family: mothers, daughters, aunts, grandmothers, etc. One wife was quite enough for him, he said, in assuring them of his love and respect for me.

Before we became formally engaged, Ali very thoroughly went over again all that I would be required to do as the wife of an Arab and all that I would find different in the life and the living in Arabia. Instead of sweet nothings our engagement night, I heard another rundown of what was in store for me. We had discussed this many times before, of course, but Ali wanted to be absolutely sure that I knew all there was to know — an action I considered most honorable.

Thus I knew that I must wear the veil and that I would have no social life as I knew it in America — no mixed parties, no movies, no chance to dine out in restaurants, no walking through the streets (under any circumstance), no way I could go to a store or do any of my own shopping. Life for me in Arabia would be almost wholly within the home, and even then not in my own home. I would live with the rest of the family with my widowed mother-in-law as head of the house, my brother-in-law Mohamed and his wife Hayat and their five children. Zainab would be there, too; she was the oldest sister (just fifteen years younger than their mother) who had returned with her son to the big house in Jeddah when she separated from her husband. During the day or in the evening I could go visiting, but visiting and partying would be among family only or with other women.

The social life — or lack of it — was not all that would constitute a drastic change for me. The weather would be uncomfortably hot and humid, our water supply would be scarce, the city was not electrified, there were flies and disease, mosquitoes and malaria, and inadequate sanitary measures. Doctors were few, medical facilities were practically nil, recreation parks and playgrounds were nonexistent, and even if they did have them I wouldn't be able to enjoy them. Swimming in the sea, even, was one of the many privileges reserved in those days strictly for men.

The picture Ali painted was black indeed but I said yes anyway and wedding plans proceeded. The only one who apparently suffered qualms after that was Mohamed. Having made it possible for us to marry, he then started to worry about my maiden name, Likowski, maybe being Jewish (which it wasn't), and about the type of person I was. His fears on the former were dispelled, but to make sure about the latter he sent an American diplomat friend, Mr. E. Burke Smith, to look me up and over when he got to the United States and report back his findings. Subsequently Ali and I had dinner with him, and sometime during the main course Mr. Smith was apparently satisfied enough to confide in us the real purpose of his visit, something he presumably would not have done had he made a decision not in my favor. I think what decided him was my lack of eye make-up or false eyelashes, criteria of his own, no doubt, because I'm sure that wasn't exactly what Mohamed had in mind.

I graduated in June 1943 and our wedding was set for October. The original date was extended three times because Ali couldn't get away to attend. He was accompanying H.R.H. Prince Faisal Al-Saud, then Viceroy and Foreign Minister of Saudi Arabia, on an official visit to the United States, and the prince, for one reason or another, kept delaying his departure. Ali had his own reasons for not telling him then of our marriage, so when Prince Faisal kept postponing his return to Arabia we had to keep postponing our wedding.

The ceremony at my home in Long Beach was attended only by a few friends and close relatives. The majority were from the university Arab groups on the campuses of Berkeley and Los Angeles. Ali's best man, Mohamed Mohamed Moughazi, was a longtime friend and schoolmate, who was almost obliged to perform his part of the ceremony in stockinged feet, having left his dress shoes at his Egyptian friends' house in Los Angeles. A telephone call had assured him he would have them in time, but as the house gradually filled with guests and the musicians were preparing to strike up the wedding march, the best man was still padding around in his black silk stockings.

Urgently seeking the bearer of the shoes, my mother stood at the door greeting each newcomer with a smile, welcoming people whose faces were unfamiliar and whose names she couldn't pronounce, and anxiously tacking onto each greeting, sotto voce, the question, "Do you have the shoes?" Until then she had been controlling well the emotions any mother feels on the marriage of a daughter, but she admits that the Arab faces and Arabic speech which filled her living room did cause a slight weakening in her aplomb, which came dangerously close to cracking when one new arrival, a dark-eyed, roly-poly, bespectacled Egyptian named Hosni bowed formally over her right hand and slipped a pair of size eleven patent-leather pumps into her left. None too soon, either. We were taking our places and there wasn't a man in the house who could have lent Moughazi a pair.

After a short honeymoon in Russian River country in northern California, we lived happily but certainly not lavishly in a small one room and kitchen apartment near the Berkeley campus. We had to count our pennies because wartime made the transfer of foreign funds difficult, and although Ali's sponsors did arrange for an increase of $30 a month when he was married his check still amounted to only $120. Moughazi lived down the hall from us, came always for Sunday waffles, and made a nuisance of himself at social gatherings by passing around a kewpie-doll bank my mother, as a joke, had outfitted in black crepe paper cap and gown when I graduated. "For Junior's education," he'd say, and stand waiting until people deposited their small change for the nonexistent Junior. As the pennies piled up Mo teased that he was conscientiously doing his part but didn't see any signs that we were doing ours. No one could have been happier than he when told a client for his "education fund" would arrive in March 1945.

Our daughter, Hamida, whose name means "praiseworthy" in Arabic, was born on March 7, 1945. Blond and blue-eyed, she was a joy to all. The Arabian family expressed their hearty congratulations by cable, with an added note that rains had fallen the day she was born, a sign that the child would have and would bring good luck. We didn't see how it could be otherwise. Everyone was surprised at Ali's delight that his firstborn was a girl — they believed Arabs rather held the thought that boys were the thing to have — but Ali had insisted all along that not only would the baby be a girl but that she would be blue-eyed. He was right, and said, "I told you so," but my mother countered that all babies' eyes are blue at birth and that Hamida's would undoubtedly turn brown. They laid a ten-dollar bet on it and for a whole year they feuded. Mother's letters urged Ali to be sure to let her know when the eyes turned brown and Ali in turn urged her to admit defeat and pay her debt. Once Hamida and I were home visiting while Ali was on a business trip and on long-distance telephone

one night Mother turned Ali's gloating to an agonized yelp by telling him that during Hamida's bath that morning she had noticed that one eye was blue and the other brown. But Mother had lost and she finally paid. Under Ali's dinner plate one night she slipped a ten-dollar bill on which she had written the words: "The Eyes Have It." It stayed for years in a small corner of his wallet and as far as I know it is there yet.

Ali worked hard at his studies but he was not destined to graduate. History rang our doorbell one morning with the arrival of a cable from His Majesty King Ibn Saud of Saudi Arabia appointing Ali a delegate to the San Francisco Peace Conference convening on April 25, 1945. The cable was addressed simply "Ali Alireza, U.S.A.," but it reached us by goodness knows what means and effectively upset our lives for the next few days. The initial thrill we both felt at Ali's being singled out by his king grew into a more sober excitement as we realized the full import of what lay ahead. The collective principles, hopes, and endeavors of a world seeking peace were to be funneled into this organizational attempt to formulate a working plan, and if the people of the world were participants by representation in this great effort, then direct participation was a tremendous honor and an awesome responsibility.

From the news angle, Ali's appointment had all the makings of a great feature story — 23-YEAR-OLD ARABIAN STUDENT APPOINTED BY HIS KING or YOUNGEST DELEGATE TO PEACE CONFERENCE — and the lone reporter who got the scoop had just these things in mind when he rang for the interview. I shall never forget his face when he realized that he had two stories all wrapped up in one. This Arabian was not only the youngest delegate to the conference, he also had an American wife, was the father of a three-week-old daughter, and what a story! The amazed reporter almost fell over me getting to the phone to call his editor: "I've hit the jackpot — get a photographer over here quick!" So the photographer came, and the story was published, and we spent the next few days under a deluge of more reporters and photographers too late to beat the scoop but intent on getting stories and pictures of their own.

Those news photos were the last pictures of a clean-shaven Ali, and I was never again to see him without the beard which all Saudi men must wear and which he was obliged to grow if he were to represent his country. The plan was for him to meet the Arabian delegation, headed by H.R.H. Prince Faisal Al-Saud, when they arrived in New York and then accompany them on their flight to San Francisco. He had first to arrange a leave of absence from the university, and as he explained to the dean why he would be cutting classes for a while he was very conscious of his grubby appearance and felt an explanation was needed. The apology he gave is surely unique in university annals. He rubbed his fingers over the stubble on his chin and said to Dean Deutsch: "Please forgive my unshaven appearance, but my government has ordered me to grow a beard." Grow it he did, and like it or not it was there to stay.

Much color and pageantry accompanied the opening of the Peace Conference. Hopes were high for the success of the meeting and San Franciscans were aware of their honor as hosts and held enthusiastic welcomes for each successive delegation. Without a doubt the most sensational group was the one from Saudi Arabia. Coming to take their part in the making of modern history they looked more like figures from the past in their gold and black headdresses, their long white robes and camel's wool cloaks bordered and tasseled with gold. The bearded men, whether royal princes or Nubian bodyguards, aroused tremendous interest. Photographs of them filled the newspapers and people flocked to their hotel in the hope of getting a glimpse of them.

There were those who assumed that these Arabs did not know English and once, the story goes, as Prince Faisal and entourage filed out of a hotel elevator a lady was heard to gush: "Oh, they are so fierce, so romantic!" with scarcely a flutter of his headdress, and keeping his eyes straight ahead, Ali answered her out of the corner of his mouth: "Tch, tch, madame, you should see us on horseback!" The jauntiness got taken out of him a few days later, however, when he was halfway down the hotel stairs before realizing he was wearing his short shorts instead of the long cottons under his semi-sheer Arabian dress and it was too late to go back. The rest of the delegation were ahead of him and he had to follow.

I kept in the background like a good Arab wife and never joined him or his compatriots in any official function. I observed and joined in the general excitement over the fascinating Arabs without most people suspecting I was in any way close to them. A saleslady and a fitter in a San Francisco department store were all agog about the exciting activities in their city as they were helping me into a new suit one day and picked me of all people to tell: "You really should go to the St. Francis. They've got *Arabs* and *everything*." Arabs and everything indeed! I was married to one of them and it would have been fun to watch their mouths drop if I told them. But I kept silent — they probably wouldn't have believed me.

My greatest excitement came when Ali said Prince Faisal had expressed the desire to meet me and was overriding the Arab custom which normally would have prevented our meeting by agreeing to come to lunch, whereupon I became so nervous at the thought that I panicked. He was the talk of the town and the oohs and aahs he caused were proof that any hostess in San Francisco would have given her eyeteeth to entertain him. But I was scared to death! What to say, how to act, what to serve? Of these, the menu was the least of my worries. I had learned to cook rice and lamb and could prepare vegetables Arabian style with meat and onions and tomatoes, and I knew which spices to use, but every time I remembered that an

Arabian prince was coming to lunch I shook my head in wonder and marveled at the turn of events that was bringing him to my door.

"My door" because Ali, a personable young man in anyone's language, was after all an Arab, a fact I tended to forget in the comfort of our American home and in the routine of university life. Ali was a young man I had fallen in love with who just happened to be from Saudi Arabia, and my mind's eye had not yet formed many scenes depicting me in any fabulous Arabian setting. I knew what I knew of Arabia but only occasionally did the interest of friends and the wide-eyed amazement of new acquaintances impress on me the unique aspects of our marriage and the adventurous, romantic ideas the magic name of Arabia seemed to conjure up. I blithely said to all who asked, "Oh yes, certainly I'll be going to live in Arabia one day." But Arabia was a someday place and far far away. Faisal's visit brought Arabia really close to me for the first time, and the magic carpet I was supposed to be on finally got off the ground when this Arabian prince came to call.

Faisal's fine face and gentle manner impressed me greatly. His English was far better than I had imagined and a good-humored atmosphere of informality was soon established. He was almost boyishly proud of having succeeded in slipping away from Mr. Tubbs of the U.S. State Department Security Force and settled back on our couch to relax. With him was Shaikh Ibrahim Sulaiman, Raiis Ad-Diwan,* whose warm brown eyes were young looking and in striking contrast to his prematurely white hair and beard. He had less command of English than Prince Faisal, but showed a willingness to learn by whipping out a little notebook at each turn in the conversation to jot down the words he did not know. Both men looked just as distinguished in western business suits as they did in their robes, and Prince Faisal told me how good it was to have this free time at ease in a private home. He held Hamida on his

* Chamberlain.

lap for half an hour and astonished me by discussing at great length such things as infant feeding schedules, sleeping habits, the age at which solid food is given, and when a child usually gets its first teeth. He was so charming and congenial that I wondered how I ever could have been afraid of meeting him.

I had to excuse myself at intervals to check on things in the kitchen, and my frequent disappearances before and during lunch puzzled the prince so much that he felt compelled a few days later to ask Ali the reason. He was flabbergasted to learn it was because I had been doing everything myself. It had never occurred to him that our house was not staffed with servants, and he had wondered at the time why I kept them all hidden in the kitchen.

For three hours we sat together, and the visit was a memorable one. I told myself, I did it, I did it! and in fact felt so superior to that other self who had quivered in dread of the encounter that I vowed never to divulge that I had fallen downstairs in nervous haste when the prince's car pulled up. That was not what Ali had meant when he had said, "Just be yourself"; but the wonder of it was that everything did turn out all right and I discovered that royal highnesses and noblemen could be themselves, too.

Ali liked to bring his other Saudi friends in the delegation to the house, but their hours of leisure meant frantic moments for me. Just the amount of time it took to cross the Bay Bridge was all they ever gave me to "whip something up for lunch." In Arabia I would not have been allowed to meet these men, but we were not in Arabia and since Prince Faisal's visit had opened the door, as it were, they too became my friends. I would discover on occasion that I was the only "foreigner" in the room and that there was nothing in the babble of conversation that filled my house that was intelligible to me. But I was grateful that they accepted me so wholeheartedly, and if communication was a problem it put no dent in their good humor or their friendliness.

Thanks to Shaikh Ibrahim, who talked about it all the time, I acquired a reputation for the excellence of my rice; so even if the main course was toasted cheese sandwiches, a side platter of rice was a must. Self-service was a novelty to my Arab friends, but they were good sports and pitched right in, their sportsmanship extending to kitchen duty if time permitted. When time did not permit, they would eat and run, expressing sincere thanks for the respite from official engagements and committee meetings.

With the Saudis we had music sessions in our home, picnics in the park, drives in the country, and evenings out at San Francisco's numerous and excellent restaurants. One Sunday as we were saying good night, Prince Faisal made a point of telling me that the day we had just spent together was the most enjoyable of his trip to the United States. For this and other reasons it is not a day I am likely to forget.

It had all started when Ali burst in the previous afternoon with the word that the group had planned a picnic and that all preparation — naturally — was up to us. There was much to be purchased and I let him do the shopping, forgetting that his marketing sprees almost always left us with an unrealistic supply of such things as pickled herring, Camembert cheese, rollmops, caviar, fancy stuffed tidbits, chutney, and other exotic concoctions. And sure enough — he came home with all the above items, plus the more usual picnic fare of hot dogs (all beef of course because Moslems do not eat pork), potato chips, buns, baked beans, and dill pickles. The following morning I made potato salad and hamburger patties, packed the baskets, and all was ready by eleven o'clock when the jolly picnic crowd arrived.

We loaded the goodies, took our places in the chauffeured limousines, and off we went to Tilden Park, with a prince on each side, a bearded diplomat or two on the jump seats, and a sprinkling of State Department folk and their friends. Piling out of the limousines under the stares of fellow picnickers, we unpacked the cars, chose our tables and deposited the food, and went for a spin around the lake in the boats piloted, respectively, by Prince Faisal, his brother Prince Mohamed, and His Excellency Shaikh Ibrahim. Around and around we went as the princes flashed and splashed their oars, leaving us passengers thoroughly doused when rental time was up. They told us later it was the first time they had rowed a boat, and we believed them.

Lunch was another experience. It was a happy milling of guests new to the task of grilling their own meat and filling their own plates. We knew beforehand that we'd likely have to explain at one time or another about "hot dogs" with assurances that a product's name is not necessarily — and in this case, definitely *not* — an indication of its contents, but we did think it strange that the really exceptional food that Ali had bought went unquestioned among this commoner picnic fare. Their enjoyment resulted in some weird combinations. I watched in amazement as Prince Faisal "built" his favorite sandwich of the day: a hot dog on a bun topped with cheese and lettuce, and the whole nicely held together with, of all things, caviar! He said it was delicious and managed to down two of them before rain moved the party to our house, where cake and coffee ended the meal but not the fun. One of our dignified Arab friends, known far and wide in his own country for his skill as a sword dancer, treated us to a jitterbug demonstration to the tune of "Jersey Bounce" and the cheers of all. Later in the evening Prince Faisal made sure I got help with the dishes, thus adding another memory to my collection, that of true Arab gentlemen doing their duty as they saw it, decked out in some of my best kitchen aprons.

With the Saudi delegation was a religious *Shaikh,* a man versed in the Koran and its laws and therefore eligible to perform marriages. It was decided to take advantage of the *Shaikh's* presence by holding the Moslem counterpart of our civil marriage, and so arrangements were made. Our 1943 ceremony was said by Judge Martin DeVries of Long Beach, California, and the Moslem rite in 1945 was performed by Shaikh Khalil Rawaf from Saudi Arabia, the witnesses this time being members of the Arabian group under Prince Faisal. Notwithstanding the fact that the occasion should have been a solemn one, our Moslem wedding somehow got out of hand and quite rivaled in gaiety our previous impromptu gatherings. My attempts to follow and then repeat the words in Arabic made them all laugh in spite of themselves, and when our child Hamida's cries could be heard accompanying Shaikh Khalil's pronouncement that we were man and wife all attempts at solemnity were abandoned. Arabs have a custom whereby the groom hands money to his bride as a token guarantee of their bond, so Ali gaily presented me with a mere penny, and Hamida was brought in and bounced from knee to knee while the guest book was signed. Shaikh Ahmed Abdul Jabbar, a published poet and scholar, observed another Arab tradition by composing poetry on the spot and inscribing it to the happy couple. He ad-libbed a few oral poems, too, and if the one he wrote in the guest book was serious and beautiful, the others were not, but most assuredly did attest to the humor of the situation. It would be interesting to know how much they lost in translation.

When finally the guests returned to their duties in San Francisco I collapsed on the cushion of stillness they left behind and felt I had been dreaming. I picked up the guest book with its page after page of Arabic, just as unfamiliar in its written form as the speeches I had heard but proof at least that it was real. Ali had not even had time to transcribe the half-page that Prince Faisal wrote the day he came, and goodness knows when I'd know what it all said. Shaking my head at my own signature in Arabic at the bottom of the marriage contract, I felt that I had just been initiated into some secret club and left alone to decipher the rules by myself. Across my living room for the past few weeks I had seen men whose garb was authentic in Biblical times, I had watched a Nubian bodyguard lay off his cartridge belts and push his jeweled dagger to one side so he could hold my child on the other, and I had received a princely gift of a necklace which could have been Cleopatra's own. Real happenings but so unreal to me now, and the full page of Arabic before me could have been the Rosetta stone for all I understood of it. It was funny that in my life's recent events all that glittered *was* gold, but that the ceremony which bound me to the life of an Arab had been sealed with one copper penny. If the penny had been for thoughts, I would have said that a living room in America was a difficult place to flight-test a magic carpet from Arabia.

Changing from an ordinary American housewife and mother by day to a jewel-bedecked dinner companion to Arab chiefs and desert princes by night was a switch that was wearing on me. Being on home ground tempered the strangeness but it also served to emphasize it, as I went from routine to glamour and back again. I kept telling myself I was enjoying privileges not permitted the veiled women of Arabia; if these men came to my house in Arabia I should have to hide my face. These were fantastic conditions to fantastic happenings, with more than a touch of make-believe. So far, my sorties into the Arab world had begun and ended in my own familiar rooms, but serious thoughts broke often through the crust of thrills and I sometimes feared what Arabia held in store for me. The ready friendship of the Arabs I knew did much to allay my doubts, but I began to wonder what it would be like when I was no longer able to switch back to things American. Once in Arabia could I, would I, adjust when the veil hid my face and the walls around my house enclosed me as surely as the walls enclosed the desert city in which we would live? I didn't know, but I usually settled for letting the excitement of the known outweigh the worries over the unknown, and it was a good thing I did.

Chapter 3

ALI'S PLANS to return to the university were never carried out. After the Peace Conference Prince Faisal and his two brothers, H.R.H. Prince Mohamed and H.R.H. Prince Khalid, his son H.H. Prince Abdullah, his nine-year-old brother H.R.H. Prince Nawaf, and the rest of the delegation stayed in America for another month. Ali was with them in New York when it was decided he should return to Arabia to work under Prince Faisal in the Ministry of Foreign Affairs, and he telephoned me from there the end of July to tell me the news and instruct me about getting to New York to meet the August 6 sailing date for London on the *Queen Mary*. Stunned by this unexpected turn in my life, I protested that Hamida at four and one-half months was far too young to travel, insisted I was far too inexperienced in travel matters to handle everything myself, and then grew hopping mad that I was forced to do so.

It had to be, so I did it, but what a hectic race it was to pack what I could and arrange to ship what I couldn't, to sell the car, run around with one arm dead from the combinations of inoculations I had, get birth affidavits and notarizations, file passport application, pay closing bills, make reservations, and pick up tickets. Somehow, bag, baby, and baggage, I made it to the train on time, but once safely aboard my feelings had a chance to catch up with me. I had not been out of the state of California since my parents took me there from Oklahoma when I was two, so now I was hit and hit hard with the realization that I was really leaving home, family, America for so far-off a place as Arabia. My mother was with me those last few days, but when the time came to go I asked that she not see me off at the station. We took simple leave of each other on the porch — she for Long Beach and I for the train and points east. At no time could I bring myself to say the actual word *good-bye.*

After the trouble I took to reach New York on time our departure was delayed four days, and the bonus in time we spent shopping, buying gifts for Ali's family, sundry articles for ourselves, and baby foods which were hard to find in the Middle East. It required special help from the State Department to get my passport processed in time, and we enlisted their help too in getting one hundred cans of evaporated milk, still rationed in America. When the passport came by special messenger from Washington we left to board the *Queen Mary,* aided by Mr. Brown and a liaison officer who took charge of formalities. We were but a handful of civilians compared to the large number of troops shipping out with us, and our steward told us how strange it was for them to have a child on board. For six years, he said, they had carried troops, and only for the last two trips had infants been accepted as passengers.

The princes, Shaikh Ibrahim, and the genial, gold-toothed Murzug, once royal executioner and now Prince Faisal's personal bodyguard, were regular visitors to our stateroom throughout the trip, but we soon caught on that Hamida was the drawing attraction. Prince Faisal came in Arab dress one morning, and as he held Hamida the gold-threaded royal *igal* struck her fancy so he took it off and gave it to her. She dropped it a few times, then clutched and yanked his white *sumada* until the cloth hung crookedly over his face as far down as his nose. Obliged by now to peer out from underneath, Prince Faisal continued as if nothing was amiss but Ali and I could not help laughing at the sight of him. He ignored our giggles and made no effort to hinder Hamida, even telling us "mind your own business" when we tried to stop her. It was he who finally called a halt to her fun, though, when she switched her interest to his beard, got a good hold on it, and proved that it was real.

Our trip on the *Queen Mary* happened to be her first homecoming voyage in six years of war, and as we steamed into the harbor the sight was wondrous to behold. Many small, medium-sized, and big boats were near to greet her and each tiny toot of welcome from them was answered magnanimously by a mighty blast from the *Queen*. An honor guard was on the dock, the Lord Mayor was there resplendent in red uniform, and a band struck up as we glided in. Officials from the British government were there, too, ostensibly to greet Prince Faisal, but if they had planned any special ceremony of welcome for him it was caught up and lost in the general demonstrations of joy.

Government cars took our party the seventy-four miles to London where we spent the next two weeks sightseeing, theatergoing, accepting invitations, and being feted as dignitaries. I was getting used to being the only woman as I tagged along in the company of Arab royalty, but everyday matters kept my feet on the ground. Although Ali and I shared a suite at the Savoy with our good friend Prince Abdullah, I still had to wash Hamida's diapers in the washbowl and beg or borrow the soap to do them with. It was difficult to get help in the evenings too, and more often than not our baby sitter was the hall porter.

It was the fasting month of Ramadan for my Moslem friends, so all normal daytime activities were curtailed. The Koran exempts its followers from fasting during actual travel, but once a traveler arrives anywhere and stays even temporarily the fast must be resumed, and for a whole month neither food nor drink must pass his lips from sunup to sundown. In Moslem countries a cannon's boom announces the exact break of day when fasting must begin and the precise moment it ends when the sun sets, but no such signal was available in London. There the sun — up or down — was rarely visible to the naked eye, so official sunrise and sunset times had to be gleaned from the daily newspaper and it was my job to pass this information on to all interested parties.

It was difficult for them to fast all day, but it was a trying time for me, too. Hamida kept her regular daytime schedule and the others slept all day and celebrated all night, so the pace was upsetting. It was nothing compared to the consternation caused in the hotel kitchen, though. Producing decent food even at regular hours was already a problem of some magnitude, harassed as they were by wartime shortages, but our request for one full meal at sundown and another just before dawn was too much. The headwaiter almost lost his starched correctness, and goodness knows what turmoil it caused the chef. Actually, the problem was never quite satisfactorily worked out. The best the hotel was able to provide on occasion was a platter of cold chicken, and that was delicious, but most often the men's daybreak meal consisted of dainty tea sandwiches of watercress and cucumbers. Whole trays of them were left on a sideboard in our rooms before the waiter went off duty and I can still see our men hopefully lift the napkin to see what was to whet their appetites after an evening out on the town. In the hope that the sandwiches would become more substantial, we ordered the crusts left on, but there wasn't much we could do about the filling — such as it was. Those sandwiches couldn't have given much sustenance for a whole day's fast, and you could tell as the men munched them that their enjoyment left much to be desired.

Our happiest moment in London was shared with the rest

of the world when Prime Minister Clement Attlee went on the air at midnight to announce the end of the war with Japan. Prince Abdullah and Ali and I left the hotel as soon as we heard the news and with arms locked together we pressed along with the crowds as they surged toward Piccadilly Circus. We bought British and American flags to wave and we sang and hurrahed merrily, wildly, with the rest. When fruit vendors appeared from nowhere, we were happy to buy two pounds of grapes and peaches for three pounds sterling, and although the manifestation of victory that night was crowd delirium each of us surely had his own thoughts about what peace meant to him as an individual.

To a man, the Saudi princes called on me the following day to offer their congratulations on the victory of the Allies and to express the hope that my brother Boyd, a Navy officer in the Pacific, would soon return home. I was very touched by their act, representing as it did one more instance of their graciousness.

Protocol and dignitaries, foreign or otherwise, had not played any part in my life until now, but I enjoyed my new position. Sheer bluff saw me through situations which were new to me and I had a good eye and a good ear, which helped me to play the great lady when occasion demanded. There were some things I was not willing to give up, however, such as taking my baby out for a walk, and I must say it caused more than a few raised eyebrows among hotel personnel and guests when I personally wheeled the carriage through the swank lobby and out toward the Thames.

Heads turned, too, when I left with the Arabs to go to a reception or a dinner or a weekend in the country. It was a big moment sauntering out to waiting limousines knowing for sure everyone was watching the tall, dark, and handsome Arabs with the greatest of interest, and probably wondering who the devil the tall blonde was and where she fit into the picture. I was not so obvious when the men wore western clothing, but when they surrounded me in their Arab finery even I could wonder what I was doing there.

It was nice to be included in so many of their activities, but added to their sincere interest in me as a person were their almost gleeful inquiries into my progress as an Arab. My mastery of Arabic had proceeded no further than the knowledge of a few common words and a shaky ability to sing one verse of an old Egyptian national anthem taught me by Ali's Egyptian roommate at Cal. The laughter caused by my rendition — by request only — of said anthem never failed to topple a few *igals,* but laughing with princes is a wonderful antidote to practicing protocol with them, and I was more than glad that my friendship with these good people could level off from the so-called sublime to be just as valid at the ridiculous.

August 29 was departure date from London. A chartered British aircraft took our party to Cairo where we checked in en masse at Shepheard's Hotel. Time could never dull the memory of my first touch with the Middle East in Cairo, a moving, heaving, screeching mass of a city whose beauty, ugliness, wealth, poverty, modernity, antiquity merged into patterns for living which have not changed in history but were ever-changing to the eye, forming and reforming in color and shape like the views in a kaleidoscope. Cairo was incredible to me, overpowering in what met my eye and what dinned on my ears. It is a weakness, perhaps, to let the things you see stay as visions to trouble you, but some of the things I saw tormented me. The beauty and wonders and utter charm of Cairo affected and awed me, but so also did the beggars in rags and the babies with fly-encrusted eyes, and the lame and the sick and the blind. It was impossible to see one and forget the other.

The balcony of our room at Shepheard's overlooked the screen of an outdoor cinema, but there were far more interesting things to see. Roaming the great halls of the old Shepheard with their Pharaonic designs and arabesque motifs was an experience in itself, and there was a saying that if you sat long enough on Shepheard's front terrace you would eventually see everyone you knew. In the center of the city modern shops and department stores had goods imported from Paris and London, but for local color the bazaar óf old Cairo was the place to go. There in the *musqy,* as it was called, articles of gold and leather, silk, reed and raffia, silver, brocaded stuff, wood, muslin, brass, enamel, amber, clay, and ivory were displayed, or hung, or dangled, or stacked, or just left in piles. which cluttered the path and dazzled the eye. I cannot remember why it was so, but my one and only purchase out of all the wondrous things I could have bought was a most uninteresting piece of material for a veil — a one-meter square of black georgette which I would soon need to cover my face in Arabia.

The plane which took us to Jeddah in Arabia was a spanking new DC-3 which was a gift to King Ibn Saud from the California Arabian Oil Company (later Arabian American Oil Company). We left Cairo very early in the morning, and during the seven-hour trip Hamida made her usual rounds of lap-sitting, some of us played cards, and others talked or slept. After crossing the Red Sea the plane followed the coastline of Arabia and we could see the reefs below showing through the water in pale and dark patches, with the waters varying shades of green and blue running all together like the fused colored glass in an antique paperweight.

Long before we started our turn in from the coast Ali urged me to start fixing the veil, which would have to be in place when we landed. Every man in Jeddah would be at the airport to greet the homecoming princes, and my face must not be seen even from the plane's window. I suddenly resented having to cover my face, and besides, I did not have the slightest idea of how to do it. In those days there was a special way of pinning one part of the veil as a base and fixing over it a kind of flap for the front part which could be lowered or thrown back as needed, but it was all new to me and I was at a loss to know how. Since my companions were beginning to cover their heads with *sumadas* and gold *igals* and the bodyguards were strapping on their cartridge belts and gun holsters and jeweled daggers, I knew the time had come for me to do something.

I made several self-conscious efforts to afix my veil with pins and tucks, but to no avail. I struggled quietly with it until one of the men espied me and started a ripple of amusement which spread in a matter of minutes to a great wave of hilarity as they all converged on me in a concerted effort to help. The trouble was that their women wore a different kind of head covering so they were just as unfamiliar with my veil as I was, and Ali was no help because he had left the country too young to be concerned with such things. It grew more hilarious as each tried his hand and I sat patiently through the drapings and twistings and pinnings. Sometimes it appeared someone had succeeded, but then either one end or all ends of the veil dangled loose, or it hung lopsided and fell off when I moved my head, or slid backward and left my bare chin sticking out or fell forward like a bib in front, baring the nape of my neck in back. The men invariably burst into laughter after standing back to view their handiwork and watching my face, one way or another, keep reappearing. No doubt part of their amusement was due to the fact that I, an American, was required now to veil from them. They had traveled in my country and knew our customs, and we had come many miles together with my face uncovered. Now that I had come to their home I was obliged to hide myself, and if I failed to see the humor in the situation, they did not. The merriment ceased when the warning to fasten seat belts confined us to our places and I sat there in dying commotion barefaced as ever and twice as upset.

When we landed I peered out to nothing but desert, but

taxiing in I saw the great crowd of men — a striking sameness in their robes, their headdresses, and their bearded faces.
The scene was completely foreign to me, as if I had landed in a
separate world. There was nothing with which I could identify
— men, plane, or desert. There was not even a proper runway,
nor airport buildings, nor signs of anything on earth but us.
My world was behind, or ahead, or off to the side, anywhere
but here, and I knew, I felt, before I set foot on it that this was
true for more than just the physical aspects of the land. This
was a closed square of other world for which I had laid aside
America, England, Egypt, and all the rest, as a child at play
lays aside outer layers of a nest of boxes to reach at last the final
small solid block. I had gone as far as I could, and the feeling
there in Arabia was one of finality. I felt I could reach
the world I knew only by building outward again.

Chapter 4

Soon I was to step from that plane and settle in this country as one of them, meriting acceptance of the people by observing their customs and conforming as I had agreed to do. For the first time I was afraid, really afraid, of my ability to do this as I alternately viewed the strange Arabian scene out of my window and watched the Arabs on the plane prepare to leave. I tried to respond intelligently to their good-byes, knowing that the veil none of us had been able to fix was already in place in principle. They left then and were absorbed by the throng while Ali excitedly spotted members of his own family and I waited in the plane.

As soon as the royal party was gone, the men of our family came aboard to meet me. The first one was Uncle Yousuf, a kind-faced man of sixty years or more, whose beard was white and whose dress was in the old Arab style of *jubba* and *umama*.* He greeted me in a hearty manner and I tried to kiss his hand as Ali had instructed me, but Uncle Yousuf would not allow it. I started to shake hands with brother Mohamed,

* *Jubba* is the long overcoat worn over white duck trousers and *umama* is the turban worn over a stiff white cotton skullcap.

but he quickly bent over and kissed me on both cheeks and bade me welcome, and then I shook hands with several of Ali's cousins. I was just thinking how nice for me they all spoke English when a number of our servants and drivers came forth and kissed my hand and I bogged down in confusion. It was unbelievable that I was in Arabia and incredible that these Arabs around me were there on my account. I did not belong here, but some of these men were part of my new family and had come to take me to my new home. I suddenly felt like the woman suffering labor pains must have felt when her frantic husband blurted, "Emily darling, are you sure you want to go through with this?" I may not have wanted to, but the moment was fast approaching when I would have to, and I dreaded going out in front of that tremendous crowd of men with that ridiculous piece of black material over my head.

We had finally just thrown it over my hair when the Alirezas came aboard, and I smiled a little smile when I noticed that Mohamed had brought a veil along in case Ali and I had forgotten. I thought he should have seen his countrymen and me a few moments before! His obvious relief that I was not going to be difficult about wearing the veil could never match my dismay at having to do so. While still aloft I had jokingly suggested to Ali that I just saunter off without it, and the look of horror which came over his face left no doubt as to the importance they gave it. For me it was not just the idea of the thing — I really couldn't see from behind it, and I was afraid I would fall flat. I envisioned myself slipping as I went out the door and sprawling there for all to see the first time I made an appearance, and I worked myself into such a fear they almost had to push me out the door. The unfamiliar long black cloak — as obligatory as the veil — flapped around my ankles and I started to tremble when I was told to proceed.

In those days the plane's ladder was just that, a ladder, and never never will I forget groping down. The minute I stuck my head out a breeze threatened to lift the veil away so I had to clamp one hand down over it. The heat came at me in a great blast and I felt that despite my coverings all eyes were upon me. If only, I prayed, the powers that be would get me safely down I could bear all else. What the "all else" was I did not know, but it would not have surprised me if it had meant waking from a dream.

My heels sank into the sand for a few steps before I was mercifully led by some kind hand to a car brought near the plane, but then relief turned to panic when the car roared off with me as soon as I managed to sit. No one else was with me, Hamida having been taken from my arms long before I started from the plane, and no one had bothered to tell me what was happening. It was hard to believe that I would be sent off like this without an explanation, so I had some wild thoughts that I was being kidnaped as an intruding foreigner and would never see my husband or Hamida again. The driver did not address me at any time as I sat bouncing around in the back, and I could not have understood him if he had. I dared not push back the veil or even peek lest he turn and shout, "Off with your head," a likelihood which at that moment I thought possible and even probable.

Actually, the driver had been instructed to get me out of public view as quickly as possible and he did it so well that no one had a chance to join me on the trip to the house. But I did not know this then. I felt abandoned and alone and frightened and tried to believe that my day had started normally enough in Cairo that very morning. It was unreal that I should be a veiled Arabian lady driving around the desert with what appeared to be a wild Bedouin at the wheel. "Rescue is at hand," I breathed, when I heard a wild tooting of cars behind, but they just passed by and kicked back a few miles of desert sand on us until all cars swerved recklessly, horns blasting, through a gate and into a walled enclosure, and I saw the house that was to be my home. Ali's mother came running down the steps as we pulled up and tearfully, joyfully, greeted the son she had not seen in five long years, the granddaughter born in America, and the daughter-in-law whose fancied fears were dispelled by her heartwarming hug and overjoyed face, expressions of love which needed no translation.

We hurried inside to escape the terrible wet heat and my veil and cloak were removed as we passed into the tearoom. For someone who had not even known where Saudi Arabia was a few years back I was assuredly now in a unique position. No one of my kind had entered this country before as a member of one of its families. I belonged; I wasn't just a visitor passing through. This great high-ceilinged, many-storied desert house was my home, the woman who guided me was my relative, those who waited to see me inside were my friends, and I was mistress to the maids who tended the samovar in the room we had just entered. Strange and stranger, and the impact of it all hit me at each turn, in waves as constant as the heat.

The tearoom scene which met my eye looked like a page out of a book whose figures came to life as we approached, for the women were wearing the old-fashioned clothes of Arabia, pantaloons and long overdresses with high collars fastened by gold studs on a chain, and no make-up on their faces except for a lining of *kohl* on their dark eyes. Their heads were covered with sheer cotton cloth partly wound in with their braided hair, and another light headscarf on top which dangled tiny tassels and lace. All wore their hair parted in the middle and pulled back tightly from their faces, and along with that it struck me odd that they all had very high foreheads. It was not until months later that I learned the Hejazi* women pluck their hairline back about "two fingers' width" to give them this desired mark of beauty.

* Hejaz is a province of Saudi Arabia. *Hejazi* means "of the Hejaz."

Barely over my surprise that they were not all wearing western dress as my mother-in-law was, my next discovery was that my attempts to be sociable were hampered by more than ignorance of the language. At the first handshake I was left standing there with my hand outstretched but unshaken, for in Arabia the women do not shake hands, they touch fingertips and then raise their index finger to their lips and kiss it. It took me the whole round to get the hang of what they were doing but not until I had tangled fingers on every greeting and waged a small battle to get in at least one slight handshake. Questions were asked me which I did not understand and they were replied to by others speaking for me as I sat among them on the *carawitas*, upholstered benches along the walls. I realized too late that my shoes were still on — I should have left them at the door — and I felt like Humpty Dumpty with my legs dangling while everyone else had hers neatly tucked out of sight.

Looking around, my eyes swam with the clash of colors in the materials, in the brass, the fancy carpets, and the glass and gold and lace. The samovar bubbling in its corner on the floor imposed itself on the strange talk so that sound joined with sight to lead me astray. My day was far from over, but it seemed like a century since it had started. The flies and the heat were my only contacts with reality, while women kept coming from town and my mother-in-law kept filling in for me as I sat helplessly by, watching dumbly all that was going on around me.

It was quite a surprise, therefore, when Ali's sister Zakia ignored all normal procedure by bursting through the door and jolting me right out of my seat. She grabbed me, flung her arms around me and kissed me, wished out loud that I have many children, hung a beautiful gold-encased locket Koran on the one child I did have, pinned a diamond brooch on me, and left the two of us standing in the middle of the room as she beamed at one and all. Immediately behind her came Uncle Yousuf's daughters who had been raised in India and South Africa and, glory be, knew English and could explain things to me. Even then, it was all so new and strange that I could not sit for long before feeling the need to be alone and, using Hamida as an excuse, went frequently to the room on the third floor which Ali's mother gave up for us.

Venturing into a new world was fascinating, but when it grew unreal the fascinations became trials and I had to go off by myself to try to clear my head and reassure myself that I was I and that this was my home. Looking out from the upstairs window I thought the barren desert matched my feelings, for the sand seemingly stretched to nowhere as my mind did in the search for something familiar. But all I found was myself and all I could go back to was myself. It would have helped if I could have found Ali, too, but he had disappeared shortly after our arrival and indeed I was not to see him again until long past midnight, and long after I had already coped as best I could with my new experiences and undergone the strain of trying to understand and make myself understood.

One of my getaway trips ended in my falling asleep on the bed after thinking I would lie down for a few minutes of rest. My mother-in-law awakened me hours later and I was terribly embarrassed. She had come earlier to see why I had not returned and found me asleep with Hamida in my arms. She didn't have the heart then to get me up, realizing how tired I was, and goodness knows what excuses she gave the good ladies who had come expressly to see me. But whatever she said or did, she covered for me throughout and left me alone until it was obligatory that I join our guests for dinner.

It was dark by then and the room was lit by a kerosene lamp which Ali's mother had carried upstairs. Zainab's boy, Hussein, about eleven years old, was at her side and could tell me in English how upset his grandmother was about the lack of electricity. She had wanted so much, he said, for everything to go well, especially my first day there, and was upset that their generator had chosen that of all days to break down. Hussein had trouble understanding my American English, having studied English English for such a short time, but he was a willing and helpful translator between his grandmother and me. "Never mind about the lights," I told him, "and please tell your grandmother not to give it another thought."

But it is certain that those lanterns affected my impressions that first night. They cast shadows throughout the house, and when we joined the others in the dining room and I saw in the flickering light the platter upon platter of strange food, and had to sense rather than really see the movement of the people and the expressions on their faces, I was overpowered once more by feelings of fantastic unreality. I believe I almost fainted, perhaps from the heat, but I can still recall every detail of that dinner and the emotion it caused me. The party was in full swing, which means that everyone was talking at once, a phenomenon I observed time and again through my years in Arabia. I was continually astonished at how the women kept so many conversations going at the same time and still managed to follow the one they were engaged in.

We sat around a table groaning with the weight and variety of food — roast meat, boiled meat, ground meat, stuffed pastries and stuffed vegetables, fish, seasoned curds, oily salads, cheeses, olives, three kinds of rice, pastes and dips for the bread, eggs, macaroni, nuts, custards, cakes, melons, dates and date cookies, short fat bananas, grapes, and hovering over the whole the combined smells of cardamom, saffron, cumin, cinnamon, and pepper. I groaned, too, just looking at it, more in disbelief than anything else, and I had no appetite for anything. The heat and humidity had not abated with the coming of night, and the odor of the spices and the exotic foods fogged my head. My body fought a growing unease, and I was getting plain mad at Ali, who was still out paying the visits required of him in town.

His mother had certainly done all she could to make my first day in Arabia easy for me, which was more than I could say for him. Funneled into a few hours had been a series of situations which took me far from my moorings and I had gotten through them more or less successfully only because of the kindness and good humor and understanding thoughtfulness of my Arabian mother-in-law. We did not have much in common but she showed me from the start that if I was willing to learn she was willing to help. I knew it would be a long time before I could take as calmly as she did the relegation of women to the background and I could not help being shocked that Ali had not spent more time with her the first day of his return. She sensed more than understood my attempts to put my shock into words, and her answering shrug eloquently expressed the patience that is part of the heritage of eastern women. In later years when we discussed the lot of Arabian women, she was wont to say, "Wallifna, al hayat kidda" — she had "grown accustomed, for such was life." But that first day I refused even to acknowledge the fact that if Ali *had* been there he could not have been with us. Of a certainty, most of the ladies present would have dashed for cover if he had so much as stuck his head in the door.

After our guests left and the house was quiet Mother* and I took our lantern and climbed the stairs together. In the hallway outside my room she showed me the drinking water in a big earthenware jug, its usual ordinary metal stopper replaced for my benefit with an extraordinary antique silver one which she had retrieved from one of her trunks. The base was solid but with beautiful filigree on top and tiny silver birds tinkling around its rim. After what I had been through that day it

* Literally, *marat-ammi*, "wife of my uncle," when expressed by a daughter-in-law.

seemed quite natural that a clay pot should have a pretty silver top. Entering my room I saw the gifts she had laid out for me, colored crystal decanters of cologne from her own collection and a lovely new ivory-colored nightgown and matching negligee ready to slip into on my bed. What good will there was in this manner of presenting gifts, open and ready! It would not have been the same if they had been wrapped for me to unwrap, and it typified the open welcome and the desire to include me that I had felt all day, however short I had fallen of feeling at home and at ease.

I still could not believe anyplace on earth could be so different and that I would end up the only stranger around, but now with the first day over maybe the next would be easier. Surely it had been a hard day for my mother-in-law, too, but I felt that for two women who had never met before we had made a good start despite dissimilar backgrounds and ever-present language difficulties. Luckily our humor smoothed the rough edges and when all else failed we just threw up our hands and laughed.

The time had come to call it quits for that day, however, so she showed me how to turn down the lantern for the night and said, "Tisbahi-alla khair."

"Good night," I replied, "and thank you for everything."

Her great dark eyes twinkled as she thought to try a little English on me and managed a passable "Gooed night." Not to be outdone by her bit of extra effort, I tried the Arabic counterpart, but lisped through the first part and finished with "kare" instead of "khair," so the last laugh of the first day was on me.

The good feeling which enveloped me at bedtime was effectively dissipated when Ali finally came in past midnight and wakened me with the shattering news that he had to leave for Riyadh at dawn with the five princes. I had gotten through the first day feeling secure in the knowledge that at least Ali would be there to help from then on, but not so. The king had cabled he wanted them present at the big feast, Eid al-Kabir, which follows Ramadan, so that was that. I could not believe it, but when I opened my mouth to launch a tirade I was told to put a robe on and hurry downstairs. His brother and mother were already there, he said, waiting to show us around the house. Dumbfounded, I could only obey. I put on my new negligee and a pair of clopping wooden sandals I found in the bathroom and joined the others around the fountain on the main terrace.

The heat had held but there was a calm clear beauty over the desert which was almost ethereal. Pattering around desert palaces in the wee small hours and holding conferences around the mosaics of an Arab fountain was asking a lot of me at this point. I met again my red-bearded, green-eyed brother-in-law who had first seen me in a veil and now saw me more than a little unveiled. It was unreal that I should be standing where I was in a white nightgown and downright eerie wandering through the house carrying hissing high-pressure kerosene lamps called *electriques* to gaze at high ceilings and furniture piled in the corners. Mohamed had just finished building the house and was extremely proud of it, and lovely it was indeed with airy rooms and spacious halls and patios and the like, but I was not fully to understand his joy and pride until I visited the old houses within the walls of the city proper.

After the tour we gathered once more around the fountain and Mohamed made a speech about how glad they were to have me and assured me I was loved as they loved Ali. I was very touched and thanked him but could not help shaking my head at the time and the place. I knew it was because Ali had to leave and because it was the first opportunity to get together, but it pushed my wonder to its limit and what happened next dropped it over the brink. Mohamed reached down into the pockets of his dress and presented me with a string of pearls his father had selected pearl by pearl for "Ali's bride," and I turned in a daze while he clasped it around my neck. What a combination, pearls and nightgown, but they did match in creamy glow, and sparkle was added when Mother fastened to my wrist her gift of a diamond-encrusted watch set in platinum. For the other wrist she brought out eight beautifully chased gold bracelets, four from Ali's grandmother, who before her death asked that they be given to the girl Ali married, and four from the old Negro nanny who had loved and cared for Ali when he was little. Mother had promised she would personally put them on when the time came, but the women of the East are much smaller boned than I and the bracelets were too small to go over my hand. A promise is a promise, and finally, with the help of many soap bubbles and much painful easing, all eight slipped over my fist. There I stood, everyone chuckling at my bedazzlement, and I thought Arabia was certainly living up to its reputation. As the desert was my witness, where else could I have gone to a post-midnight gathering in a nightgown and wooden clogs and come back with diamonds on one wrist, gold on the other, and a perfection of pearls around my neck?

Back in my room thrill and fatigue finally surrendered to sleep, but not before my mind mulled over and over what had happened and what would be happening to me. I had discovered in just one day that there were many things that were fascinating and thrilling in Arabia and many things that were neither. There was a great gap between outward luxury and confinement of body and soul. As I was to continue to discover, I found little to make me feel that I was leading a normal existence, and that of course was just it — I wasn't. Arabia was too new and too old, and my ears were to ring often in days to come with my own silent shouts: I am an American! What has all this to do with me? But trying to pierce the strangeness with the weapon of nationality was no good, and getting that shout down to a whisper was an accomplishment that took months. While thrilling to the glamour and jewels, I longed and often cried for freedom. Things got better when I realized that nothing was going to change on account of me and that what was difficult and strange for me was established and commonplace for them. But such conscious thought was not my guide at first. Starting with my entry at the airfield when I had to veil for the first time, I went into a kind of shock and floated from situation to situation without really understanding, language-wise or life-wise. I conformed as well as I could and followed where I was led, but I dragged behind me for a long time the anchor of my old familiar, wonderfully free pre-Arabia existence, and was to make myself, as well as those around me, quite miserable at times until I became better adjusted to all that was new to me.

Chapter 5

THE NEXT DAY the sticky, breathless heat of morning drove me
to the balcony to see what I could see, and what I saw was my
mother-in-law sleeping on a wooden table which a fortnight
before had served a banquet to the king. She opened her eyes,
sat up and said, as she searched for her glasses, "Sabakhilkhair." *
"Good heavens," I exclaimed, "did you sleep on the table? Do
I have your bed? You shouldn't have done that. I'm sorry."
"Ma-alaish, ma-alaish," † she said, and we were both soon laughing at her efforts to assure me that she often slept out on hot
nights and that she had given up her room because it was increasingly difficult for her to climb the stairs. Besides, she said,
she was used to sleeping on a hard surface. I could vouch for
that — the bed I had slept in was hers and it was nothing more
than a thin cotton mattress over a solid wooden baseboard.

The heat — indoors or out — hung heavy on us, refusing to
diminish. Mother had little trickles of perspiration running
down her neck which she blotted with her handkerchief as she
looked at me and shook her head. "Har," she said, and I agreed.

* "Good morning."
† "Never mind, never mind."

It was very hot. We went downstairs to breakfast on tea, cheese, olives, flat bread, and jam while I fought the layers of flies circling and circling over our food before coming in for landings. If someone had ever told me how many there were I would never have believed them, and I waged war against them from the start. The big house with its many verandahs, rooms, halls, and balconies literally hummed with flies, although our square of desert was fairly isolated and we were far from town.

While Mother performed ablutions for morning prayer I wandered through the downstairs rooms until I heard Mohamed's voice and someone else's coming from the tearoom. Goody! People! People speaking English! Carried away with anticipation of holding English conversation, and completely forgetting that I should instead have turned tail and stayed out of sight, I burst in unannounced and then stood there with my bare face hanging out. Mohamed gaped in disbelief for a second, then graciously saved us both from embarrassment by introducing me to his friend, Sayed Hussein Alatas, Jeddah representative of the Netherlands Trading Society banking firm. While Mohamed probably wondered darkly if this was the way his new sister-in-law intended to keep, or not keep, their customs, Sayed Hussein and I had a very nice chat. He told me about his wife in Singapore and his children in school in Egypt, and I told him about our trip to Arabia and my first impressions (some, at least). Both men were amused at the extent of my annoyance with Ali for having gone off so soon after our arrival, and Mohamed said, "Never mind, we are all leaving for Taif this afternoon to join the rest of the family and they will keep you busy enough." Later he had something else to say to me, that whereas I had luckily chosen a good family friend to show my face to I had better not do it again, eh? Many times in the years to come Sayed and I laughed about the blithe way I walked in on them, and he never forgot to mention that he was the first Arab in Arabia (outside the family) to see me, a distinction he always considered worthy of note.

As if to soften the blow of restriction he had earlier imposed on me, Mohamed called me back that same day to introduce me to another male visitor, and it was directly evident why this visit was considered all right, too. The old man who peered out at me from twinkly, crinkly eyes must have been a hundred years old or more, and the only thing he was interested in was the sack of gold in Mohamed's lap. I was reminded it was the big feast day (as if I could forget), the day money is distributed by those who have to those who have not. "This old fellow was a freed slave of my father," Mohamed said. "He has come every year for as long as I can remember, collecting his gold pieces and going his way until the same time the following year." Mohamed put his hand in and pulled out some sovereigns which clinked as he dropped them into the wrinkled old hand. The ex-slave nodded happily and smiled toothlessly and included me in his benediction, "May God protect you and give you long life." His life had already been so long he was past worrying about custom, and likely neither recognized me for a foreigner nor wondered why I was there, a woman sitting among men. But the whole thing certainly made me wonder. Slaves, and veils, and sacks of gold indeed! How had I come to where the Red Sea shimmered to the west of me, the white turrets and mud walls of Jeddah lay to the south, Bedouin tents patched the desert north of me, and the holy city of Mecca lay eastward over the hills? I belonged only because I was there.

The courtyard was by then a bustle of drivers and servants making ready for our trip to Taif, and I peeked, taking care this time not to be seen. Mohamed approached to mention again how anxiously I, "the bride," was awaited in Taif by his sister, wife, children, and the staff. I was pondering being a bride when a strange voice close by startled me and I went to the terrace to investigate. There waddling toward me from the living room was a bright green parrot squawking "Inal abouk, inal abouk" as it marched around the fountain in its funny clipped-wing walk. Mohamed came up laughing and said the parrot was uttering curses, and I laughed too as I thought That figures! Where else would one day's events bring down on my head the blessings of a charming turbaned old genie freed from his chains and the raucous cries of "Curses on your father, curses on your father," uttered by a cocky footloose-and-fancy-free green parrot?

"Yallah, yallah," * Mohamed yelled some hours later, and it was time for Mother and me to adjust our veils and take our places among baskets of food and water jugs in the waiting cars. Four autos and a truck carrying luggage, bedding, and foodstuffs gave one the impression we were starting on a long trek so I was surprised to discover that our destination was only five or six hours away. It was my first lesson in desert travel, which requires that food and water and signal lights be carried and if possible that drivers be qualified mechanics. No trip in the Arabian desert is undertaken matter-of-factly, but this one was to be unusual for everybody and it was my presence that was making it so. Any caravan leaving Jeddah for Taif would normally take the regular route through Mecca, but Mecca is a holy city forbidden to non-Moslems and I am a Christian. With me along, our caravan had to travel instead the seldom used other road which by-passed Mecca. So I caused a touch of adventure for them, too, more than I knew at the time. There was only one man in the party, I discovered later, who knew the way well enough to act as guide.

When we finally got under way, the heat was less dread but still stifling under the veil. I tried to dispense with it because we were far from houses or streets, but we had to pass through the outskirts of town and several small villages on the way out; so Mother advised I cover until we were well in the open. I

* "Hurry up, hurry up."

peeked at Bedouin women wearing peculiar nosepieces and headdresses ornamented with coins and beads, but there was nothing else to see after we turned off the regular road to take our almost uncharted path into the mountainous area where the so-called road was really rough. Hamida thought we were bouncing her in fun and got a case of hiccups that persisted well into nighttime.

In the dark the markings of the road were fainter yet when sand from the car ahead swirled before headlights and one of our cars got lost. A search party was formed which backtracked and beamed and crisscrossed lights until the errant car was found. All our vehicles bogged down at one time or another, and we women watched as the men, servant and master, hiked up their skirts and put their shoulders to the bumpers to push the cars free of the sand. Chanting as they struggled, fitting the rhythm of their chants to the work at hand, or vice versa, they almost seemed to be enjoying the challenge. Then when the car train moved again, wending its way up, one could sense the never-slackening strain to get just a little farther on, in great contrast to the rest stops characterized by a peace and quiet that was almost scary.

Then our surroundings had no beginning and no end and the star-filled sky was like a top-heavy tent threatening to collapse over our earthly emptiness. At one wayfarers' station during a meal stop the effect was different; we seemed to crowd the desert. I jumped to sit on a high rope-webbed bench to watch the hustle and bustle accompanying food and drink preparation, my feet dangling, a cloak pulled tightly around me and my veil wrapped around my head and chin and tucked in so the brisk desert breeze would not blow it away. Someone brought my meal and I drank with it the heavy sweet brew the servants called tea while I watched the fascinating scenes taking place in the dark around me. The Arabs milling around respectfully kept their distance from us women and some resembled busy stagehands hurrying to rearrange the set for the next scene. Here and there a few fires provided the only lighting effect and then died as little by little the pace of activity slowed and died, as we packed up again and soon left the place as barren as we had found it.

I was bursting inside, bursting with wonder, but the calmness of the desert must have acted as a safety valve to keep me calm too. A sort of acceptance, a wait-and-see attitude was mine. It was all I could do, really, no matter how hard I found it to believe that I was where I was. After eleven hours on a trip which normally took six, I finally got out of the car and passed through the ancient gate behind which I was to live for the next two and one-half months, and I knew with one look that my bewilderment had only begun.

"Alhamdulilah, alhamdulilah alla salama," * and it was Zainab, waiting and trembling with excitement behind the latched gate, who hugged me first. I knew she was the oldest of Ali's full sisters, but she looked like a teen-ager. After her came Hayat, Mohamed's wife, who burst from behind to gather me in her arms and swing me around a few times. "Sistair, sistair, I verree happee; I tell everyone Ali bring American arusa home." Hayat had studied English and French as a child in Lebanon but she forgot now and then and inserted Arabic instead, making conversation with her a charming mixture of all three. She was trying to impress on me the fact that she had bet Ali would come back with an American girl and she had been right. There I was, and her pleasure was such she felt compelled to tell me the first minute she saw me.

The maidservants were next. They formed a line down the hallway and as I tried to shake their hands they tried to kiss mine; I was certainly having my troubles with handshakes! I remember how rough and dry their hands were, and under the cuffs of their long cotton pantaloons I noticed that the skin on their feet, too, was so dry it was cracked.

* "Thank God, thank God, for your safe arrival."

As we passed through the old house on our way to my quarters, the rooms and stairs looked like sets from the movie *Ben Hur*. We opened a creaky latched wooden door into a wing which Hayat gaily informed me was mine. I looked around in desperation while a servant brought the baby's things and our hand luggage. Directly in front of me was a well, of all things — an honest-to-goodness well set into the wall. On a small wooden table near that were a tin plate holding a squash or two, carrots, a tomato, a potato, and a saucerful of uncooked rice. Next to that was a can of powdered milk with Arabic print all over it, and alongside that was a three-legged contraption which looked like it might be a stove. Hayat, not knowing what I had in the line of baby food, thoughtfully put these things out for my convenience. Little did she know! Tired, baffled, and distressed by the look of this ancient house, I could only nod dumbly as she and Zainab led me around.

The next room was a step down — after we stepped up over two inches of door frame — and to my tired eyes the carpets covering the floor seemed to undulate. Built-in cupboards divided one room from the next, where two large alcoves had already been made into sleeping platforms. The mattresses covered their stone surfaces, with sheets, blankets, and pillows of different sizes and shapes placed on top. Boxlike mosquito nets formed a rectangular tent over the whole with the netting tucked in around the mattresses and the four top corners of each held up by tape or string attached to four strategically placed nails around the room.

So *this* was the ex-palace of Turkish potentates during the Ottoman Empire! The big *electrique* lamp hissed louder than I could have, and one of the women pumped it to restore pressure. When it seemed about to explode I thought I would too. Wearily, I tucked my baby in under one of the mosquito tents, my in-laws verified the arrival of the last of our luggage, and *tis-bahu-ala-khair* was said by one and all. And so to all a good night! I crawled under the other net and fell almost immediately into the deep sleep which utter fatigue induces. I dreamed no dream that night to rival the one I was living.

With the dawn came Hamida's cries for her bottle. The wooden shutters blocked what early morning light there was so I decided to turn up the small kerosene lamp sitting by the well. Stubbing my toe on the way because I forgot to step up before stepping down, I fixed the lamp, found the bottle and boiled water, mixed the formula, and took it to the contraption to heat. I heated nothing but my temper as I pulled every strange knob, then pushed them, even unscrewed a few, but after nothing worked and I had burned a whole boxful of matches, I gave up. Later, much later, I learned. One had to pierce a hole in the burner first with a little wire gadget that was always getting lost, pump an initial fine stream of fuel, light, and pump again like mad until the fire caught with a roar.

Hamida drank her milk cold, but I minded more than she did. My stubbed toe hurt, the kerosene lantern's glass chimney was totally blackened from the flame turned too high, and I wanted to cry every time I looked at the stove. To top it all, I let a whole squadron of mosquitoes in with me when I crawled back to bed and spent the rest of the dark early hours swatting blindly until it was light enough to see. Then I could corner them and squash! In one such moment a too mighty swat aimed toward one at the top of the net brought the entire northeast corner down on me. Hayat, of course, chose just that moment to bring me her wedding gift. Tamed by the netting draped over my head I stood there and Hayat stood there and finally, by way of explaining her presence, she silently proferred the diamond brooch in her hand. It was too much! She started to laugh uncontrollably and I crumpled inside the net and became hysterical at the incongruous times Fate had picked for me to receive my wedding jewels. Added to the comedy mosquito act I had put on, Hayat had also seen the smoked-up lantern and the pile of burned matches and surmised correctly and with great amusement my predicament of the night before.

Accompanying our laughter was a quite extraordinary cacophony of noises made up of Hindustani records going full-blast in Uncle Yousuf's courtyard below my window, the braying of donkeys somewhere near, calls to and from servants, and other various house noises. I thought there was even the sound of horses thundering past, but I shook that thought away and came down off the bed to receive my gift. Hayat hugged me and told me she loved me very much already, and we sat together while I drank the bowlful of coffee and milk the maid Rogaiya brought. Tea was the usual morning drink, but they had heard that Americans drink coffee and that was what I got without fail each morning. How they made it I'll never know because their brews are different — a special pulverized grind of roasted beans for the Turkish type and green beans for the native coffee — but however it was done the result was delicious and the thought much appreciated.

Rogaiya was asked not to leave until she took our laundry, and to get it Hayat flung open our suitcases and picked out numerous things, among them a few pairs of my hard-come-by wartime nylon stockings. Bundling everything together, she instructed Rogaiya to return the lot by nightfall. The neat pile of clean laundry was dutifully brought with my beautiful nylons on top in a new shape — neatly wadded balls of string. The baby things were scrubbed clean, too, but not spotless, dotted as they were with burn holes. No one had told Rogaiya, who had considerable fame as the best washerwoman around, that nylons are not washed like sheets, and to be honest, the burn holes were not really her fault, either. Old-fashioned irons, heated by live coals in a special compartment at their base, were still in common use and cinders quite unavoidably fell out now and then through the air vents and burned through clothes.

Getting the laundry inspired Hayat to continue unpacking,

and it would have been akin to stopping a runaway freight train to talk her out of it. She never asked, she just went ahead and did it, emptying with frightening alacrity each suitcase and putting belongings in those lopsided blue cupboards which tilted crazily along the walls. It was useless for me to try to help so I spent the time inspecting our rooms, three in all if you counted the anteroom where the well was, and where three wooden gates led, respectively, to the outdoor hall, the toilet of the hole-in-the-floor type, and to the living room-bedroom.

The well had a rickety ill-fitting wooden cover and the water was drawn from a faucet no more than a foot off the floor, besides being so close to the wall that the rim of any receptacle would not fit underneath. Water splattered our feet when we brushed our teeth, and the tiny trough on the floor which carried the waste alongside the wall, under the wooden gate and down the drain in the toilet, almost never was big enough to contain the flow, so that it overran and left a patchy design of dried residue on the rough floor.

The sitting room was interesting, too. It had a small window seat covered with a carpet and a brocaded bolster for each elbow. The floor which had appeared wavy the night before was, in the light of day, more than wavy. It sagged and dipped and the beautiful carpets actually did seem to have motion. They covered a floor so worn in spots that the dirt foundation showed through, but the carpets appeared none the worse for it. They were already old as carpets go, but the colors were vivid still, and age and use had only made them prettier. The bright blue cupboards Hayat was stuffing could be opened from either side of the two rooms. The carpentry was crude and the wood roughly hewn, their iron latches were old and heavy and their big keys would not turn in the locks until the doors were propped up from below. The locks themselves were also installed upside down, a phenomenon so common in the Middle East that it ceased to be one. The bed platforms under each window wall were now in daytime great Oriental couches covered with carpets and gaudy pillows and the narrow windows set along the outside walls were numerous but had, alas, no glass. The only view out was through shutters levered upward or downward or straight out, depending on where you wanted to look.

All ceilings were high and walls were thick. Wind roared and whistled constantly through the paneless shutters, in one side and out the other, slamming doors that were not hooked and pulling out both hook and plaster of those that were. They told me there were whistling snakes, too, but I never saw any and only pretended to hear them.

For breakfast that first day we had crispy flat soda bread and a softer flat dark bread which was coarse and chewy. We had *gishta,* the creamy, crusty product which forms on the top of boiled milk cooling in a kettle, and black honey from Hadhramaut in southern Arabia, tinned butter, quince jam, white goat cheese, and tiny green olives from Lebanon (distinguished by the split up their middle) which we scooped from a crock of lemon-seasoned oil. Delicious, but we had to fight the flies for it, and the mosquitoes which had holed up during the night in the dark corners under the table now started their day by coming out to breakfast on me. My imported blood appealed to them, and Zainab got me one of her cotton *shershifs* to wrap around my legs for protection. That *shershif* was henceforth folded at my place like a napkin.

Because the dust and sand and wind made any day a cleaning day, that morning as most mornings we heard the *swish-thud, swish-thud* of the Tukroony* handbrooms as the maids swept on hands and knees from one end of each room to the other. Before we finished our breakfast the children, who had long since had theirs, were at their lessons and we could hear them and their teacher, Eustaz Aish, in the adjacent room intoning

* The name for a certain area and tribe in Africa.

verses from the Koran. Zainab's Hussein topped the list of family students, followed by Essam and Abdullah who were the only two of Hayat's five children, aged nine months to seven years, old enough then to have regular lessons.

After breakfast each lady had some private mid-morning activity, praying, writing letters in her room, sewing, instructing servants on the day's activities or meals, but Hayat had me under her wing and returned to my room to finish unpacking. She had wanted to give Hamida a bath but the child had dropped off to sleep and the idea was dismissed until Hayat got the welcome idea I might like one. There had been no sign of a bathtub, but the suggestion delighted me and even mild approval was all Hayat needed to shift into high gear. She clapped her hands for her maid, dashed off with me at her heels to get towels, soap, cologne, talcum powder, and something that resembled an over-sized Shredded Wheat biscuit. She marched me up one hallway, down another, through an arch, into one tiled room and then another with a dome that was like nothing I had ever seen. Niches and arches made up the character of the place and painted cherubic faces peered down from walls and ceiling. A single brass faucet protruded from the wall, and off to the side was a tiny cubicle for changing clothes. The tiled floor was bare except for one short-legged stool and an oversized tin cup. One wall was emitting steam and I stood flabbergasted at the overall effect. I could hear water bubbling somewhere and it almost didn't amaze me when I learned that the wall itself contained a well filled from the other side and heated by a wood-stoked fireplace below it.

So fascinated, I wondered almost as an afterthought where one bathed and with what. Surely not in the tin cup or under the brass faucet! As if to answer my question Hayat's maid appeared with three buckets, of which one was empty and two full of cold water. Hayat filled the empty one from the hot-water wall, and took the *mograf*, the big tin cup, to mix and splash water in and out of the three pails, spilling in more hot water from the faucet, testing, feeling, changing her three pails' contents with all the intensity of a timpanist working over his drums. Then she turned to me, putting the tiny stool near the buckets, and said, "Okay, come now! Sit!" Well, I certainly had not bargained for that, but it was clearly her intention to bathe me herself and I had no choice.

I sat naked on the stool while steam swirled around me, the painted cherubs watched, and I was soaped and scrubbed raw with the Shredded Wheat biscuit, otherwise known as a *loofa,* a spongelike tropical gourd. After half drowning me with her pitiless bucket rinsings, Hayat finished the deluge with cologne and powder and was as soaked as I was. This was only partly due to steam perspiration; the rest could be attributed to her utter abandon in hoisting those water pails. As for me, I was squeaky clean now, and Hayat, with this mission accomplished, was already looking for new worlds to conquer. What a way to establish rapport with one's new in-laws.

Chapter 6

ALI'S FOUR-DAY TRIP to Riyadh became eighteen instead, so I spent my first few weeks in Arabia without him. There I was with an instant family I had never seen before and there they were with a foreigner come to be one of them, and we couldn't even talk to each other. Everything was new to me — new, different, frustrating. It had been easy to say I would accept the need to be veiled, but I had not been prepared for the confinement I felt as we lived each day within room walls, within house walls, within garden walls. The one man we did have around, Mohamed, was gone most of the time, and we only saw Uncle Yousuf for an occasional greeting or a short visit, although he lived on the same grounds in a separate guest house. I felt so cooped up that I could hardly stand it, and I found it hard to believe that my life now revolved around women and children and that there was really no out-of-the-house place to go.

Men with men, and women with women, that was the way it was, and unaccustomed as I was to the social separation of the sexes, I fussed and fumed about it. Every time Mohamed had a separate meal table set up in the house for him and his friends, I angered; and squinting through the wooden shutters of my bedroom at the older men of Uncle Yousuf's group who joined him each and every day for talk, tea, coffee, backgammon, chess, and meals — I called them "the regulars" — I could almost wish a pox on them for what I considered usurpation of the garden below. If it weren't for those men, I thought, we could walk outdoors and roam through the orchard (all within the confines of our walls, to be sure, but at least outdoors), but only occasionally did we have that privilege. It wasn't granted to us specially; it would just happen that the regulars would meet elsewhere that day and Uncle Yousuf was always considerate in sending word that the garden would be free to enjoy if we wanted to.

Wanted to? He could never have known how much! I longed for just a pane of glass somewhere, anywhere, in that big rambling house — longed for a clear view out of just one window. Those shutters jailed me and I resented the barred view they gave me of the world outside. Any release from that house, even temporary, was welcome, and from the time dear Uncle Yousuf started his day, and mine, calling mightily for his manservant ("Ya Awad, Ya Aaaaawad!") until the time I crawled onto my stone bed to sleep, I pondered and ached for my lost freedom. Never, never again would I take it for granted.

We had activities, of course, which were useful and gratifying, companionable and fun. The Arabian women and I established far more readily than one would imagine a rapport and compatibility that worked for us in spite of our difficulties. But freedom is special. It is the element mixed with everyday duties and pleasures that makes the whole tolerable and enjoyable, and in Arabia, we lacked freedom. We women sewed, cared for our children, cooked up a pot of something now and then, made jam, talked, played games and wrote letters, but we were not free to come and go. Visiting offered an outlet, but it just meant exchanging the confines of our own rooms for the confines of those of some other lady. A male had to get us a car, a male had to drive us, and in between, cloaked and veiled from the time we left our door until we reached the upstairs parlor of whomever we were visiting, we had no contact with anyone or anything. We were the original "in-group," and our particular in-group usually got its kicks from watching the goings-on in the streets from our upstairs windows.

The living room windows offered the army barracks across the street at the intersection where desert road and town met. The tearoom looked down on the gates of the city, and the dining room had a longer view of the city walls and the street leading to the town well. Our bedrooms on the other side of the house looked out over the enclosed garden, where a plodding gardener could sometimes be seen walking his primitive plow down one row, lifting it, and walking slowly back to start another row. Nothing ever seemed to grow there and every time I saw him I wondered why he only plowed in one direction, but maybe it made sense to him, and if I could believe that, then I was truly making progress.

The army recruits who drilled in the desert enclosure across the street were obviously new at the game. The Saudi government had recently brought in foreign advisers to teach and train troops, and Taif was one of the training centers. Most of the soldiers we saw were barefoot Bedou whose long hair fell in thick curls beneath their checkered *ghutras*. The army had put these men into trousers for the first time in their lives and anyone watching could tell they were uncomfortable in their new attire. We saw one fellow who must have been having an unusually trying time adjusting to the hang of things; he was marching through his maneuvers with his pants on backward!

From the windows on the city-gate side the one thing you could always count on getting was sand in your eyes. The dust never got to settle there because of the constant stream of Bedou, townsmen, autos, soldiers, trucks, donkeys, and camels; and once in a while even a woman could be seen — a veiled

Hejazia with a cape around her, or a Nejdia whose headdress was part of the long cloak sweeping the sand in a trail behind her. High-spirited horses belonging to the army put on a show morning and evening as their cavalry grooms rode or drove them to water, and the house shivered and shook as they galloped by — proof that I had not been hearing things after all that first morning when I thought I heard thundering hoofs.

One of my first-learned obligations was to keep a daily lookout for the water carriers. The other women knew to stay out of sight when strange men were around, but I consciously had to remember the necessity of doing so. The water carriers, balancing two ten-gallon water tins on a shoulder pole, shuffled upstairs in their peculiar running gait crying "Tareek, tareek" * to let us know they were in the house, but at least twice I either did not hear them or wasn't thinking and got myself caught in the open between rooms. The only thing I could and did do was hide behind the hall door until the coast was clear, and I was properly furious with myself the rest of the day for allowing myself to be reduced to such evasive tactics. It hurt my pride to have to hide from men and I tried always to avert it by staying clear of any area where men for the moment held priority.

There were so many things to learn that my thought for the day, every day, was that I'd never make it. And things had to be bad if one day I was reduced to amusing myself by counting all the mosquito bites on my two legs. As it happened, I forgot about being amused when I passed the one-hundred mark and went to my room and cried the rest of the day. Flies were even more frustrating. I couldn't bear to see them on our food so I was a two-armed windmill flailing at them, particularly at mealtimes. When no food was around they picked on people as the next best thing and were so persistent they almost had to be plucked off. They liked to settle around the eyes, and when stronger than usual winds drove them inside in ever-increas-

* "Make way, make way!"

ing numbers the battle with them was fierce. The stronger the wind the more flies, but since wind and flies were constant in varying degrees it was actually their permanency rather than force or number that shook my nerves.

The air was dry, too, so dry that our lips and the knuckles on our hands cracked and bled, a condition no amount of hand lotion or slave could prevent or cure. We got some amusement from the wind, though; it made our nostrils so dry and at any given time we could whistle through our noses, and Hayat and I loved to get two-note duets going which we played back and forth until it made us laugh too hard to blow.

Games not so dependent on the whims of nature included our favorite, carom. Its board was placed on a pillow on the floor and we shot the red and green rings into corner pockets for hours on end. Hayat and Zainab were expert players and they taught me, the novice, while Mother, well, she played more to amuse the rest of us than for her own enjoyment. She could never get her fingers and hand in the right position to make a proper shot, and when she thought we weren't watching she scooted the marker in, pushing it all the way to the pocket with her thumb. We always caught her at it, and although she feigned indignation, she didn't fool us — we knew she did it to give us a laugh. There was a certain amount of skill in carom and a good game was a challenge, but most of all I remember the hours we spent playing it as times of great good fellowship.

Our most lived-in room was the tearoom. There we played carom or cards, talked, sewed, and cared for the younger children during the day. The old brass charcoal-burning samovar bubbled from early morning until night and another familiar sound came from the other much-used fixture, the ancient-looking but brightly efficient hand-cranked Singer sewing machine on which the women turned out clothing for their men, dresses for themselves, and various garments for the children and the maids. Somewhere in the room were always folded prayer rugs and *shershifs* ready for use, and scattered here and there or tucked under the bolsters of the *carawitas* were *mirwahas*, fans which looked like straw mats with bamboo handles. Since the heat didn't bother me as much as it did the others, I used the *mirwahas* for whacking flies.

I cannot remember any wall decorations, but never could I forget the pile of footwear which decorated the doorways. I learned to take my shoes off like everyone else when entering a room, but one of my pet annoyances was having constantly to step over and around the ever-present pile of assorted footgear thus left in the way. It was like running an obstacle course on days when we had visitors.

Other decorations were few, and there were no lamps in the rooms because they were only brought in, hissing and sputtering, as dusk fell. A radio connected to the big car battery which powered it sat across the doorway, and when possible the English news broadcast was tuned in for me. Listening to what was going on elsewhere made me feel more separated than ever from what I was already referring to as "that other world." The telephone we had wasn't much help, either. So far all it had done for me was impart the information that Ali was delayed again, and it was just as old-fashioned and produced more static than the radio.

It was the crank kind, both in its mode of operation and in the effect it had on anyone using it — getting the operator required many turns of the handle, more cranks to get a ring, and after all that the connection was generally so bad that the operator had to act as go-between. He first gave the parties a chance to make sense of the garbled words, then relayed the messages himself. The operators also made a good side business of informing clients of the airplane arrival times of loved ones returning from a trip. They made it their concern to find out who was on an incoming plane and when they would land, and anywhere from a quarter of an hour to an hour before arrival they put calls through to interested families. Cables giving the same information more frequently than not didn't arrive until after the person sending them did, so the voluntary information service was generally appreciated enough to warrant a good tip. As the number of flights going in and out of the main cities increased with the growing number of travelers, the most ambitious of these public servants no doubt tapped a substantial source of revenue.

One morning I walked into the tearoom and saw a strange lady, and when I bumbled the greeting she thought I was strange too. Her dress was different from any I had seen and her hennaed hair was striking by its brightness and the haphazard way it was semi-contained under an equally bright cloth tie. There were just the two of us in the room, and we must have made a great pair, for she was clearly not from Saudi Arabia and neither was I. Our attempts to be sociable to one another were not exactly scintillating. She probably wondered more about my presence there than I did about hers, because she at least could speak the language. When Mother came in with one of our maids who handed some bundles to the lady, I guessed that she was some poor soul who had come for a handout and that the bundles contained our contribution. But she was a lady peddler (in Saudi Arabia?) and the bundles contained her wares. She was Circassian and had probably come many years before to perform the Pilgrimage and like so many others decided to stay.

The goods she had were mostly notions and cheap toys, some bangles and trinkets, and one *buksha* full of materials ranging from cheap gaudy fabrics to fine broadcloth and even two cuts of Swiss lace. Partly from a real or imagined need, but mostly from the sheer pleasure of making a purchase on our own, we bought almost everything she had. I hadn't held even one piece of Arabian money since I arrived, so I didn't really "buy," but I picked out what I wanted and Mother doubtless paid for it. Since I had been in Arabia anything I needed or wanted was gotten for me by one of the others — or at least it was ordered by them, for we were dependent on our servants for the actual purchasing from the *suk*.

The procedure there was for shopkeepers to release goods to known house servants for home examination and those articles chosen for purchase were kept and the rest returned. In case nothing was suitable or desirable, the whole lot would be returned and another taken on approval. The poor fellow who did our buying rarely had the same taste we did, so he sometimes made the trip three or four times before he managed to return with something we liked. And he not only had to keep at it until we were satisfied, he had also to avoid coming under verbal fire for failing to inform us ladies of what was available and new in the *suk*. It was not to his advantage in any sense of the word to have us hear from outside sources that some new article or product was in town, or worse, that an interesting item had come and gone, bought up by other ladies, and was no longer available to us. Thus a good marketing servant learned as best he could the tastes of the women for whom he shopped, and he tried to keep them apace of the market and one step ahead of the other women in town.

Day in and day out situations formed in my association with my in-laws that went just so far and then were blocked by language difficulties. Laughter was the one thing we all understood and that's what we did when all else failed — we laughed. They tried to reach me and teach me and I tried to pretend we were both succeeding, but I always did something to give myself away and the joke was usually on me. It was natural that the words I heard the most were the ones I picked up the quickest, but some I had to lay right back down again because they were wrong.

I thought for the longest time that *ma fee ahad* meant I didn't have to veil — a case of wishful thinking if I ever saw one. I'd march out the door carrying my veil, not wearing it and thinking they surely must like to wear the veil if they did it even when it was not necessary, and then halfway through the garden my bare head would be noticed and everyone had to wait until I was properly attired. It really means "there is no one around," that we therefore didn't have to be ultra-careful in veiling, but never never did it mean, nor was it ever to be, that we ventured forth unveiled.

My ear, quick if nothing else, detected another expression which I took to be another of the many salutations because women said it to me when we met. "Mashallah,* tawila," they'd beam at me, and I'd silently mouth the words and practice them in my mind so one day I could say it too. Luckily, my tongue was not as quick as my ear, for the good ladies had just said I was tall. I cringed later thinking how upset an unusually short guest might have been if I had come out with a cheery "My, good gracious, how tall you are!"

When I did learn a good and authentic welcome word, *marrhaba* or *marrhabtain* ("double"), I tended to confuse them with the word *marruba*, which means "jam," so I guess telling ladies coming up the stairs "Oh jam, oh double jam" was just as bad.† In everyone's interest I learned it was better most of the time to keep my voice to a non-discernible murmur and to stay close to my in-laws whose adeptness at rescue grew in direct proportion to the number of my goofs. There were times, nonetheless, when I was on my own during visits and I was expected to answer the initial rounds of question-and-answer in the customary way. Expected, but not forthcoming, as I consistently broke up the traditional formulas of specific replies to specific questions and broke up the company in the process. "Fine, thank you," I said, instead of "thanks be to God," for whatever health I was in, leaving even more genteel niceties of speech like "I am

* *Mashallah* literally means "it is God's will" but in this sense is used rather as we use "knock on wood."

† It is customary to say in greeting: "Welcome, double welcome" (*-tain* is a derivative of *ithrain*, meaning "two").

fine, may God save you," or "fine, may God leave you, your husband, and your children" far into the future.

I have championed the cause of politeness for years but my
distinct impression was that Arabic had far too many polite ways
of saying essentially the same thing. It was discouraging to
stammer and falter through weeks of learning common expressions only to have new ones crop up constantly to stump me. I
had reached a smug point of self-satisfaction that I could at least
answer satisfactorily all questions on my health, when one good
soul from the inner regions asked me one day "Ish lonik?" *
and I couldn't even begin to tell her — I hadn't learned my
colors yet! And when a perfect stranger sailed up to me and
announced, "We've missed you," I could only think, how could
they have missed me if they didn't even know me? If I replied,
"I've missed you, too," I would have felt altogether too silly
and I was reasonably sure that was one time I shouldn't bring
God into it. Perhaps it was their way of including me among
them and their twinkle escaped me.

Everyone wanted to know about America but all I could do
at first was spread wide my arms and say, "Kabeerah." † This
seemed to confirm their own thoughts on the subject and they
asked the next question, had I *salemt?* Had I become a Moslem? My family told them quite openly that I had not, they
nodded understandingly, said, "Oh," and that was the end of
that. The fact never seemed to upset anyone, and if anything,
it was I who felt left out when everyone but me got up to pray.

Their prayer was fascinating to watch. Performed by faithful, sincere people, it is impressive and infinitely graceful.
Before prayer, all Moslems must first perform ablutions — washing face, feet, hands, and arms up to the elbows, after which the
women must also cover themselves from head to toe with the
light cotton *shershif*. This sheet of material is first laid over

* "What color are you?"
† "Big!"

the head and then draped around the entire body, the ends brought up and tucked tightly around the cloth bordering the face so that no hair shows. Prayer begins by pressing the open palms over the face and eyes to shut out all evil, an initial bow is made eastward toward Mecca, and the prayer sequence begins, bending, kneeling, touching the forehead to the ground, and resting back on the heels while the lips move in silent recitation.

The Moslem prayer is a physical as well as a mental exercise, and it is almost certain that while the prayer serves to help purify the soul the act also helps to keep the body limber. I watched women of eighty pray with nary a crack of their knee bones, while my much younger limbs went dead asleep just watching them. The *"carawita* tuck" they had all grown up with was giving me lots of trouble and I'd hate to know how much time I spent the first few weeks trying to untingle my legs without looking like a victim of St. Vitus's Dance.

Leaving the house to pay visits were, in Arabia, drastic new experiences. A car and driver had to be reserved; it required making up our faces and dressing our persons so we could then cover up with cape and veil; it meant sitting behind those veils in the back of a car while the driver took us through narrow streets to be deposited finally in front of a doorway and some ancient-looking stone stairs, which invariably smelled of antiseptic and were unbelievably uneven. Stretching to reach the high steps, we jarred our teeth by the shock of suddenly having our heels come down on an unexpectedly low one; and visibility was never improved by holding our veils out from the face, because the stairwell was always dark and we had to grope in any case. Met at the proper landing by a maidservant or lady of the house who took our veils and capes, we were led to the sitting room, where one by one the other ladies of the house joined us.

Hospitality is a genuine source of pride with the Arabs and

although the gestures, the speech, the actions involved in any visit conform to patterns long established, there is nothing false in them. Every visit the same things may be said, the same routines followed, the same niceties observed, and the traditional serving of coffee and tea is still a must, but the feeling of genuine welcome is always imparted and the visitor feels he is truly an honored guest.

Because of my dumbness and general inability to follow in depth anything that was going on, I did my best to stay in the background, which was ridiculous because, like it or not, I was very much to the fore. The presence of an *Americania* among them had evinced a certain curiosity and as I tagged along behind my Arabian family on visits I was anything but unobtrusive, and not altogether for the reason that I towered over most of them.

Hayat's practical jokes did the trick, her favorite being to tell a hostess the reason I didn't smoke their cigarettes was because I preferred the *shisha*. (All of them smoked American or British cigarettes or rolled their own, but I was supposed to smoke a water pipe!) *My* first inkling of it was when suddenly set squarely before me was a jumbled contraption of hoses, water chambers, colored tassels, and fuming coals which I was expected to do something with. I had never seen one — let alone smoked one — and the only words I could muster were a few well-chosen non-Arabic ones directed at Hayat, still prolonging my predicament by insisting my protests stemmed from nothing more than shyness, renewing their determination to "make me feel at home." I struggled to be at once lucid and diplomatic in my continued refusal, but what really astonished me was their surprise that I didn't smoke cigarettes and their utter lack of it when called upon to provide me a *shisha*.

From what I "saw" on our trips through town it was regrettable we could not get out and walk. There was much of interest and I would have liked to roam at will. Hole-in-the-wall shops whose owners perched crosslegged somewhere near their goods were bunched together in some areas, and there were small cafés whose tiny tables were set practically on the street, where men sat smoking small water pipes and sipping glasses of coffee. Boys with their *tobes* tied up around their waists wobbled down the street on bicycles too big for them, and here and there a henna-painted donkey or two jogged down the road, bells jingling around their necks and riders sitting far back on their mounts' softer backsides. Old and poorly constructed buildings gave a ramshackle appearance to some quarters but larger structures had many fine architectural features altered but not erased by time, and which attested to the fact that they had been good quality in their day. Artfully carved wooden doors and gates, etched still more by desert sun and wind, guarded walls and courtyards, and from any point in the city you could look up and trace the skyline of flat roofs, sun-baked turrets, domes, and the minaret tower which was always the highest point on the horizon.

Taking the place of windows were overhanging enclosed balconies made of filigreed wood, intricate and lacelike, ornamental from the outside but functional from the inside as a place for women to sit and watch the goings-on in the street without being seen from below. The local grapevine being what it was, we were reasonably sure our presence and identity had been noted and the news passed on, so we took care when sitting in these rooms to keep our voices and laughter low. The men in the streets knew us by our cars and drivers and if afforded the chance they let us know they knew. It pleased them to prove we weren't fooling them, veil or no veil, so they called our family name as we passed in the streets.

It was my contention that they were curious *because* of our veils, not in spite of them, but that didn't change our comportment. We always sat quite primly in the car, not daring to move our heads one way or the other and in unusually congested areas we were unusually sedate. Wending our way once through heavy pedestrian traffic, Mother suddenly exclaimed, "Well, for heaven's sake," when her veil slipped back, exposing a bare portion of her lower chin and neck. When out of a wall of black all you can see is a chin and a collared neck the effect can be, and was, disastrously funny. Hers had slipped, but we almost blew ours off laughing while Mother, restored to anonymity, kept saying, "Well, for heaven's sake, girls, is this the time for laughter?" Well, yes, it was, and none of us calmed down until arrival at our destination forced us to compose ourselves.

When we three younger women set off to do something on our own, Mother was always fearful. She never stopped us, but she did caution us. She tried to tell us one afternoon it was too late for a drive, but we were fed up with the house and went anyway. Our driver Saleh took us some miles out in the desert where we left the car and walked around while he waited far enough away to be out of our immediate view but close enough to hear if we needed him. I gathered some desert plants which were scrawny and dry but interesting as survivors of the attempts of desert winds to beat them down and we, interesting survivors of the same thing, munched the few pastries we had. When the sun went down everyone prayed except me (I thought a prayer) and the peace that is the desert at dusk spread over us. We were loathe to leave, but they'd have a search party out after us if we stayed too long, so we donned our outer garments and started home.

We didn't go far. There was no real road and it was easy for the driver to misjudge the terrain in the dim light of early evening, so very soon we were stuck in the sand. Saleh had to stay at the wheel, leaving the job of getting behind the car and pushing to us girls. Picture if you can the silhouette we made: the automobile down to its rear hubcaps in sand, the Arab driver behind the wheel, and three black-caped females straining with all their might to dislodge the car and at the same time keep their cloaks about them.

Back and forth, forth and back we rocked the car, wheels

spinning each time Saleh gunned the engine, until our mighty final push gave the tires the needed traction and the car not only shot forward but it kept right on going for more stable ground. The three of us, already leaning far forward in our effort, suddenly had nothing to hang onto so we ended, one two three, flat on the ground with our faces in the sand. We lay there laughing till we cried. Then we glanced up to see Saleh leaping like a jack rabbit toward us over no man's land. We jumped up, sandy and wrinkled, to let him see we were all right, because the poor fellow had had the fright of his life when he looked back to see his three charges lying prone and still in the sand. He was beside himself with fear that we had injured ourselves and downright petrified about what would happen to him if we had. He was the only quiet one in the group as we continued home without further incident, and he would not be cheered.

Our hilarity, though, was full-blown by the time we reached the house. It was decided that if we were going back in the house at all we would do so barefoot, which we did. Carrying our sand-filled shoes we traipsed out of the car and up to the gate, through the yard and up the stairs, refusing on the way to explain our disheveled state or our crazy actions. Odds were that before we reached the third landing the servants would know the complete story anyway, so we hastened to present ourselves to Mother so she could see for herself we were all right — not very sane perhaps, but safe and sound. She was a worrier at heart, but our silliness would dispel any concern. She pleased us by doing exactly what we surmised she'd do when she got her first glimpse of us; she clapped one hand over her mouth and said: "Well, for heaven's sake, have you all gone crazy?"

With the possible exception of Saleh, the outing had done us all good, and our high spirits continued throughout the evening. Dinner was good as usual and I was beginning to notice that dishes I particularly liked were showing up regularly on our table. After dinner Hayat treated us to one of her movie-story enactments, playing all parts with great dramatic flair, and in-between times I helped Zainab's sewing efforts by ripping seams. Zainab sewed like the girl in the fairy story did her weaving — she worked all day and ripped it all out by night. But when finally she finished, the something she made was perfect and exquisite.

With all the noise Hayat was making it was hard to see how anyone could relax, but Mother would have her after-dinner snooze on the *carawita* if the world was falling down around her ears. That night she was lying as usual with her glasses off and her eyes closed, her Turkish coffee cooling by her side with the saucer placed upside down over the tiny cup, when Hayat cut her dramatization short, peered over toward Mother and said: "Well, you cute little thing, you!"

Mother wasn't all that asleep, and assuming rightly that Hayat's talk was directed toward her, she peered back and said, "What's the matter with you, girl?"

It was even worth putting her glasses back on. When she did, she discovered that Hayat was not looking at her but at a point directly behind her. She turned and there on the *carawita* pillow was a tiny mouse looking straight back at her. Before the poor beastie could blink, Mother was already standing on the highest point of the farthest *carawita* on the far north wall yelling, "Cute little thing, my eye — how can you say cute? Blindness in its eye!"

"Why, Mother, it's a tiny little thing."

"Tiny or big," Mother replied. "Get it out of here without a lot of empty talk!"

So the mouse was chased away and maybe even killed, after which none of us could think of fun, so off to bed we went. Dear old Rogaiya plodded in with my warm milk shortly after I went to my room and my simple "thank you" was a kind of thank you to them all. It had been a good day.

Other days were not so good. There wasn't much I could do

for them — and precious little for myself — except try to fit in better, but in those early weeks I was never quite sure in any given situation just what that entailed. Routine duties and habits in households such as ours were long established, so it remained for me, the only one foreign to it, to settle down and become part of the whole. My place in the life there was the same as the other women's, but for me the sameness was strangeness. Those near and dear could only try to help during those times when I couldn't help myself, when near panic swept over me when I encountered difficulty in communicating a need, in fulfilling a request, following an action or understanding a conversation.

The family did the most they could do in shifting their lives around to include me, but I balked on the whys and wherefores and was not always able to be comfortable in the place provided for me. Sometimes I got downright nasty, and once I flatly refused to go to dinner. The real reason was that I felt I could not face the same trip down the same hall, sit at the same place at table in the same room, and go through the same after-dinner routine, going to bed afterward looking forward to another morrow which would be just like today. But I couldn't tell them that, even if I had the vocabulary, so I just said I was tired of fighting mosquitoes — true enough — and to prove it I sat inside my mosquito net, which Rogaiya had already rigged for the night.

I must have looked ridiculous sitting there and I felt ridiculous, too, when Mother and Zainab and Hayat came bouncing in to join me, followed by a servant carrying our dinner on a huge tray which was set in the middle of my bedroom floor. Not wishing to be fed alone in my "cage," I gave in to the powers that be and came out to be part of things again. We sat around the tray and made great good fun out of a potentially sticky situation, while I silently admired their super-finesse and thought I might make it yet. Nowadays, and it isn't quite clear why, this incident reminds me of something that happened to Joha, a character famous in Arab folklore. The story goes like this:

One day Joha was given charge of ten donkeys to drive to market and started off on his journey riding the lead donkey. Everything went fine until he turned to count the donkeys and discovered he had only nine. Perturbed, he jumped down to the ground to count them again and this time there were ten. Much relieved, he remounted and continued his way, but farther on he checked again, and again there were only nine. As before, he jumped down to recount them and happily found ten. He then decided to continue his way on foot. "Better to walk to market," said he, "than to lose a donkey."

Chapter 7

IF TAIF WEATHER kept our hands in a state of chronic red-
ness and dryness, it was nothing compared to what happened to
them the day we helped Mother make her famous quince
preserves. Anyone who has tried to get a knife through raw
quince will agree that somewhere in its lineage someone
grafted in a little concrete. It took us the better part of the
day to peel, halve, and quarter what seemed like half a bushel
of fruit, the better part of the night to cook the stuff, and the
better part of the week to unkink our sore fingers. Mother
tended the simmering, bubbling fruit from a short-legged stool
set in the least windy corner of the big hallway, and the noisy
dafur — the very same stove I had such trouble with my first
night — could be heard but not seen, it was so dwarfed by the
huge kettle above it. I was volunteer official taster when
Mother ladled syrupy chunks onto a saucer to test, and since it
took an inordinately long time for the mass to become chewy-
soft and apple-red I must have eaten a pound before it was
even done.

Not long after the quince session I awoke once more to the
sound of the *dafur* hissing in the hallway and thought: Oh no,

not again! We still have three gallons! But it wasn't quince; this time Mother was boiling goat cheese, a particular kind of goat cheese available only from the Bedou and only at certain times of the year (something to do with the nannies dropping their kids, I think). Mother bought a basketful — one of those big floppy African baskets — and since the cheese tended to be full of animal hairs and grit when we got it, she trimmed it clean, cut uniform patties of it, and plopped them piece by piece into boiling salted water. Rubbery at first, boiling softened but didn't crumble the cheese and purified it in the process. Baskets and bowls and trays of cheese in varying stages of preparation surrounded Mother, and off to the side was a large aluminum tray where the finished cheese cooled. The process was continuous until the last morsel was scooped from the milky liquid in the kettle and, to finish, Mother pressed *habba soda,* black bits of spice whose name means just that, into each warm, soft piece. I know Mother saw that I was not packing all of the cheese into jars when I helped, because there was a plateful of it on my bedstand when I retired to my room that night. Even though my enjoyment of the cheese was silent — it squeaked but it didn't crunch — Mother noticed that I liked it and in good Arab tradition made the thoughtful gesture of sending me more.

It must have been while bargaining for the cheese that Mother remembered that the Bedou of Taif had, in days past, performed a kind of pageant called a *gaysa,* a very special Bedouin theater performed by this tribe. Awad, our major-domo, was sent to inquire if it was still being given as a spectacle, and he was successful in engaging a local troupe to perform for us as a special favor. The *gaysa* was to be held at our house and it was so special Mother planned a real gala around it. She invited many guests but was particularly pleased that I would be getting to see it and promised it would be like nothing I had ever seen.

How right she was! I fell sick the night before with a raging fever and on the big day was confined to my bed while everyone else was actively involved in preparations for the big affair. The Bedou arrived just before dark, started the charcoal fires to tighten their drumskins, and made a final check of their costumes before setting the stage on one of the large side balconies. They beat a few warm-up rhythms, and it annoyed me when they stopped. But it wasn't long before the beat was established and became an all-penetrating constant which varied only in its ever-increasing tempo. Those drums could always affect me, and whether it was my fever or something else that magnified their unrelenting insistence on my very being, I soon knew I couldn't stand solitude any longer and, guided by the sound waves, staggered shakily out to join the party. My family jumped up in shock when they saw me, feverish and disheveled, in the doorway, and I stood there in shock too at the scene that met my eyes.

Like a vision conjured up by my delirium, the balcony whirled with color and action as strangely garbed creatures with human bodies and animal heads stalked and were stalked by sword-wielding hunters dressed in the old styles of the desert. With the drums beating an even faster signal, they leaped and struck at each other and sometimes fell. Softening the drums but heightening the effect were tambourines and tiny brass finger cymbals played in perfect accompaniment to the stage action by a swaying, stomping group of players off to one side. Between the various acts depicting the hunt and the pitting of human cunning against animal cunning, the drummers stopped to hold their drums over heat rising from braziers of red-hot coals, heating and testing, heating and testing, and I was amazed how this changed the drums' resonance. Satisfied at last with their drums, another act would begin.

I have no idea how long it lasted. All I know is that, seated and bundled up against the night air, I sat transfixed, all conception of time and place lost to me. Completely and fascinatingly caught up in the extraordinary hum of whirling bodies, merging colors and shadows, and stirred by the soul rhythms and musical sounds, I stayed until the performance was over and wouldn't go even then, discouraging all attempts to return me to my bed because I wanted to see the people under those extraordinary costumes who had performed so splendidly for us. Doubtless the *gaysa* is now truly a thing of the past and I daresay that, thanks to my mother-in-law, I am one of the few westerners, and maybe the only one, to have seen this Bedouin spectacle. It lived up to all the promise Mother gave it and I would not have missed it for anything.

For many days afterward I was confined to my bed, and I'm told I was a very bad patient. I had high fever and delirium and upset everyone around me by dripping great tears of self-pity when I was unable to communicate my feelings, my hurts, and my needs. Mother cried, too, turning away from my bedside saying, "Dear God, I can't understand the girl," and when Hayat and Zainab tried to help me I fought their ministerings, and babbled and ripped off the medicated throat packs they applied just as soon as I thought I could get away with it.

More family had arrived from Jeddah while I was sick and they occupied the upper floors of our house. All came to see me, and it's certain I greeted more ladies from my bed than I ever had before. The most faithful of my visitors was a grand old lady we called Steta Oma, or "Big-sister-aunt," the title given to the oldest and therefore the highest ranking aunt in the family hierarchy. She, God rest her, visited me daily in spite of her age and the fact that she could hardly walk. A servant had to help her down the stairs each day, setting a chair at each landing for her to rest on until slowly, slowly she made her way to my bedside.

Steta Oma's dress was the old kind, long-sleeved and to the floor, and her snowy headdress almost but not quite covered her white hair. Her eyes were deep brown and I always thought I detected in them an almost urgent wish to exchange real talk with me so we could tell each other what we knew of the world. We were both new experiences for each other but were limited, alas, to exchanging formal niceties, which I couldn't even do properly.

Each afternoon she had her servant place her chair next to my net tent, reached under to grasp my hand, and said ever so gently: "Kaif halik alyom? Inshaalah taiyibah. Salamtik." *
I knew enough to give thanks to God in reply to the first two phrases, but not having been sick in Arabic before I made the guess that *salamtik* is a way of saying "get well soon," which it is, meaning literally, "May you be saved." "Ashkourik," † I'd say, smiling back, and then she would nod her head and chuckle.

This chuckle of hers always happened, along with a kind of approbation in her nod, as if to assure me that no matter what I said she would understand. It amused her that I didn't turn her wish around, as I should have, to ask God to save her and give her long life. In her already many years it was probably the first time she had ever heard anyone answer these expressions incorrectly and she got a big kick out of it. In later years when I visited her in the "Big House" in town in Jeddah and said all the right things at the right times, we could have been any two Arabs meeting — that special something was gone. True, she had become very forgetful by then and lived mostly in the past where certainly I had played no part, but we were never as close as we had been at first when our only line of communication was human warmth.

Ali finally returned from Riyadh and walked into my room just as they, not I this time, were taking off another throat compress. It would have been hard to say who looked worse, he

* "How are you today? Well, I hope, please God. May you be saved."
† "I thank you."

or I. To all appearances he had not shaved since he left Jeddah, and I shuddered and said, "You're not the man I married!" He started to ask how I had gotten along but detected storm warnings and tacked immediately, assuming rightly that any and all answers would inevitably lead to mention of his glaring absence from my side when I had needed him most. He told me instead stories of his own rather unusual experiences in the palace in Riyadh.

I wasn't exactly regaled with his first one, which had to do with someone offering him his pick of "fine, young slave girls" for his very own, but when my hollow laughter died down he told another quite delightful and completely credible story about how he alone had usurped the entire palace's total supply of bath water for one whole day. We could imagine him doing that, because in some respects Ali, who had left his country as a youngster to go to school, didn't know much more about living in Arabia than I did.

At the old mud palace in Riyadh he had to depend on the servants to take him here and there, guide him to his appointments and take care of his needs, and when he couldn't find a place to bathe he asked the valet. He should also have asked how to take a bath, because when he walked into the bathhouse he thought the two supply barrels, one filled with hot water and the other with cold, were all for him. Thinking how nice, he climbed into one for a thorough soaking and then nimbly out and into the other to rinse. Leaving the bathhouse, he saluted cordially the assorted ambassadors and privy counselors waiting their turn as they told him, "Naiman," the polite thing to say in Arabia when someone has freshly bathed or shampooed. I bet they could have eaten their words when it was discovered Ali had given both barrels the treatment and there would be no more baths for anyone until the barrels were scrubbed down and filled twenty-four hours hence with the next day's supply. One of the men in line was His Excellency

Shaikh Hafiz Wahba, then Saudi Arabian Minister and later Ambassador to the Court of St. James's. He was an old-timer in the country and it was he who, during the *majlis** that day, took Ali aside and told him, "Look, son . . ."

Returning with Ali to Taif were Shaikh Ibrahim and Prince Faisal, and in the weeks that followed both of these men sent me their unopened copies of the magazines *Life, Time, Post,* and *Asia,* which my eyes and mind devoured and practically memorized before I returned them. A bouquet came each day from Shaikh Ibrahim's gardener, rosebuds, jasmine, and pretty, small geraniums bound so tightly with string wound all the way down the stems that the clustered tops formed a tight pattern of color with all the fragrance of Arabian perfume. The flowers always came with the message, "If there is anything I can do for you, *tahadomarik,*" † and each time I thought, here is a friend, a close friend, and a good friend, yet so far away in this Arabian society. The offer was there and he meant it, but not much could be done by him or anyone else to get me out of the prison of Arabian customs.

With things as they were, a simple stroll or a simple ride became a thing of joy, and once the family and I picnicked in a borrowed private garden oasis where our desert-oriented eyes feasted on the miracle of a running brook. This was the first real picnic we had had since I had been in Arabia and it made me almost as happy for the children as I was for myself. Places to go and things to do were limited for them, too. Except for a few card games and marbles on the living room floor, their leisure seemed terribly aimless to me and I determined to teach them group games and show them the fun of physical competition within the range of their years. So it was that at the picnic we played blindman's buff, drop-the-handkerchief, pussy-wants-a-corner, and a wild game of hide-and-seek in

* Court audience.
† "Your wish is my command."

which even the adults participated. In foot races the older children magnanimously allowed the younger children to win. Searching in that garden spot for throwing stones for hopscotch was as much fun as the game. Only one game got out of hand, an impromptu one of popping watermelon seeds at each other. Also not in the plan was an unscheduled fifty-yard dash to reach Hamida when an errant donkey suddenly appeared at one end of the garden and started galloping toward the spot where she lay sleeping in her carriage. We headed it off all right, but were unsuccessful in talking it into giving rides to the kids and consoled ourselves by eating another piece of Abu Ali's delicious Lebanese pastry called *konafa*.

Abu Ali was Mother's Lebanese cousin, a mountain of a man with a big booming voice, marvelous humor, and talents in commerce, story-telling, slipping across borders and other intrigue, and cooking. At the picnic he had to stay pretty much in the background because there were women guests from other families, but we could see him back there helping prepare the dozens of things we had for lunch that day. When we sampled his dessert, a delectable pastry fashioned from mild white cheese and honey and golden shredded wheat on trays so big they had to be baked at the local baker's oven, I could hardly believe it was his handiwork. Abu Ali looked like a professional wrestler and had a reputation for other things, like exciting escapades and dangerous cloak-and-dagger ventures during the 1940s when Lebanon was struggling for independence, so it was interesting to know he could also turn out works of art, which his *konafa* certainly was. In the ensuing years Abu Ali was to become one of my favorite people.

I thought the picnic was our ration of excitement for a while, but not so. Excitement of a new kind came a few days hence in the person of a Turkish lady named Shamsia Hanam, a member of Prince Faisal's palace household and a longtime friend of Ali and his family. She had heard Ali was back and came to see him and his "bride" as soon as she could hitch a ride. We were rocked out of bed by the sheer force of the commotion she caused when she got there early one morning. It was unbelievable and so was her name — "Lady Parasol" — and when I went out to see what was happening everybody in the house, mistresses and servants alike, was congregated in the hallway. The noise she generated was in itself sufficient to convince me that she was special and Ali, having heard snatches of words expressing her horror that we were still in bed, hastened to go out and greet her before we all got pulled under by the tow of her tidal-wave personality.

It was natural she should greet Ali as the golden-haired child she thought him to be, but I was unprepared for the extent of her straightforward, no-holds-barred exuberance over everything in general, including me, the bride. Whereas most ladies I met in Arabia held back not exactly in shyness but, shall we say, in curiosity about me, Shamsia Hanam clapped me on the back and boomed some earthy remark, lost on me to be sure, but causing everyone else to giggle their heads off and "forget" to translate. Moving along with her until she hauled herself onto the *carawita* in the tearoom in a manner anything but prim or proper, we got a volley of questions fired at us, but she never waited for answers. That suited me fine! She would have ripped me and some of my more famous replies apart!

She was fair, round of face and body, and her age might have been forty or it might have been sixty. For the next ten hours we survived an ordeal of hectic fun that left us limp and enervated. One felt busy just sitting with her. She kept conversation and people moving at a frantic pace, maintaining a running banter with the maids who brought her tea and coffee all day and with the few of us who tried to match her whim for whim and activity for activity. Complaining about the way we rolled cigarettes, she snatched the tin of fixings and rolled her own. She cheated shamelessly at the card games we started in desperate efforts to get some order in our day. And her Arabic was atrocious. I was no one to talk, but hers was not improved by the fact that although a set of false teeth had been provided for her she much preferred to go toothless. Indeed, part of her fame lay in the fact that she could and did tackle the toughest meats with her bare gums and enjoyed with relish anything and everything which required thorough mastication by any of the rest of us. She was fond of telling stories, as we learned throughout the day, but I am certain she never told them the same way twice.

When Ali joined us, something he could do because they were friends since he was a child so she didn't veil from him (and probably wouldn't have anyway), things really started popping. She had just been fooling around before. The two of them kept a steady stream of mock insults directed at one another, which usually ended by Shamsia Hanam screaming at Ali that he had no respect for his elders, and his yelling back, "Aha, so you've finally admitted your age!" To quiet things, we hoped, someone suggested a game of carom, but the skill those two contributed was that of educated toes rather than finger dexterity. She started it, naturally, surreptitiously dumping loose men in pockets near her by pushing them in with her toes, or when her opponent's piece landed in the nets her toes sneakily pushed from under until the offending piece slipped back onto the board. When Ali beat her at her own game she called foul and the ensuing verbal fencing provided the best entertainment we had had in a long time. We were exhausted when she left, but she galloped downstairs seemingly just as fresh as when she had started our day for us.

Life was picking up interest with the picnic and Shamsia Hanam and the children's enthusiasm over things to do and constant insistence that we do them, but all was topped by the dinner invitation Ali received from Prince Faisal, which included, wonder of wonders, me! When Ali said both of us, we, had been invited I could not believe it. The short time I had spent in Arabia had been sufficient to condition me to the idea that men and women do not mix socially — enough so that when we left the house together on the appointed night, he in his robes and I properly veiled and cloaked, I actually had a fear of being found out. Our driver took us through the dark streets of town and I was in a complete dither when we descended at the outer gate of Prince Faisal's palace. A doorman let us in and I, still veiled, felt first like the Count of Monte Cristo's black lady as we slipped through an inner door, upstairs and down a corridor and then, as I groped my way behind Ali who helped me as best he could, more like someone with a sack over his head being led to his doom. The servant showing the way waited for us to approach and then opened a door into a brightly lighted room. Prince Faisal was standing there, and after one startled look at my veiled face he burst into laughter.

"Why are you still veiled?" His Royal Highness said.

"Because my husband told me to," I said, pointing an accusing finger at Ali.

"Well, you don't have to cover here inside; you could have removed your veil as soon as you entered the building." He motioned us in and I heard him turn back to Ali and say, "Shame on you for being so strict."

My wraps (now I know where they got that word) were taken by a Sudanese servant and I was introduced to the other guests. Shaikh Hafiz Wahba, the very same who had missed his bath in Riyadh, was there; Dr. Ramesy, the doctor who had brought Ali into the world; my old friend Shaikh Ibrahim Sulaiman; and several Turkish gentlemen, in-laws of Prince Faisal. Princess Iffat, Faisal's wife, was still in Alexandria, where I had met her briefly during our stay in Egypt, so I was the only woman among all those distinguished gentlemen. What a twist that was from the previous weeks I had spent in

Arabia, and how great to be out in the big bad world again, even if once the evening was over I would have to retreat again. I felt like a school kid playing hooky on an outing organized by the principal, and I settled back to enjoy myself.

Sudanese waiters resplendent in their *galabeeyas* and turbans stood at assigned posts until dinner was announced, and then we dined at a table beautifully set with exquisite china and silver and ablaze with three gorgeous flower arrangements picked that day from the royal gardens. I was seated on the right of Prince Faisal, who read the printed menu to us before the first of eight courses was served, and I floated through it all as in a dream, giddy with the joy of being at a party instead of practicing purdah in the seclusion of my home. Arabia really sparkled for me that night, and I was pleased and forever grateful to Prince Faisal for planning the evening. Such high-level consideration proferred through friendship by this truly great and kind man did more than soften the bonds of his country's customs. It made me proud and I went home that night with the resolution to stop catching flies, as it were, and start catching a few of the marvels.

I knew I could not count on many parties like Prince Faisal's, but I was glad I had that experience before I attended my first big women's party, which we gave at our house in honor of Madame Ibrahim Sulaiman. All the prominent womenfolk in town were invited, and I anticipated even more new sights and sounds and observations.

The main job of food preparation was done by town cooks and bakers, but certain specialties were prepared at home and I helped when possible. We had no table large enough to accommodate the great number of guests so we placed a long white cloth on the floor, and I learned to set a table Arabian style by placing two plates, one on top of the other, a knife, fork and large spoon, two or three rounds of bread, and a napkin as big as a diaper at each place, but no water glasses. If a guest wants water or juice it is asked for at mealtime. Small dishes containing bread dips made of mashed garbanzos and sesame paste and another made of eggplant mixed the same way but seasoned with garlic, parsley, cumin and salt — and both kinds covered with oil — were spaced all over the table, with spinach and meat pastries, goat cheese, cracked wheat and meat patties, puffy crispy fried shrimp crackers, black and green olives from Lebanon, small saucers of *doogoose*, a fiery hot pepper relish, flaky cheese puffs, raw beet and turnip pickles and spicy pickled lemon halves (more of Mother's specialties we hadn't yet helped to make), lemony salads of diced fresh cucumbers, tomatoes, and carrots and parsley. There, I thought, a real feast!

By then guests were arriving, clapping their hands on their way upstairs to announce their presence, and we went to meet and welcome them on the landing with many a greeting, many an over-the-shoulder embrace, and many a finger-tip-touch-and-kiss. First greetings over and capes and veils whisked away by maids, we crossed the hall, shoes were removed and left in the usual pile at the door, and the guests walked in to seat themselves in the salon, whose everyday look had miracu- -lously changed to one of bright brocades and fringe and shiny pillows. The slipcovers had been removed to reveal very Arabian-looking materials and I was delighted with the effect. Quantities of brass trays, cigarette boxes, and flower bowls, which were new to me, decorated the room and soon to join them was my old smoking favorite, the *shisha*. Several of them were brought in but this time none were for me.

Some of the elderly women had asked for them and I saw them actually being smoked for the first time. I watched enthralled as the complicated-looking contraptions bubbled and gurgled when the smoker inhaled from the wooden mouthpiece on the end of the colored hose which curled around the apparatus. The burner part, where a small mound of *toombac* rested on a few pieces of charcoal, reddened with each pull of smoke and the fruity odor — most good *toombac* contains dried apples or other fruit — insisted its way into our nostrils. Looking around, I was again envious of the Arab ladies' grace in tucking their feet under them or sitting crosslegged with ease, because I still lacked the necessary suppleness and had difficulty tucking my big feet anywhere. I always tried to find a wall corner to lean against, a better place for me anyway to watch and listen and be less conspicuous when I did the wrong things at the right times. It seemed a pity with all the interesting personalities around me that I had to sit there unable to get a decent conversation going. But lacking that and other common ground as we did, the guests and I still did not want to miss anything and it was downright comical the way we eyed each other but tried to pretend we weren't. At times like that it was a source of recurring pleasure to remind myself that despite my shortcomings, I was nonetheless one of the ladies of that Arabian house, and the thought still held enough of the incongruous in it to cause a wide grin to spread over my face each time it occurred to me. Then the good ladies who were watching smiled back and for the moment all was well with my world.

When lunch was called I filed in with the guests and gaped at the table I had left nearly ready a short hour before. I was totally unprepared for the display of food before me, even knowing as I did that some food was being catered. Two tremendous trays contained a whole lamb each, heads and all, and both roasts were stuffed and fairly bursting with macaroni and hard-boiled eggs and slivered almonds. Mounds of white rice laced with raisins and pine nuts stood next to mounds of saffron rice, and here and there were plates of okra stacked pod by pod with tomatoes in an artistic design. There were green beans stewed with lamb and tomato and onion, spinach, and squash, tomatoes, eggplant, and green peppers all stuffed with rice and ground meat. What a good thing we were eating on the floor! No table would have supported such quantity and variety. Mother was watching with undisguised pleasure my open-mouthed wonder and amazement at the assortment and beauty of the food on our party table, and I knew by the way she was watching that she had planned and hoped to surprise me in just the way she did.

Surprise followed surprise. For the first time in my life I saw people eat with their fingers, and I admit to being shocked. Some of the ladies went so far as to take something on their plates, try it, and return it to the serving plate if they did not like it. The same spoon was used for serving and eating so that a dish was dug into from all sides as the guests helped themselves, and some even ate directly from the platter. My stomach was already a bit queasy from staring at the lambs' eyes and having them stare back, but my in-laws carried me safely through the situation by demonstrating once more their ever-present concern and thoughtfulness for this American daughter of theirs. They made no comment, but they saw to it that the food I got came from an untouched side or a fresh platter, and this was much appreciated, because the food was sensational. Zainab feared for me when some after-dinner belching began but she needn't have. I was too busy stuffing myself to react negatively — which caused her to be pleased and me to be smug that I was making this passive sort of progress.

I was just getting to the point where I could identify all the goodies on my plate when some ladies surprisingly got up to leave. I remembered then the Arabs' custom to leave the table as soon as they are finished eating, never waiting for others to finish, but I hadn't known some women make it a practice to appear not hungry at parties and to toy with their food instead of eat it. They even go so far as to try to be the last one at table and the first to leave, and I think there were some like that at our party. Murmuring "Alhamdulilah," a grace said after rather than before the meal, they appeared to be satisfied (Zainab said they probably ate before coming) and left the room. I wasn't following that custom; I stayed on through the sponge cake and custard and sectioned pomegranates and cold sweet grapes and watched the servants remove what was left of the main meal to serve to those behind the scenes. Such lavish meals thus are not as wasteful as they might seem, serving the two necessary purposes of honoring the guest with a sumptuous display and feeding the rest of the household and drivers and personal servants accompanying the guests.

Mother had arranged for several old-time courtesies to be observed. Servants stood outside the dining room door with special brass basins and pitchers, soap and clean towels, and as each guest left she washed her hands and rinsed her mouth, which was very genteelly done. The basin had a very artistically perforated top, crescents and stars, through which the dirty water disappeared without ever being seen, a very fine point which impressed me. Mother kept an eagle eye on me during these proceedings and I thought then and still think that one of the main reasons she gave that party — besides the obvious one of feting a local personage — was to acquaint me in one fell swoop with many of their customs and traditions having to do with hospitality and hostessing.

And it wasn't over yet! After lunch, coffee and tea were served in the salon, and then a goodly number of our guests curled up on the *carawitas* or on the floor or off in a side room for a nap, and when the time came everyone prayed and we were soon all gathered together again. More coffee and more tea were served, and that was no surprise, but I was astounded when Insaaf, one of the least assertive *jarias* belonging to my mother-in-law, walked in swathed literally in a cloud of smoke. Except that it wasn't smoke; it was incense emanating from a small metal container she was carrying, which resembled a dome with holes in it. I watched bug-eyed as Insaaf stopped in front of each of the ladies and held out the fuming burner so the incense could be fanned toward her person with her hands. When it came my turn I did as I saw them do and thought up the bad pun that among other things that day I had been taught how to get properly incensed. My bug eyes became pop eyes when Insaaf placed the incense burner in the middle of the floor and one by one the ladies stepped up to it, raised their voluminous skirts to form a tent of sorts over the incense, and stood there shaking their clothing to allow the smoke to circulate freely underneath. That was the pièce de résistance of the whole party for me, and I bet it was for them, too.

The party began to break up when Insaaf returned with a big bottle of French cologne, but she didn't do anything spectacular with that. She just went down the guest line splashing a little in each upturned palm, and that, I learned, is the signal in any Arabian home that the party per se is over and that one may, if one wishes, feel free to leave, without specifically implying that he must. A very polite and very enjoyable way to end a meeting, and it was thus that ours ended.

Helping to put the *carawitas'* everyday slipcovers back on that night, I had the feeling I was doing the same thing to myself — slipping on the everyday covers of my existence. Back tomorrow to everyday living, I thought, and then I laughed out loud, and to whom could I tell why? For almost two months I had been living an extraordinarily strange existence for one of my background and already I dared consider it everyday? They had been hard, fascinating, unbelievable months where the only familiar occurrence was that day followed night, and when I awoke some mornings even that surprised me. I wasn't adjusted to life here — I just went along with it when I could and had a good cry when I couldn't. Or a good laugh when that was the greatest expedient for extricating myself or others or all of us from some predicament or malentendu. The family was wonderful; that was the main thing. They waited ever so patiently for me to come to grips with my problems with the veil and confinement and physical discomforts, and rejoiced with me when we had our many, many good moments. These became more frequent as I came to the realization that these people got along, and had for some time, with what they had and that their methods suited them and their life.

I could wish for a modern kitchen but I could not say that it would produce better food than their beds of coal did. I could decry the housecleaning methods and try to get the servants to do things my way, but if our beautiful carpets still looked the way they did after having been swept for years with simple straw handbrooms, then who was I to say my way was better? Piped water we did not have, but on a hot day the water in· the long-necked earthenware jugs tasted better than anything else and was pure and cold. And, I ask you, what modern bathroom ever had a functional hot-water wall and smiling cherubs to watch you bathe? I even came to prefer the stone-hard surface of my bed platform, it was that restful. And I didn't stay mad too long at the primitive old floor toilet because someone — I'm not sure who because no one confessed to having done it — had a sit-down one concocted especially for me. I walked in one day to find a wooden seat rigged with three spindly iron legs sitting over the toilet. One just has to try a little harder when others around you will go that far to make you happy.

Chapter 8

In early November we prepared to leave Taif for Jeddah. The job took days and I marveled that such trouble was taken each year for a few months' stay in the mountains. Bedrolls, boxes, suitcases, trunks, foodstuffs, water, fruit baskets, dishes, kitchenware, and sundries were piled high in the trucks by servants who then at departure time scrambled to places high atop the load for the grueling, hot, jolting trip to the coast. It was worse than being seasick for most of them, but the real wonder was that none ever got sunstroke, their only protection from the pitiless sun being that furnished all too inadequately by their own head coverings. One good thing, they were all Moslems so they could take the shorter regular road through Mecca. The caravan that had me along was once more obliged to use the longer seldom-used road which by-passed the holy city.

Ali had already left on business, so brother Mohamed was in charge of our trip. The morning we left I was mad at him for fussing angrily at us women far too soon, I thought, about lowering our veils and for yelling impatiently at us to move along faster to the cars. "Bet he couldn't walk at all, let alone *see,* with two thicknesses of veil over *his* face," I muttered to no one in particular. "Yallah, yallah — emshu." "Come on, come on, get a move on," he prodded, and I burst out, "We're not cattle, you know." He either didn't hear or pretended not to, and it was just as well because I was in a bad mood.

Already annoyed because he had rarely joined the rest of us during our stay in Taif, I felt he had continued to avoid me, and I found out later that was indeed true. Painfully aware that the facilities in Taif were far different from anything I was accustomed to, he was embarrassed that my first impressions of Arabian life had to be formed in that old house. And rather than explain, or apologize for what he knew was lacking, he let me muddle through on my own. Perhaps he preferred not to watch me struggle through new situations each day, thinking: Well, if she gets through this, she'll get through anything. Whatever it was, the time had come to leave Taif, and my spirits immediately rose at the thought that later in the day we would be somewhere else.

A modern smooth highway now links Taif and Jeddah and the trip is made in a few short hours, but not so in 1945. Then it took long hours of rocking and bumping down a tortuous, winding road in cars whose drivers were hard put to maneuver the rough spots. Rocks and pebbles beat an almost steady *rat-a-tat-tat* against the floorboards, wheels spun, and chassis lurched this way and that. Passengers never got a chance to rest, bounced as they were straight up or into one another, and it was enough to make anyone carsick.

A wayfaring site halfway to Jeddah was our scheduled stop, and upon arrival we separated into several groups, men with men and women with women even there in the middle of the desert. My group took its share of water and food into one of the huts where we knelt on the crude straw mats and started to set out bread, cheese, olives, and fruit. In seconds the uncovered food was colored black by hordes of flies that swooshed in from the nowhere of the empty land, and when we tried to shoo them they whirred into our eyes and up our nostrils. I covered Hamida's face with my veil, but to her that was a fine game of peek-a-boo and I soon gave up trying to protect her. No one could win against them, anyway, so I did the next best thing — I relaxed and enjoyed the food, flies or no flies.

In the relatively quiet rest hour that followed I sat there and thought about where I was and about the scene before me. Mother had taken out the black leather case which contained her coffee-making paraphernalia and set the tiny alcohol burner on the mat, mixed the coffee with water in the *jezwa** and brewed her after-meal cup. Saada knelt at a small brazier fanning embers to a red heat so our tea water would boil, and Hayat and Zainab prepared to pray, but only after a short and slightly heated argument on which direction was truly east. The land outside and all around showed no evidence of life anywhere and I could think of the world as curving emptily down, down back into its own circle. Extraordinary, I thought, that our little group formed the one evident knot of humanity there and that each of us had come from different places to be together at that particular time at that particular place — I and the slave girl, the kind-faced lady sipping coffee, and the wrapped-up figures now touching their foreheads to the ground in prayer. How near to each other we were in that spot of nothingness, yet how far apart in our histories.

"Sitti Marianne, etfadhali . . ." † and I looked up to see Saada proffering a glass of freshly brewed tea. It took a moment for me to focus back to reality and Saada misunderstood my look. "Ma tibghi shahee?" she said. "Yes, yes, indeed I want tea. Thank you." And I had to smile. Tea was always such a civilized custom, to be enjoyed in swank parlors and fine drawing rooms, and there we were sipping it in a crude desert hut and being called milady as nicely as you please. How many

---

* The special pot used to brew what is commonly called Turkish coffee.
† "Mistress Marianne, please . . ."

travelers before us, Bedou, Arab tradesmen and merchants, hunters, desert warriors — or their women — had sat there sipping tea as we were now? My mind's eye pictured such a group and I suddenly wondered what their reaction would have been if I had appeared unexpectedly among them? And then I knew what would have happened, because I was still the first of my kind to become an Arab and live among them and they accepted me and my living there as naturally and completely as if I had been born there.

I had to remember that the situation was as new to them as it was to me. Fretting as I did about the Arab world shutting me in, I had failed to appreciate the very important fact that at least it had not shut me out. Closed in I was, but still "in" and the big point was that I could make that closing-in an opening-up. I was still at the stage where self-congratulation was in order when another day passed and I had gotten through more new experiences in a wholly new way of life, but this new feeling was a start. The easterners have a proverb which says, "Everything comes and passes, but it makes a hole and passes." Maybe I had begun to make a hole, but only time would tell. Adjusting to a life so vastly different was no overnight thing, nor was it a clear-cut thing. It was varying effort meeting with varying success, and of all the factors involved only the people remained the same. No one changed to suit another, yet all of us worked to make a go of it. And since the bonds of custom held fast no matter what, my prime discipline was to do what I had to do in spite of my shackled freedom. It was not fun to get dumped regularly into sink-or-swim situations, but I kept my nose up by learning to tread like mad.

Jeddah was a delight after Taif. Our life was still centered in and around the home but at least we could see through real glass windows, look at the Red Sea in front of us, see the mountains behind us, and have the pleasure of walking in our yard in relative freedom. Ours was one of the few compounds outside the then still walled city, and the calm and quiet in our area was broken only occasionally by the jingling of donkey bells as a lone rider passed outside our walls, by an auto horn's signal to open the gate, or at nighttime by the drumming of the Rawais* Bedou who lived just north of us. Before that year, every one of our family had lived in the big Alireza house in town in a many-floored maze of rooms and apartments situated above the ground-floor offices of the family firm. If that had been my first home in Arabia, I feel most certain that I never could have adjusted. Instead of buckling down to the task of making a home within a home, I would have just buckled, which I did anyway at times, getting all emotional about America, about my difficulties with the language, about my frustrating relations with the servants and occasional misunderstandings with my in-laws.

My first exodus from Arabia came during the first year, and as the plane lifted up and away I was tempted to toss that veil of mine out the window. I could have done it, too, through the small circular openings some planes' windows had in those days, but of course I didn't.

We were going to London, where Ali was to join Prince Faisal and the rest of the Saudi delegation for the United Nations Conference. With that trip Ali set a precedent that he was to keep for a long time — that of taking me and the children (child that first time) with him on trips outside of Arabia. Until regular airline service was available, we had to arrange passage on planes going in and out of Jeddah airport (or the strip of sand so-called where camels often trespassed) and sometimes they would be British craft from Aden, or maybe United States planes, where we had to sit in paratroopers' bucket seats and share brought-along lunches with other hitchhiking passengers while the non-commissioned members of the crew curled up and slept on the metal floor. We had our choice of fly-

* The Rawais was a district.

ing catch-as-catch-can in that way, or of taking one of two old British steamers, the *Taif* or the *Talodi*, which plied the Red Sea to Egypt and back, a one-way trip from Jeddah to the nearest Egyptian port taking five days. On those boats (as a later trip proved to us) open-deck passengers sometimes enjoyed being peeping Toms through stateroom portholes, rats as big as cats made the rounds each night, the sleeping bunks were full of bedbugs, and even a guest at the captain's table was served bread with weevils in it. We flew whenever possible.

In Cairo on the first leg of that London journey we found that all air traffic was still controlled by postwar military regulations. Ali managed to get A-1 priority for himself, but Hamida and I would have to go, if at all, by boat. That was a blow. I was so helpless still in travel matters and felt so much the foreigner in a foreign land that I cringed at the thought of setting sail in mid-winter with a child, but when a British troopship with some accommodations for civilians was found leaving Port Said for Liverpool on December 21, 1945, Ali booked us first class and comforted me by saying he would not leave until Hamida and I did. The choice, however, was not his to make. He had to leave when space was available and one did not toy in those days with A-1 priorities. He was very soon gone, but Ahmed Yousuf had happily arrived in Cairo and it was he who made overnight reservations for us in Port Said and took us there by train the night before sailing.

The hotel had no record of our reservations when we got there so we spent hours clop-clopping around in a horse carriage until past midnight looking for other lodgings in the passenger-filled city. The streets were deserted by the time Ahmed found rooms that he considered passably acceptable, and even then he was not satisfied to let Hamida and me go in until he had first made the night man change the sheets for our miserable beds in his presence.

After spending a fitful few hours behind lockless doors

worrying about the way I had groped down the dark hallway searching for the unmarked w.c. and how I had opened the wrong door to the rough oaths of the rough man I awakened, I worried even more that dawn would not come soon enough to light my way to the proper door. When we finally arose and prepared to venture forth to the next adventure, I had the distinct wish that I were back home instead.

At the ship Ahmed saw me through the formalities and then left it to the steward to show Hamida and me to our quarters. Ahmed had a few errands, he said, but would return before sailing time for final adieus. Well, my "quarters" turned out to be almost "eighths." My first-class passage meant that I was to share a cabin normally meant for two with five other people, and they were already there when the steward ushered me in. Six bunks, three and three, were in the room and we were to share a bathroom with the adjacent six-bunk room. Being the last to arrive, the only bunk left was a top one, but one of the ladies, although not overjoyed at the thought of a nine-month-old traveling companion, kindly exchanged her lower one for ours.

My heart sank to my toes. I put Hamida in the bunk and endured with numbed feelings the looks of the others, too shocked to sit even if there were room to do so. I stood until the stewards started bringing in my luggage and then my worries really began. The others' luggage and belongings already crowded the room, and I had far more than I normally would have because Ali had given me his excess weight and Ahmed had loaded us down with cases of chocolates from Groppi's, Cairo's famous chocolatiers. "Sweets are rationed in England," he said, "and if you can't eat them all, you can give them to people!" Each bag brought more questioning looks from my companions, and then I got a strange look on my own face when a crate of tangerines with my name on it appeared — a cagelike crate whose straw packing dribbled out the sides at each movement. Then another crate was brought, bananas this time, the little finger-size ones peculiar to Egypt, and then another and another, thirteen in all, of assorted fruit.

I didn't know a thing about them except that I would have to do something, as they soon took up the remaining space in the room and were queueing up in the corridor. I caught my stocking on the rough bamboo sides of one cage as I tried to get by to yell "Stop!" to the baggagemen, and then tipped them well to put the cargo of fruit and whatever else I would not need in the ship's hold for the duration of the trip. "It's all Ahmed's doing," I muttered, when the place was clear of fruit but not of straw, and I went on deck to see if he had returned. I fixed him with a bleary eye when I tracked him down and asked if he knew anything about any fruit.

"Oh good. It arrived, did it? Fruit's so expensive and hard to get in England now, so I got you a good supply."

"You certainly did," I said, "and I want you to come with me now and see where we were supposed to put it *and* Hamida *and* me."

When he saw the room he couldn't believe that my first-class ticket did not entitle me to anything better than that, and he stormed to the purser so the mistake could be corrected. But it was we who were mistaken in our thoughts of luxury and comfort in those trying times. Ours was essentially a troopship and if we thought we were crowded perhaps we should visit the other decks. We got the message. Ahmed was very sorry it had to be that way, and I was sorrier, but soon the gong sounded, signaling all visitors ashore, and we set sail.

That was a voyage! The military regulated our days; I had to hang Hamida's laundry somewhere down in the ship's bowels where all the pipes were; afternoons we were issued coupons for a cup of tea and two sawdustlike biscuits between meals that were adequate, I suppose, but not much else; and the weather throughout the trip was abominable. For days our nerves were strung tight (tighter?) with the relentless sound of our foghorn going off every few minutes, as we lumbered through heavy seas, and almost everyone on the ship except Hamida and myself was sick. I think the only reason I wasn't was because I simply could not afford to be.

We had resigned ourselves before departure to the necessity of spending Christmas somewhere on the high seas, but come New Year's we were still there. Besides the weather factor, we had two unscheduled stops, one at the shambles of Malta and one at the wreck-ridden harbor of Naples, where we were not allowed at either place, understandably, to go ashore. When we hove to in sight of Liverpool, we were five days behind schedule and even then could not sail in to the dock. As I understood it, we arrived too late to catch the high tide and had to wait outside port until the ship could safely navigate the channel.

Then I was not sure that Ali would be there. I had received a cryptic cable on the ship from Ahmed telling me not to worry, they had found Ali safe and sound, and I hadn't the slightest clue what that was about. But he was there, standing on the dock, wearing of all things a Homburg hat — as much of a surprise to me as if he had been wearing his Arab headdress. He looked very much the diplomat, in fact, with his tailored topcoat, briefcase in hand, and I thought how different we humans look under different situations, remembering the time he came home to Taif from Riyadh looking like a lost nomad.

Ali had wangled permission to board, so we first suffered a happy reunion on deck before he gave me his briefcase to hold and went off to take care of getting me disembarked and into the country.

In the excitement I forgot to tell him about the fruit, but perhaps it was just as well that he discovered it for himself. He rushed back to me, having quite lost the diplomat image, and said, "What in God's name is all that blasted fruit they say is yours — how do you expect me to get it cleared and onto the train and into London and the hotel with it?"

"Don't yell at me," I replied, "it's all Ahmed's doing! He thought it would be nice for us to have while we are here. Isn't that sweet?" I could be flippant now that the worry of it had shifted from my shoulders to his.

"Sweet, my eye! Good Lord, you have thirteen crates of it down there."

"Yes, I know; how well I know!"

On the train to London Ali explained about the cable I had received. After leaving Cairo their plane was hit by lightning and their radio was knocked out, so they were lost in a storm somewhere out over the water and droned around the skies until land was spotted below and they looked for an air-field — any old airfield — on which they could land before their fuel ran out. They finally went down in Germany, and then had to get to France and England by a combination of train, car, boat — everything except bicycle. No one had known where they were for a while and Ali said that during the emergency in the airplane there were few of them who thought they would ever make it at all. Ali, however, re-acted with relief that his persistent efforts to get permission for Hamida and me had been unsuccessful. While the others with him remained pensive and quiet, Ali had made a nuisance of himself by ordering sandwiches and settling down happily to the meal for which no one else had the appetite. He was so obviously happy about something that it caused the others to wonder if he was not quite right in the head.

Ali cringed as porters at the London station unloaded our belongings from the train and got us several taxis. Our emptied compartment bore a slight resemblance to a cattle car, and Ali was sure the taxi drivers were laughing at us even though there were no evident signs that they were. But the truly last straws fell at the grand Claridge's Hotel, where they were strewn the length of its hallowed halls. I think that has to be the only time a check-in at Claridge's was followed by a broom and dustpan, and my trials were not over yet. Upstairs I discovered that the briefcase which I had been guarding with my life contained only a pair of pajamas and a toothbrush and that sent me out in search of something to read to calm my jangled nerves. At the hall porter's desk, which resembled a magistrate's bench, I asked, "Would you please tell me where the magazine stand is?" The hall porter, looking like a magistrate, answered, "Madam, *Claridge's has* no magazine stand."

One would like to end the story there, but there's more. First of all, people did not laugh long about my fruit. Our chambermaid had a good cry, in fact, when I gave her a few bananas, they were that rare and precious. Then I thought what a nice gesture it would be to make gift baskets and send one to H.R.H. Prince Faisal, one to H.E. Shaikh Ibrahim as-Sulaiman, and one to H.E. Shaikh Hafiz Wahba, our minister in London, so I did. I bought the baskets, cellophane, and ribbon, and using a box of Groppi chocolates as a nucleus, made some very artistic arrangements, attached our card to the basket handles, and had them delivered. Prince Faisal, recognizing a golden opportunity when he saw it, replaced our card with his, confiscated the other two baskets and did the same thing, and sent one to Buckingham Palace with his compliments, one to Prime Minister Clement Attlee, and the third to some other high official. Ahmed Yousuf's thoughtful gift had started as a headache but had ended as a gift fit for a king and was, to all accounts, appreciated as such.

I guess Ali forgave the trouble it caused him, too, because he had kind words for me later in an incident that happened during one of the committee meetings. He was shuffling some papers when he looked up to see Mrs. Eleanor Roosevelt sitting next to him. They struck up a quiet conversation. She asked him some questions about himself and then about his country, expressing an interest in both, and then Mrs. Roosevelt said: "And how do you like the Americans?"

"Oh, I like them fine," Ali said, "and as a matter of fact I not only like them, I love them — I married one!"

I attended quite a few meetings using Shaikh Ibrahim's delegate pass and I was glad to be a part of them, even as a spectator. Behind the scenes I listened long and carefully to the accounts of the men on the progress of the session and to their sometimes amusing sidelights in a day's happenings. One night Prince Faisal was teasing Ali dreadfully, calling him Your Royal Highness This and Your Royal Highness That, and I finally got the story out of them. That afternoon His real Royal Highness and Ali had been standing in front of the lift at Prince Faisal's hotel waiting to go up to his room when a well-dressed woman rushed up to the two of them, took a quick glance and then grabbed Ali's hand and said: "O-o-oh, Your Royal Highness, I'm so glad to meet you," and so forth and so on; whereupon Prince Faisal looked away as he told Ali in Arabic, "I'll break your head if you tell her I'm the prince, not you," and sauntered into the now open lift, leaving Ali, alone to respond gracefully and graciously to the thrilled woman.

We stayed in London until the end of the conference, working hard during the week and going on weekends to the legation's beautiful country house, which I remember for its cold bedrooms and the maid who awakened us faithfully at dawn to serve us our morning cup of tea, its beautiful grounds, the big fireplace in the dining room, the superb billiard and game room, and the one egg Hamida got every Sunday morning. Luckily, Ahmed hadn't known how very scarce eggs were, too.

Then it was time to pack away the business suits and Ali's Homburg hat, get out the headdresses and the veil, return to all my male companions the penny poker stakes I had been holding for them, and take the airplane back to Arabia and to the house where I had made a little progress since my first trip. I would have to resume that other life where I had left off but where was that? I thought it might be like starting all over again on some things, and I knew I had forgotten some of my Arabic vocabulary even in the relatively short time we had been gone. The look of Arabia and the sounds of the house were needed to recall those words — so many of them pertinent only to the life we lived there.

For a long time it was hard for me to think of the house in which we all lived as my home, and Hayat and I had great discussions on the subject, as well as we were able. It was easy for her to conjugate the house into "mine, yours, his, hers, ours," but I was not accustomed to communal living and insisted that although I lived there it was not *my* home. "How nice it would be," said I, "if I had my own home." And how wrong I was! Wrapped up in myself and my problems, only gradually did I come to see the thousand-and-one things a household such as ours demanded of the person running it. Even on a small scale I never, never could have managed an Arabian household those first years. How could I have known how to order or buy food or goods, keep accounts, oversee anything and everything, manage servants and hire and fire, assign chores, and do the constant checking and double-checking necessary to keep a house running well? I was having a hard enough time as it was with a minimum of duties, and no real responsibilities other than child care.

It was Mother who ran things at our house, and she did it with what I now consider genius. She was Sitti Kabeerah, the "Big Lady," and her natural business sense and true executive talent more than compensated for her lack of formal schooling. We younger women did what we could to help, but it was precious little in comparison to her responsibilities. We managed only a small segment of personal affairs within the full circle of our life together and, speaking for myself at least, we took much for granted.

Buying and planning and keeping accounts on food and all the other things our household consumed or used must have been a real headache. No wonder Mother often pulled herself up from the *carawita* at night with the words, "Ya oomie, yarate-ik my jipteeny,"* when the houseboy came after dinner to go over accounts with her. Lists and receipts were methodically checked, and when Mother was satisfied the totals were correct she shuffled off to her room, sandals flapping, to unlock the large teak chest where among other things she kept the house money. From the strong canvas sacks full of silver riyals she counted the proper amount and handed them to the boy in payment for that day's expenses. The procedure was the same the next day and the next. I never knew how our individual accounts were kept, or paid; maybe they were lumped together and drawn from a general fund, or maybe an accounting was made to our men. However it was done, I do know I never handled money that first year. There was nothing to do with it anyway, for someone always took care of my needs, something the whole family apparently had been doing even prior to my arrival.

Mother had many things she had bought and tucked away for me in the inner recesses of one of several teak chests, and every once in a while she would remember some long-forgotten item and rush off to get it. Zainab had hand-sewn articles for Hamida and me, and both Zainab and Hayat had set aside at one time or another many cuts of yardage they had chosen as presents. Mohamed had bought for me a fine new short-wave radio which he hid in the garage so as not to tempt others, but, to hear him tell it, he was pestered to death as each in turn found its hiding place and petitioned him for it. "It's for Marianne" was his flat refusal each time, and when he finally placed the carton in my hands I had the distinct impression he was glad to be rid of it.

Mohamed also got a refrigerator, but not to give to me. He

* "Oh mother mine, I wish you hadn't had me!"

just gave me the job of taking care of it. Home refrigeration was a concept new to Arabia in those days and not many people had a refrigerator or any other kind of modern household or kitchen appliance. It had never occurred to me to consider any kind of icebox, modern or not, as furniture for the dining room, but that was where Mohamed instructed the servants to put ours. He made a sweeping gesture toward the shiny-white new model with the words, "Well, Marianne, it's American like you, so you take charge of it, eh? And please show the others how to use it."

So what's to show? I thought. You plug it in, open and close the door, fill the ice trays once in a while, clean it now and then, and that's about it. If I had been thinking, I would have remembered that we had electricity only at night, and that a refrigerator that melted all day and tried to catch up at night would have been worse than none at all. No, ours worked on kerosene — something I hadn't known existed until then — and it was up to me to learn the mechanics of the thing, study diagrams and customer instructions, and get the works assembled. Then I fueled the fill jar, adjusted the wick (and became very good at trimming it, too), regulated the flame, and — lo and behold — it worked. What's more, with only minor breakdowns now and then, I kept it working, thereby establishing for myself a quite unmerited reputation for proficiency in mechanical matters that I never quite lived down and barely lived up to as through the years it caused me to be brought, among other things, vintage typewriters and sewing machines, odd kitchen gadgets, and various models of cigarette-rolling contraptions to repair.

Heretofore, perishable food was rarely, if ever, kept a second day because heat and humidity spoiled it so quickly, and what a job I had convincing the staff that dishes left under refrigeration overnight would be safe and good. Saada, for instance, was adamant in her belief that leftover watermelon was poison — to be eaten the day it was cut or not at all — so it was to protect me from myself that she tugged one day for possession of a watermelon slice I was trying to shelve for future enjoyment. I won the tussle, stored it, and then invited her to be there to watch me eat it the next day. She was there all right (with the attitude that *someone* had to be there to catch me when I fell) but I did not consider it a victory when I lived to tell the tale, because in the final analysis she was right. Leftover watermelon was *not* safe! It disappeared! With everyone, Saada included, convinced at last that refrigerated watermelon was as good as fresh and twice as cold, the chances of finding *any* became almost nil.

There were far too many of us using that poor refrigerator to allow it to function properly. The door was seldom shut for more than fifteen consecutive minutes and after some early bird always got the night's undisturbed output of ice, the trays for the rest of the day were in an almost constant state of liquidity. Tiny marbles of ice floating around were all it could muster in the daytime, so the home supply was bolstered with thermoses full of ice from the one local ice plant. People started leaving the ice trays alone then, and I got to carry out my wish to make ice cream, if you could call it that.

"Ice slab" would have been a better name for the frozen milk crystals I got time and again, and I know now that its great success could only have been attributable to the fact that it *was* cold. I would so have liked it to be creamy and smooth, but the results of my efforts were frustratingly foolproof — same cold slabs every time. Moreover, flies flew in from miles around to watch and tried so desperately to get into the act that great care had to be taken not to whip a dozen or more into each batch. Not that it whipped! Fresh cream was unavailable and the chilled evaporated milk substitute never stayed cold long enough in the hot room to form anything more than a mushy froth. The resultant icy concoctions were well

liked but never took the place of the regular cold delights of
chilled cactus pears, molds of burnt sugar custard, melons
mashed with sugar and crushed ice (as available) and pomegranate seeds floating red and pretty in bowlfuls of sugared
ice water. After ice cream, I tried to introduce ice tea, but
failed to make even one convert. Tea drinkers preferred hot
tea even in dead summer, and it was just as well. There was
never enough ice anyway.

We subsequently made a deal with the ice-plant owner to
make good ice cream for us. He had the proper equipment and
agreed to do it if we furnished the ingredients, allowed him a
full day, and brought our own take-home containers. His
plain vanilla was great — and I can still remember creaming
my elbows as I scooped it from the very bottom of a tall wide-
mouthed thermos — but our all-time favorite was mango. Our
friend transformed tins of Indian mango pulp into the most
gorgeously tinted, most delicious cream I have ever eaten. A
thermosful of that made any day a party.

I had a soft spot in my heart for that ice cream man but he
was just one of many townsmen with whom our household dealt
that we women never saw and never would, and it didn't seem
right that we knew only their names. True, our men likely
never saw them either, because most errand-running and contacts with tradesmen were made by servants and office helpers,
but that was different. Even the doctor was taboo for us females unless one of us was his patient, and if it was a child who
was sick, we young mothers never talked to the doctor or sat
with him on his bedside visits — Mother did. She was not
veiled at these times, but custom did demand that she cover
her head with a light scarf. Eventually these restrictions relaxed to allow us to be in a mixed group of men and women if
a good family friend was visiting — and that certainly included
the doctor — but such was not the case at first.

A sometime pastime of the women was to hide behind the

windows to get a glimpse of a man visitor coming up the driveway or to peek through the arabesque designs of an upstairs balcony to watch the men partying in the garden below. I am glad that I got to Arabia in time to see and live these things, but I was less than enchanted at the time and full of shock and resentment in the name of womanhood the first time I saw our women do it.

"No one is going to catch me sneaking around just to get a look at a mere man," I said, except that the first time it happened it was no mere man, it was H.R.H. Prince Mohamed bin Abdul Aziz come to visit. I snorted anyway. "Humph, he rowed me around a lake once and I've seen *him* without *his* headdress" — whatever that was supposed to mean. "I refuse to stoop to peek at him!"

With haughty dignity I stood there while the others scrambled for better viewing positions, but my so-called dignity got properly fractured when very soon I had either to do what I had flatly stated I would not do, or leave the room to avoid being seen myself. Pondering my predicament shortly thereafter from the solitude of my bedroom I thought, what a far cry from home! Almost immediately this became a far far cry from home, and my mind was faced with the task of picking its way back to where my body was.

When men came that I could see, like dear Uncle Yousuf and his son, Ahmed, brother-in-law Ahmed Zahid, cousins Abu Ali and Om Abdullah Abul-Hassan, to name a few, there were other bewilderments. I was puzzled as to why on some occasions their greetings to me were readily accompanied by hearty handshakes and on others by an evasive jig to avoid my outstretched hand. "Mutawuddi," they'd say, and surmising that to be yet another form of greeting, I shook hands anyway. The poor souls were trying to tell me they had performed their ablutions and were thus purified for prayer, but even if I had understood the word, no one had ever told me that between washing and prayer men must not touch a woman. My handpumping unpurified them, as it were, making them repeat the whole washing process, but it speaks so well for their nature, I think, that these good men always returned my hellos graciously, *mutawuddayeen** or not.

I adjusted to these things as they occurred, but my life had changed so completely it was unbelievable. The other women had been born to this modus vivendi but I had to work up to it and in the meantime fought the bonds, wanting reasons when any reason that might be given was small consolation for keeping my face and my place behind the veil, regardless. Because the limitations were many and so very binding, resentment came easily and flexibility about the lack of freedom came hard, but I rarely suffered in silence, attempting most eloquent trilingual speeches on what I considered women's rights, when my spirit should instead have been quashed by the other women's seeming apathy on the subject. They brushed aside any serious thoughts of the veil being abolished and when I was calm enough to look at it from their side, I was staggered by all that would have to be done before the women themselves could accept it.

In those days, the number of Arabian women who had seen anything outside their own country, or who knew through education what the rest of the world was like, was very small. Most older Arabian women had never been to school, public schools existing still for boys only. Whether or not a girl was taught depended entirely on the wishes of her family and on their ability to pay for a private tutor. The women in my immediate family had all traveled and Ali's father had seen to it that his girls learned alongside his boys, but this advantage was not shared by many others their age. Arabian fathers were just then beginning to provide better educational opportunities for their daughters, with a very few sending them to foreign

* Plural form of *mutawuddi.* See the Glossary.

boarding schools, so the most an Arabian girl usually learned was to read and recite from the Koran. Other than that, her home was her school and indeed her whole life until she married, and the very city in which she lived was as closed to her as Saudi Arabia itself was to the rest of the world.

Change was in the offing after the discovery of oil and the development of its resources, which transformed Saudi Arabia from a country whose economy was mainly dependent on pilgrim head taxes, pearling, goatskins and camel's wool, simple agriculture, and commerce to a country whose coffers brimmed with oil revenues. But change comes slowly when so much is needed. It had not been too many years since King Ibn Saud had conquered various regions and unified Bedouin tribes to form the Arabia of Saud, and oil was just beginning to give him the means to develop it, so the status of women had to take its slow advances along with the growth of industry and agriculture; the building of roads, waterworks, hospitals and clinics, ports, electric plants; the amelioration of health and sanitation conditions; the opening of schools on all levels; and the emergence of a people awakened to new concepts of living and a growing ambition to achieve them. The women I knew had seen nothing yet to give them this ambition. The life they knew was too old and the one on the way was too new, and because their life had always been behind it, the veil was security and protection for them. It was not, as it was to me, a hindrance to liberty; it was proof that their men respected and loved them and wanted to protect them in all ways.

Once when my mother was visiting us from California, she discovered what it was like to be unveiled in Arabia. She and three of us Alirezas were driving through Jeddah's streets one afternoon when suddenly she whispered to me, "For God's sake, get me a veil, too — I feel like a lost woman sitting next to all of you." If she had been going around in what I called "foreign circles" she would have felt less out of place, because the wives of western diplomats and businessmen and airline pilots never veiled, but as part of our Arab family she felt the pressure of being the only one among us with her face bared and soon joined us in public anonymity. It was easier on the nerves than being "free." None of this kept me from wishing it were otherwise but I, like other women, would have to wait.

The desire of the men to protect us from the eyes of others extended to the menservants, and with one of ours named Ba-Awad I lived a heavy drama which made me more impatient than ever with the status quo. We had workmen going to and from our quarters as they built an extra room on our balcony, and although I knew enough by then to stay out of sight when they were around, BaAwad felt it his duty to the end to close my bedroom and hall doors and keep them closed as long as strange men were around. A closed room was worse than death in that heat, so I opened my doors each time he closed them and vice versa. The battle raged for three days — no words involved, just clicking hardware. It nearly drove me to hysterics, and I accused Ali finally (who had nothing to do with it) of making me a suffocated prisoner in my own home. It's a good thing he did not laugh; I was in such a state I might have packed up then and there and gone home to Mother. Or tried to!

I never looked into the ways and means of doing such a thing in Arabia, where we women could not get to a minor visit in town without major planning, and I don't know how one bent on leaving her husband's bed and board would get out of the house, let alone buy a ticket and get on a plane or boat to leave the country. Even in our fairly progressive household, the men kept all passports, so that stopped right there any effort to flee long-distance. My two passports, Saudi Arabian and United States, were locked in Ali's safe at the office, which could have been the Rock of Gibraltar for all the access I had to it. I might have borrowed, say, Saada's passport, except that she was probably already using someone else's. Arabians follow through in their efforts to keep their women from being seen by exempting them from pasting their photos in their passports, and I suspect that this leads to their being shared, alike or not. Anyway, Ali did not laugh and he did keep his promise to talk to BaAwad. The matter was thus settled, and in good Arab fashion: both sides "won" by the simple expedient of each giving in halfway — I agreed to leave the door half open and BaAwad agreed to leave it half shut.

Chapter 9

It wasn't long before the worry of *anybody* seeing me was gone, temporarily at least, because everybody in Jeddah had left, or was in the process of leaving for the Pilgrimage. A servant or two, and Hayat to keep me company, were all that were left in our house, and after the hustle and bustle of preparation the calm of comparative solitude was eerie. Moslem faithful from all over the world had been pouring into Jeddah for days on their way to their holiest of holy cities, Mecca, forty-five miles due east of us. The harbor was full of ships and lighters discharging pilgrims, charter flights arrived by the minute, others came overland in cars and trucks, and there were some who had taken months or even years to arrive on foot. Government shelters along the waterfront housed thousands, while local agents strove to complete arrangements for their transport to Mecca.

Camel caravans, normally few in number, were brought into around-the-clock service and could be seen any time of day plodding through the city gates bearing personal effects and provisions. Time was when they carried women and children, too, in a conveyance on their backs called a *shoogdoof,* a gaily bedecked enclosed frame with tasseled curtains all around for privacy and fancy carpets and pillows on the inside for comfort. Mother told me how they rocked all the way to Mecca in the old days, trying to keep the kids from toppling out, thankful when they dropped off to sleep very soon as a result of the rocking-chair effect of the camel's peculiar gait, and how it required good backs and good stomachs to withstand the trip in good shape. (It is not for cargo-carrying alone that the camel is called the "ship of the desert.") I would have loved it, I know, and riding in a *shoogdoof* remains one of my unfulfilled desires. Imagine running over to the local oasis for a picnic in one, relaxing in the Oriental splendor of its interior and peeking out now and then between the curtains. I was so enthralled with the idea that Mother tried later to locate one, if only to jog me around the yard, but her search was fruitless. The *shoogdoof* was one thing I had come to Arabia too late for.

Pilgrims must wear special clothing after a certain point on any approach to Mecca, but our family pilgrims donned theirs before leaving the house. Women wear long, simple, all-white dresses, unadorned white cotton headdresses wrapped tightly around the hairline of the face, and no veil during this time. Men wear two long towels — one wrapped around their waists and tucked in over a belt, the other crossed over one shoulder — nothing on their heads, and sandals on their feet. Stitching or seams are not allowed on the towels, so that none can be sewn better than another, the idea being that whether a man be king or peasant, beggar or nobleman, he is outwardly the same as the next and equal in the eyes of God.

Jeddah was a ghost town during that three-day period consisting of the eighth, ninth, and tenth days of Dhul-Hijja, the month when Moslems perform the prescribed pilgrim rites. And I thought I was seeing a ghost when a bedraggled Ali walked in unexpectedly on the second day of the Hadj, or "Pilgrimage," when he was supposed to be somewhere beyond

Mecca. His pilgrim towels hung heavy and wet on his body and large red welts covered the exposed areas of his skin.

"Good gracious, you look awful!" I blurted instead of a cheery hello. "What happened to you?"

"Hailstones," he said. "Hailstones as big as my fist! And I have to go back, I just came home to change."

"Hailstones?" I said unbelievingly, ignoring the fact that he would soon be gone again. "Where in the world did *they* come from?" A stupid question, but hailstones were the last thing I expected Mecca to have, especially ones big enough to cause injury to a man as big as Ali. He told me what had happened as he rested and waited for his driver to bring a new pair of towels.

The first day of the Pilgrimage had gone well, as thousands upon thousands completed the rites at the Great Mosque of Mecca. First they visited the Kaaba,* a building almost fifty feet high that sits in the courtyard shrouded in black silk inscribed with beautifully embroidered Arabic characters. The Arabs believe the patriarch Abraham and his son Ishmael, to whom they trace their heritage, built it and that the sacred Black Stone which sits in one corner was put there by the Prophet Mohamed. They kiss the Black Stone and visit another stone in another part of the courtyard called Station of Abraham. The stone there is believed to be the one on which Abraham and Ishmael stood while building the Kaaba.

I was fascinated. The recounting of this reminded me of my Bible class days, and the stories I learned as a child became more vivid when Ali told me that within the confines of the Great Mosque are what is believed to be the course the handmaiden Hagar followed in her search for water for her son Ishmael and the well that subsequently sprang up in the desert to save his life. Moslem pilgrims must run that same course in commemoration of Ishmael's salvation, and after doing it seven

* From the Arabic *ka'b*, meaning "cube."

times back and forth between the two knolls named as-Safa and al-Marwah, they visit and drink from the well they call Zam Zam. My Bible tells the story thus:

> . . . the angel of God called to Hagar out of heaven, and said unto her, What aileth thee, Hagar? fear not; for God hath heard the voice of the lad where he is. Arise, lift up the lad, and hold him in thine hand; for I will make him a great nation. And God opened her eyes, and she saw a well of water; and she went, and filled the bottle with water, and gave the lad drink.

I got goose pimples thinking how close I was to the places representing, to me, Biblical history, and in learning in detail how sacred they were to the Moslems, but I still hadn't heard about the hailstorm and made Ali continue. After Mecca, he said, all pilgrims proceed to Arafat, a plain some twelve miles eastward where everyone camps overnight and stays until sunset prayer the following day. It was there the storm hit, surprising hundreds who were out in the open unprotected from the hailstones raining down on them. Ali and others did their best to shepherd women and children to some sort of covering, finding space for them in tents when they could or otherwise devising some form of shield or shelter. They were too busy helping others to notice their own hurts until after it was over, and it was then that Ali came home. He was anxious now to return to Arafat and complete the Hadj, which he had done many times as a child, but which has to be performed as an adult to have full religious meaning. He particularly did not want to miss the prayers at Arafat and nearby Jebel ar-Rahama, the Mount of Mercy, because there the prayer is called "the best of prayers." It must be a spectacular sight and a highly emotional experience for the thousands worshiping on that great open plain, at one with themselves and with God.

They would then start back to Mecca, many on foot as they came, stopping on the way for another rite in the village of

Mina, where they gather around three pillars representing devils and throw seven stones apiece at the pillar nearest Mecca. The number seven thus again figures prominently in the Pilgrimage — seven times pilgrims circle the Kaaba, seven times they run Hagar's course, and seven stones they throw to keep the devil in submission — but it is well that the same trend in numbers does not continue in the great sacrifice of sheep which follows. One animal for each pilgrim is killed by slitting its throat in the traditional manner, and I was shocked into asking what is done with so many slaughtered sheep. The law says the meat must be shared with the needy of Mecca, but I found out later that the need is surpassed by sheer number and the government is obliged to send truck crews to clear away the carcasses. The reason for the sacrifice is to commemorate God's sparing Abraham from making a burnt offering of his son when Abraham's willingness to do so proved he was God-fearing. The Bible says Isaac was the son to be offered, but Abraham's first son was Ishmael and it is with him that the Arabs identify the happening.

When my good Ishmaelites came back, I was pleased beyond compare with what they brought me — a bottle of water from the well of Zam Zam. It was a warm human thing to let me thus share in their own religious experience — a sharing of faith based on common ground, one might say — and I was moved then as I was each time I heard the *muezzin* summoning the faithful to prayer. The words needed no translation for me to feel their beauty and power and faith. Good words and good deeds have meaning for anyone, no matter in what language or country they are experienced.

Life after the Pilgrimage settled back into the routine of small house tasks, caring for and playing with the children, sharing morning and afternoon hours in the tearoom, waiting for our men to come home from the office, eating meals together, suffering from heat and insects, and my learning Arabic. The language is so rich that one could spend a lifetime learning it, but mine was not a scholarly approach. I had to learn to live in Arabic. Day and night, bread and butter, the time of day, needle and thread, button, button, who's got it and how do you say it, wash and iron, air, water, sea, sky, moon, hungry, thirsty, dirty, clean, good, bad, and "I don't understand" were vocabulary I had to build.

At first all sounds went in one ear and out the other, and then everyday words started piling up in my head because I heard only Arabic day in and day out, and as soon as I could I matched them with meanings and let them out as speech. This involved me in untold situations which tended to be either very funny or very upsetting, depending on whether I used the words correctly or not, mispronounced them, or wedged them into life situations I knew nothing about. It was easier than teaching them all English, to be sure, and I was generally able to learn a lot from my mistakes, but I knew very soon that it was not I embracing the life there, it was Arabian life embracing me, compelling me to do, see, hear, feel, taste, touch it before I had the ability even to put names to all I was living. And looming beyond mere word-learning were all the intangibles that make life go around, the customs, beliefs, superstitions, values, humor, manners, ways. These compounded my word difficulties, or my word difficulties compounded (and confounded) them. Only because my being there put me squarely in the thick of things did I persevere in keeping up with the action, and maybe partly because I caused a lot of it.

More than words, I needed knowledge of what made things tick so I could stop setting off alarms. My words kept hitting nerve centers in the underlying workings of Arabian life, baring unsuspected beliefs and superstitions of which I learned to take cognizance. Visitors no longer surprised me with expressions of hope that I would get to keep my daughter or by calling her "she who has the name of God upon her" instead of by her name. I realized that these were reflections on the high infant mortality rate and the ever-present concern for the health and well-being of the young. But I was wrong in letting this lead me to the assumption that my happy motherly pronouncements about Hamida's whopping appetite and her getting fat would be met with polite rejoicing. That hit a nerve and all I got were glum expressions, mumbled replies sounding strangely like prayers, and finally, a briefing on the "evil eye." One just did not say healthy things about a child's progress and growth because that was tantamount to inviting this evil eye, whatever or wherever it was, to work its malevolence and strike the child down. "Uh-huh!" said I. "So *that* is why people are always taking one look at my lovely offspring and saying 'poor thing.' " Infuriating, that was, but now I knew it was because she *was* so pretty that the evil eye must never hear of it. If already a "poor thing" it would not waste time on her, logical enough if you believed in that sort of thing. And maybe I could extend that into an explanation of why Arabs use the expression "not bad" so much, a deflating habit when you've presented something that is clearly marvelous or cooked something scrumptiously delicious.

Encouragements followed discouragements but the pitfalls were many. It was surely not evil-eye strategy I was practicing one day when I patted a visiting child on the head and told him, "Hi, hi, you little bastard, you!" I was merely using an expression I heard Hayat use every day of our lives when she played with our children, tossing them high in the air and bouncing them on her knees. It sounded so endearing when she said it I just knew it meant "Oh, you little darling, you," or equivalent. Learning the phrase, I matched it with a meaning and proudly said it in my best Arabic. Imagine my surprise and chagrin when my words fell on the room like a bombshell, causing heads to snap up and looks of surprise and disbelief to be directed my way. Oh dear, now what? I thought.

And when they told me, it was my turn to be shocked. It's one thing to call your own progeny such words, but altogether too much to apply the epithet to another's.

I was very careful after that, but who would have dreamed that telling Zainab one day how pretty her earrings were would get me into trouble? It did, though. The jewels were superb and I told her so and the first thing I knew she had taken them off and given them to me. It tickled her that my ears matched their ruby-redness as she convinced me that there was no way she would take them back. Just another old Arabian custom, but what a way to find out. Never again did I openly admire something belonging to an Arab nor did I ever let anyone else admire those earrings away from me. They meant too much and if Zainab wouldn't take them, no one else was going to get them.

In later years, we were similarly to lose a newly built house to no less a person than King Ibn Saud, when on a sunset drive along the beach one day during one of his infrequent visits to Jeddah he saw the house, asked whose it was, and let it be known how much it pleased him. Yes, an old Arabian custom, and we gave the house to him, but the only thing is, he didn't keep it. He gave it to the then Minister of Finance, Shaikh Abdullah as-Sulaiman, who didn't keep it either. "How could I live in a house like that when the Viceroy of Hejaz has not one to compare?" How indeed! So Shaikh Abdullah gave it to the then viceroy who was also foreign minister and none other than our good friend H.R.H. Prince Faisal Al-Saud who, we hope, is living there happily ever after.

One of my silliest problems was the inability to pronounce properly, of all things, my own husband's name; what pleasure Hayat got out of teasing me about that! She would wander through the halls calling, "Ah-lee, Ah-lee, oh, Ah-lee," when she knew I was within hearing distance, and I must admit it was funny. My difficulty lay in the first letter, which is not really an *ah* but an Arabic *ein*, a sound which gets its vibrations from somewhere down near the tonsils. I finally learned to do it, along with the *ghain* and the *dhal* and the *qaf* and the *kha* and several other Arabic sounds foreign to western tongues, but it took a month of Fridays — Friday being the day of rest in Arabia, not Sunday.

And I got even with Hayat, too. Mother had sent a small trick box in one of her packages from the good old U.S.A. that claimed to send your voice back to you if you yelled into it and then pressed a little button at the bottom. The idea was easy to sell to Hayat because she had seen enough U.S.A.-made gadgets to convince herself that Americans were a clever lot, so she believed every word and with great dramatic flair gave a fine speech into the little box's mesh "microphone." And sure enough her voice came back, loud and clear. More like a full-blown yell it was, as the hidden pin in the little black button emerged to give her thumb a vicious jab. I laughed loud but not long, as Hayat took off after me in a chase over furniture and all through the house that caused others to think we had both gone mad. I had no more volunteers for voice-testing, but the box did have one more victim, come to think of it. An English-speaking doctor picked it up when he was alone in our living room one day and the lady of the house walked in just in time to see him staring blankly down at his bloody thumb. All anyone could do was send for Mother's favorite antiseptic, "mer-cur-cur-o-chrome," and take care of his thumb before he could treat the patient he had come to see.

"Mer-cur-cur-o-chrome" was one of Mother's better English words, acquired long before I got there. She had that penchant for doubling syllables when she spoke a foreign word, plus certain pronunciation problems, that kept her language-learning from ever becoming a serious matter. Zainab, on the other hand, had good pronunciation and learned many English words, but she seldom mustered enough courage to use them. Zainab was too afraid of making mistakes and kept her talent hidden for the longest time, unlike Hayat who forged ahead much as I did, letting words of any language fall as they may and learning by guess and by golly. A twinkle in the eye was requisite to Mother's speaking English, because she knew it was beyond her capability to gain any proficiency and did it more for fun.

I tried to help her, but no matter how much effort we put into the informal lessons her *p*'s still came out *b*'s, *v*'s were always *w*'s and anyone watching her try to force her tongue into the proper position to say *the* would have thought she had something stuck in her throat. To spur us on we adopted the famous World War II slogan, V for Victory, but her consistent "Wee for Wictory" ended that battle, if such a wee difference can be so termed. "Love" was high on the list of words to learn and one day I caught Mother practicing it on her own. She was leaning over, her hands cupping a tiny flower pot that had just produced one of her favorite blooms, a hyacinth, and she was telling it, "I low you," and love it she did.

While I worked on Arabic good mornings and good evenings Mother liked to greet me with English ones, and for the longest time it was not evident who was doing the better job. *Good evening* to her, of course, was "Good ee-wen-ning" but that took too much lip service, so she rounded it to "Good-a-neen-ing" — much simpler. Only one problem then remained, that of using it at the right time, which sometimes she did and sometimes she didn't. Her cheery "Good-a-neen-ing" often met me when I walked in to have morning coffee with her, and many's the time I trudged up to bed with her sincere wish for a "Good morning" ringing in my ears. Substituting *toodle-oo* solved part of that problem, and it was an expression I eventually got the whole household to use. Mother loved it because of the double *o*'s and because it was suitable for day or night leave-taking; the maids liked it because it always gave them the giggles; and I enjoyed hearing such a silly word come out of their mouths.

The word was in common use around the house when Sitti Fatma Rawasa, a distant relative of Mother's on the Turkish side of her family, came to visit, becoming almost a byword between her and me as our friendship grew. She made it a ritual almost every time I left a room to twaddle her fingers at me, cock her head to one side, and say, "Toodle-oodle."

Sitti Fatma was a slight but very spry little old lady with small fine features and fair skin, blue eyes and beautiful very long white hair which we liked to see free and loose. She wore the style of dress she was most accustomed to, the long high-necked dress and pantaloons with lace cuffs and, when we let her, her lovely hair braided and tucked under the tassels and twisted folds of her headdress. Her lips complained but her eyes twinkled when we made her take her hair down, which she always did, in more ways than one. Her forte was telling stories, and when you had heard one of hers you had seen a play. Any room was a stage as she became each character in her stories, playing to perfection whatever they were — a swaggering prince, a duped village idiot, a sought-after maiden, or a downtrodden slave.

She belied her age by leaping and grimacing and gesturing through folkloric tales showing great insight into human nature and containing more morals than Aesop's fables. Others were just stories, some of which were undoubtedly true and others which unmistakably were not, stories gleaned throughout her life. Her timing was faultless, topping with a punch line when you were already bursting and so tricking listeners into laughing harder than they ever thought possible. At her best it was not uncommon to find a whole roomful of people bent double over sore stomachs, begging this wisp of a woman to stop her antics. I could never follow all the words of her stories, but her acting was so good I was misled into thinking I had, and that was true art.

The months Sitti Fatma spent with us were so enjoyable we

hated to see her go, but there were many families vying for her visits and she eventually yielded to their requests and moved on. Her belongings were meager. She was a woman of very little means, and she had no immediate family of her own, a distressing situation in any society. But the Arabs take good care of their own and Sitti Fatma, like many other women who had spent their lives behind the veil and through the circumstance of age or widowhood had come to be dependent on others for livelihood, was welcome in the homes of her relatives and friends to stay as long or as little as she liked. And with them it was true hospitality and true generosity, never smacking of condescension or of charity.

Houseguests like Sitti Fatma, who adapted easily to our daily routine and who neither expected nor required special treatment, were a joy to me and I was completely at ease with them. It was the morning, or afternoon, or all-day visitor I halfway dreaded because of the contrapuntal conversations, the conventionalities I had to remember, and the struggle at times to rise above the backward process I was often forced into — of doing and saying things wrong first and learning the right way afterward. No matter what simple thing I learned, if too often required more knowledge to allow me to use it correctly. It was not enough, for example, to know the names of the days of the week, which were "First Day" for Sunday, "Second Day" for Monday, and so forth in a logical manner except for Friday which is called "Day of Gathering." It was also necessary to know that one day ends and another begins at sundown, because lacking that information would lead you to call Monday night, for example, "Monday night," which it isn't. Monday night in Arabia is "Tuesday's Eve," Tuesday night is "Wednesday's Eve," and so forth. If you said "Monday night" and meant it, you'd be talking of Sunday night, *Lailat Al-Ithnane.* *

* Literally, "the night of Monday the second."

Moreover, sunset time is always twelve o'clock in Arabia and all timepieces are religiously set correctly at that time. It would be six o'clock anywhere else, but there it's twelve, why I'll never know. Zainab was the one in our family who usually stood by a window in the west wing to watch for the exact time the sun sank into the Red Sea, and until I knew better I thought she was just inordinately fond of sunsets. Working up from twelve o'clock, then, dinner would be at two, three, or four o'clock, midnight and noon became six o'clock, my ten o'clock coffeebreak was at a strange four o'clock, and four o'clock tea at an even stranger ten o'clock. Delving deeper into the system I found other ways in which their time was not my time. I told someone once it was twelve-twenty, which it was, and after the laughter died down I got a lesson in fractions, learning to say it the proper way — twelve and one-third o'clock. It was all right to use quarter-pasts and half-pasts, but if someone asked me for the time of day when my watch said three thirty-five I pretended not to hear. Twenty past was funny enough and I wasn't going to stick my neck out on thirty-five past. A few more arithmetic lessons and I learned to say half-past plus five, but it's easily seen how with a little imagination one could come up with endless combinations and I uttered some great ones before I told time to straight faces.

There was no mirth in any of it when looked at in the light of things to do and places to go. Time to us women was definitely not "of the essence" and how fitting, I thought, that our pretty wrist watches were set by the timeless sun! Certainly we had no urgent appointments that required watching a clock — no maître d's holding a table reservation, no hairdresser with our names in a time slot, no time clocks to punch, for no woman worked in an office. There were no trains or buses to catch; no local movie house to get to in time for the feature; no concern with opening and closing hours of parks, museums, libraries, markets, business offices, department stores, shops; no worry about getting the kids off to school on time. If we had sent our children to public schools only the boys could have gone, anyway, and none of us went to church or the mosque. For me the closest church was in some other country and Arabian women go only to the sacred mosques of Mecca and Medina for special worship or ceremony. The Moslem religion, in fact, has no formal service other than someone to lead the Friday noon prayer attended by the men. Their religion is more a simple, daily personal force than a religion of formal teaching and preaching. The women prayed in their homes and, indeed, if any great attention was paid by them to the time segments of a day, it was in the observances of the five specified prayer times — before dawn when possible, noon, late afternoon, sunset, and evening — and even then there was some leeway.

As for me, I did well if I knew for sure the day and the date, many times I knew neither. I postdated or backdated letters often by as much as a week, but at least I never sent a letter home with the Arabic date on it. My folks may or may not have known that the Arabic calendar differs from ours, dating as it does from the Hegira ("flight") of the Prophet Mohamed from Mecca to Medina in 622 A.D., so getting a letter from me dated 1300-something might have caused dire concern that I was taking the stepping-back-into-the-centuries thing too seriously. They'd really wonder if I had told them I'd get my dates squared around again as soon as the new moon appeared, but that is what starts a new month in the Islamic calendar, the new moon, and twelve of them make a year eleven days less than the Georgian year, because they have only twenty-nine or thirty days apiece. Furthermore, months have no direct reference to seasons; they rotate in the Islamic year so that any one month can and does occur in sequence in all four seasons. This maybe makes a difference only to those observing the month-long fast of Ramadan when it occurs in summer and days are longer, or to those, say, whose birth records were lost or never kept. An old-timer knowing only that he was born in the spring of whatever year could only guess his age, because his "spring" got a little later each year until the cycle started again, and how do you tell how old you are from that? Seasons did not exist in the real sense where we were, anyway. Weather was much the same all year around and the sand never changed color except a few days after a torrential rain which soaked enough water into the desert to push up a little green.

We were lucky to have more green around our house than most. Mohamed had planted acacia trees the length and breadth of our outside garden walls and set henna bushes and jasmine and *fulle*, another fragrant night-blooming white flowering plant, in concrete rings filled with good earth brought in from somewhere. Jeddah for years could boast of only one famous tree downtown but new houses like ours springing up in the outskirts were trying for gardens, shade, arbors, and flowers and solved the watering problem by bringing in tank trucks from Mecca to do the job on a regular basis. Water for personal use had to be provided that way, too, to keep our cisterns filled when rains were slow in coming. The discovery of great sources of water near enough to be piped into Jeddah's houses occurred in the early 1950s and eased the problem, but until then water stayed high on the list of things I would never again take for granted.

Chapter 10

W HEN I THINK OF how I lived my Arabian days and nights I often don't believe it. I think of how we women had to congregate out of sight in Mother's room on nights when our men had the house for a men's party and of the first time we were served our dinner from platters removed from their table. And I think about how I came out of that room to accost my brother-in-law passing in the hallway to tell him how wrong it was, between sobs of anger so full inside me I thought I would wrench apart. I remember how he listened with the most surprised look I have seen on anyone and then surprised me more by throwing back his head and laughing. He finished by kissing me on the forehead, gently turned me around and nudged me into motion back toward Mother's room, and then rejoined his guests. But the women in our home were never ever again served the men's leftovers from the many parties given in our house in the years to come, when we women had to gather in isolation far from male conviviality. Mohamed was stirred to give the irrevocable command to the kitchen and servants that men and women get separate and complete services at such times. Perhaps we all gained more than we thought by this one change in the usual way of doing things. I don't know.

Arabia confused me by knocking me down with an intolerable situation like that, rolling me around awhile to soften me, and letting me up to try again. Each time I got up it said, "See, things aren't as bad as you make them out," and darned if some of the time that wasn't true! I came to love those enforced hen-party gatherings, for it was then that Mother and Zainab reminisced of days past and I heard tales of life in Arabia before my time.

I heard about marauding bands of Bedou who made it dangerous to travel in the not too long ago and about gate-crashing soldiers who believed music was a thing of the devil and rushed into houses to smash records still turning on the old wind-up phonographs. Zainab one night told of Ibn Saud's campaign to conquer and unify the separately ruled regions in Arabia and described the massacres of Taif and the siege of Jeddah and her father's anguish when he, as Governor of Jeddah, finally had to surrender. I sat enthralled at tales of the Turks and the Hashemites in Mecca in the days before Ibn Saud and was enjoying one discussion about law and order until the women told me of the time they passed through the streets of Jeddah just in time to see a thief's left hand cut off at the wrist. Other stories described the still strong fanatically puritan influences in the country, and I heard again how crafty Ibn Saud overcame their objections to radio by broadcasting recitations from the Holy Koran, proof that radio was not an instrument of evil. Other forces are strong, too, and one evening Zainab told a charming story about a slave girl in their big family house of old (where it must be remembered whole branches lived together) who became pregnant and was called before the "dean" of family men to tell who among her masters was the father of her child. Moslem law is very strict about such things, holding a man responsible for the care of any child he fathers, so the family wanted to do right by the girl. "Tell us, very simply, who?" said the family head to the girl. After a somewhat pensive pause the girl threw the elders into an insoluble dither by saying, "We-e-el-l-l-l-l . . . there was Master So-and-so, and Master So-and-so, and Master So-and-so, and . . ."

Sometimes sitting there in Mother's room I "joined" them on long boat trips to Egypt and on stays on quarantine islands, and heard of longer trips to India in a time when travel was far different from now. I came to know through description innumerable family characters remembered through generations for traits good and bad, and other stories built around people and incidents depicting human foibles and life's little surprises. One must be classified under life's big surprises, having to do with Mother's purchase of a young male slave the same age as Mohamed so they could be companions together, and discovering the first time she bathed him that he was a eunuch. Arabia knocked me down again on that one: it just didn't seem possible I was in a place where things like that happened, but then they told me that traditionally the guards of the Great Mosque in Mecca are eunuchs. Castration of humans is no longer permitted, but in my time many older eunuchs were still on duty in Mecca and from all I gathered they were fearsome guardians, brooking no nonsense from anyone and ever wont to tell a woman pilgrim that her manner or her dress lacked the proper decorum if they felt that was indeed the case.

Zainab liked to launch hair-raising tales that put sleep out of the question and kept us glued to the spot long after we had the run of the house again. She had one about a dagger-bearing ghost on their stairway in India and another about her maid whom she saw and talked to one night in her room when the girl had not been there in the flesh at all and could prove it. She told of a servant who lived for the longest time under an evil spell and of people believed capable of casting such spells on others. Mother believed one of her children had died from a spell put on it by a notorious witch. In telling me the story

Mother said she knew the woman's reputation but had been powerless to prevent her from looking upon her son, who was in apparent perfect health one day and dead the next. Those evenings dwelt on all subjects, including the morbid, but whatever was discussed they were times when I learned much about Arabian life from stories authentic enough to be truly informative and imaginative enough to be spicy. And the one-room scene was remarkable in itself, with party fare spread all over the floor on a fancy tablecloth and Mother, Zainab, Hayat and I (I name us here in the order of seniority so important in Arabia) lounging around happily confined together. As the evening wore on props to the stories were added, things brought out of souvenir chests or *bukshas,* those embroidered squares of material used to bundle belongings or gift-wrap presents, to corroborate or add interest. Hearing about old-time weddings you could thus see Mother's wedding gown which proved that brides of old did indeed wear red. A jingly-jangly anklet showed you what mothers used to put on their children to keep the *djinn* away, and you could lay out a parade of photographs picturing people and places you were hearing about. Mostly on those evenings I felt like a child at story-telling hour with a party and a museum exposition thrown in, and my imagination soared far beyond those four walls.

Aftermaths of parties are often letdowns but ours were shoulder-to-shoulder efforts with our servants and interesting as such. Clean-up tasks were shared, ladies of the house assuming those involving good china, crystal, and silverware, and helpers among the staff filling in as needed. We had ceased setting party tables with the quite ordinary dishes and cutlery formerly brought from a stock kept in town for the use of all branches of the family, supplanting them with truly beautiful services and an accompanying fussiness that they be laid and served properly. This naturally involved teaching the servants, since we were so dependent on them, and it was interesting to watch their initial reaction to new methods and to see which of them learned quickly and which never tried. I am sure they looked askance at the innovation of my fancy colored candles, especially when hot weather arced them over to resemble more a bent mass of croquet wickets than romantic candelabra. Bending them straight and lighting them quickly at the moment of serving was one of the servants' jobs — it was up to the guests to keep them straight after that — but I think they won acceptance only as guarantees of light when the generator broke down.

Part of my survival test as an Arab consisted of learning to get along with our servants. My few set ideas for doing things were no match for the priority given centuries-old methods. It wasn't unwillingness on their part, only difficulty in changing ways. Rogaiya, she of the ruined nylon stockings episode in Taif, was assigned to be our "girl" in Jeddah. Shiny-black, strong, and just plain big, she could, depending on her mood, make short shrift of any task or make it last two days, and in any mood could jar a room just by walking through it. If the floor didn't actually shake under her bulk, you thought it had, and when something tickled her booming laugh to full pitch, pigeons were scared loose from the uppermost ledges of the house. When she was angered and her face glowered into gloomy black, even a strong man trembled.

Rogaiya was hired as washerwoman, but she accepted other tasks when she felt like it and agreed to take care of us when Mother asked her. She even humored our desire to have the one meal of breakfast alone upstairs, but it was Ali and I who gave up the planned tête-à-têtes in favor of sleep. The breakfast time we requested was 2:00 (8 A.M.) but Rogaiya, bless her heart, lumbered up the stairs about 12:00 Arabic time, rattling metal trays and shifting their contents around the whole two hours in an effort to arrange everything nicely for us. We had failed anyway in our effort to teach her the proper arrangement for knives, forks, and spoons, the combinations she could get out of a mere handful of silverware being truly unbelievable. To her it was a lot of fuss over nothing — all she ever ate with was a clean set of fingers, or a big spoon maybe, but she tried and tried to learn and I tried and tried to teach her, and never the twain did meet.

In other things she worked on the principle "if a little is good, a lot more will be better." Take bleach, for instance. We fell heir to some from the house of a departed American businessman, and I gave Rogaiya a demonstration of its power to whiten and remove stains. Thoroughly impressed, she couldn't wait to try it, and in fact didn't. Taking her Master Mohamed's newly tailored *tobes* and *surwals* (seven of each needing the stiff newness and smudges of work removed before wearing), she prepared a whole pail full of bleach to do a really good job and left the garments soaking overnight. The rest is history — not only the sizing was removed but great hunks of the material itself — and Mohamed almost had apoplexy when Rogaiya (honest to the end) took the holey mess to show him. The "words" exchanged between the two of them caused her to go home to her children for the rest of that week and we had to get along without her, a far easier thing to do, believe me, than having to get along with her had she stayed.

As for her cleaning schedule, she swept only when the spirit moved her and the first inkling anyone had of that happening was some morning around dawn when the delicious calm was scratched by her heavy wielding of the handbroom. Then you girded yourself for a whole day of it, because Rogaiya was thorough if nothing else — sporadic to start and painfully slow to finish, but thorough. Furniture was disarranged, ingress and egress blocked with obstacle courses in between, and all carpets rolled up and back as literally pounds of desert sand and dust were dislodged but not necessarily removed. Moving like a juggernaut, slowly but relentlessly on hands and knees from one corner of the room to the other, she punctuated her efforts with soulful cryings out to God and her mother, like *swish-thud,* *swish-thud,* "Ya Allah!" and *bang-bang, plop-plop,* "Ya-Oomie." * With Rogaiya, a job started was not necessarily a job finished and at lunchtime she was like as not to go off and forget to return, leaving you to pick your way as best you could through the maze of furniture and telescoped rugs. Convincing her it would be a nice gesture to get our beds out of the middle of the room and restore the original plan before bedtime was not always easy. Her hand was heavy around vases and objets d'art, but when she toppled and broke them she was the first to be sorry. Unfailingly she brought the carefully gathered pieces of a favorite Sèvres vase or a crushed Rosenthal figurine to show us, and while we wept she went off with a light heart secure in the knowledge that she was an honest woman.

Our other maids, Saada, Insaaf, Baraka, Gabool, and the retired Bushra, had all come into the family as slaves. Bushra had an abode in town provided for her, a yearly stipend, and the complete sets of clothing and gratuities given each year to all members of the staff at feast times. She came and went as she pleased, and she often pleased to come to the house and do thoughtful little chores as she was able. Saada was the one who helped more with Hayat's children and mine as they came along, and she also took care of Mother's quarters and Mother's needs. Insaaf had come as a very young girl from Ethiopia and gradually disengaged herself from house duties, preferring to work in, around, and for the house kitchen. She could do a fine job of cooking when we were between cooks and was known for keeping the work area spic-and-span at all times. Baraka was Hayat's maid, and I had none that I acquired on my own.

I was horrified when townswomen made the suggestion that I buy one, and they could never understand why it would be impossible for me ever to do so. Having slaves was a way of life for them and one could hear them complaining from time to time how the good old days were gone when a slave could be had for such-and-such a price. While I never could approve of slav-

* "Oh, mother mine!"

ery in any form, I could see that in Arabia it was, in a way, a good thing. Having already been taken by slave traders by whatever means, a slave's lot was sadder yet if he did not get into a good home, where in most cases he became a part of the family, often assumed the family name, and was so well treated and loved that it would never have occurred to him to leave even if he could. Ali's father had been one to make a practice of buying then freeing slaves, letting young ones grow up and be taught alongside his own children, and giving them high posts in the family firm if they merited it. Mohamed freed all our slaves one year, and they reacted by crying for days that we no longer wanted them. Moaning and weeping about where they could go and whom they could turn to, they had to be convinced how wrong they were and that no one had ever wanted them to leave home.

The slave situation was much as I believe existed in some old Southern homes, where a bond of love and respect held slaves and their families together far more than the legalities of ownership papers. In Arabia the slave who cares for a child from infancy on is often called "Mother ———" by that child, although this was more common in royal households where each child has his own "mother," or governess, than in other homes.

Before we moved from the Rawais house Mother bought a very young slave girl named Murgana, and I found out I was not as used to slavery as I thought. I had been listening quite calmly to slave-market talk, knowing our own slaves had been bought years before in days when people did that sort of thing, but when Murgana came fresh and new and so very young, eight or nine I think, I was jarred to the teeth that this child actually was there in exchange for money. She was to let us know through the years that she wasn't too happy about it either, and we all had to take a hand in making her place with us. Mother was her prime mentor of course, keeping Murgana close to her, teaching her manners and habits of cleanliness, giving her small responsibilities within her capabilities — like running upstairs to tell me lunch was ready, fetching things, or staying with a younger child. Her talent for devilment was prestigious, hardly a day going by when we weren't upset by something she did (or didn't do), and she disappeared as often as she thought she could get away with it to the older girls' quarters, not to commiserate but to perpetrate more devilment. Smart enough to preserve outward appearances of cleanliness and "perform" the manners taught her when it behooved her to do so, she reverted to her same mischievous, destructive, rebellious self whenever and wherever she could. The whole household reared her (which was probably her problem) and few among us ever thought we would make it. It was fitting, I guess, that she figured in one episode which remains starkly alive in my memory because in it I acted much as she might have, and she was just a child.

It was one of those times when I was myself rebelling against the life in Arabia, in particular the way we all lived together. I resented the fact I could not just get up in the morning and go through the day on my own with no one else to worry about, following any whim of activity, or any whim of non-activity if that suited me better. That day I did not want to be part of a whole houseful of people; I wanted to do as I pleased and I wanted to do it by myself; and the more I thought about the fact that I couldn't, the more I was pushed beyond the bounds of reasonableness. I decided I *wasn't* going downstairs to follow the day's routine; I *wasn't* going to go down and have all the servants kiss my hand; I *wasn't* going to go down and be dutiful and do all the things I should; I wasn't, in fact, going to go down *at all*, at least not until I jolly well felt like it. There was no other way I could fight the establishment — I couldn't hop in my car and go to the local drugstore for a Coke, I couldn't run around the block, I couldn't pretend I wasn't home, nor could I turn on the radio and listen to a soap opera, call a friend on the phone and chat, or go on a hike.

I felt trapped, not just physically, but by the requirements of living where many people had to be greeted each morning, where I was but a small cog in the whole works, and where everything was shared. We couldn't even have a good fight with our spouses without all the family and servants knowing about it! No, I was in no mood to talk to anyone that day and purposely let my usual hour of descent go by without a peep. I had known all along what would happen next, but when it did I blew my top. Little Murgana came knocking on my door looking like she had flown in on her huge hair-ribbon wings and told me, "Sitti sent me to find out why you haven't come down and to see if you are all right." Through tears of anger I burst out, "Damn it all, of course I'm all right! Just because I don't go down at the stroke of dawn and kowtow to everybody, does that mean I'm not all right?"

Poor Murgana didn't understand my angry words but she wasn't going to stand around and have them translated and so flew back to her mistress. I followed her to the landing, yelling like the madwoman I momentarily was, and repeated my words to Mother who had by then come to the bottom of the stairs. My tirade spent, I retreated to my bedroom until Ali came home for lunch, but then the whole thing came back up inside me and to my horror I gave a repeat performance. It passed over, not because I apologized, but because Mother luckily never knew what I really said, and secondly because Ali was always good at talking me out of my fits. They didn't happen too often, but once in a while I had to free in that manner or another the feelings that gripped me, as ivy climbing all over a house must be trimmed now and then to give the structure light and to let it breathe.

Because we lacked the so-called normal social and recreational outlets of modern times we had to depend for fun on one of the truly normal outlets of all time — the enjoyment of nature. A simple ride or an outing under the stars thus became a form of entertainment and the name the Arabs give such outings is apt in the extreme. "Sniffing the wind" was what we did when we left all our walls and when someone said, "Hiya, neroh nashoom al howa schwoya," * we took off as if we were going to a show, which sometimes we were. Sunsets on the sea were spectaculars of the first order and maybe it was their glory that gave the Red Sea its name.

One night Mohamed and Hayat, Mother and Zainab, and Ali and I went off to sniff the wind in grand manner, which is to say we took a picnic dinner, our old-fashioned phonograph and three albums of records, and drove to a site on a lovely lagoon famous for its sandy shores and a colony of sharks. The sea and the sand and the moon and the crazy things we did that night have always reminded me of Lewis Carroll's poem "The Walrus and the Carpenter." I half expected the dear little oysters to come prancing up as we pranced around ourselves, but we didn't even see a shark. Mohamed played a wild Carmen Miranda record and went into her famous dance, cavorting and wiggling and weaving, somewhat hampered by his long *tobe* and losing his headdress, but putting on a great show. When the Viennese waltzes he played next swelled in the desert air Mohamed asked me to dance, and one hasn't lived until she has waltzed through one whole production of Strauss on, over, and through Arabia's sand. Mohamed swooped me through great exaggerated dance motions and we were sniffing the sand instead of the wind before we were through. The evening ended after a footrace between the two men with Hayat atop Mohamed's shoulders and I atop Ali's. Mother and Zainab made up the cheering section as the men carried their neither light nor steady loads in charges across the beach and Hayat and I hung on for dear life. For us it was like jogging on a camel, and I don't think the men were exactly comfortable either. Neither of them actually won because it was too difficult trying to match the jogs from below with the

* "Come along, let's go out ["sniff the wind"] for a while."

jigs from above and we all soon collapsed in a great laughing heap.

In contrast, some nights in the desert were quiet ones where we sat silently back to back and let the very serenity soak our tensions out, and then it was a lonely peace. Everywhere we looked it was like looking at forever and the bigness of problems disappeared in the magnitude of desert stretches and the panoplies of sky and sea. Sniffing the night wind with a full moon above and more stars than anywhere cleared our hearts and our minds and made us forget that our lives had fences around them.

Chapter 11

Soon I could slip through some of the fences around me provided I slipped back inside them afterward. As Ali himself got more into the swim of things, I was allowed to be at his side for some of the entertaining his work and interests entailed. Visiting VIP's, members of the diplomatic corps, and foreign businessmen (who were usually our houseguests, partly because of Arab hospitality and partly because there were no hotels then) were regularly entertained at our house, and if no Arab men were present (or at least Arabs who would not approve my appearing in mixed company) I was invited, too, and got to play hostess.

Strangely, almost every one of the parties thus attended is memorable to me for reasons other than the most obvious, that I was simply allowed to be there.

Hamida made one party unique by swallowing enough of a well-known laxative to choke a horse just minutes before guests were due to arrive. She thought it was chocolate, and had hastened to inform her grandmother of the treat she had found (she kept the family *au courant* of such things) when I spotted the wrappers and raced to find her. I heard Mother telling her, "May it increase your well-being, darling," but the little darling would need help, we knew, and we sent for a doctor. The first one we got bounced the child on his knees, patted her cheek and said, "Well, she'll be tired certainly, but no cause for alarm," and we got rid of him in a hurry, sending a bit more frantically for a second doctor. That one, the newly arrived Lebanese Dr. Idriss, knew what to do and did it and stayed with us until all was well.

Our neglected guests were not served dinner until close to midnight, but they hadn't minded. They had fallen back on their own resources and were by then, as the saying goes, "feeling no pain."

On another occasion an evening-gowned, white-suited, Arab-tobéd group of us went off in jeeps to end a party with a midnight spin on the desert. We spotted a wee kangaroo looking at us in the beam of our headlights and played a game of follow-the-leader behind him. Then there was the night of the rain (it either rained not at all or tended to burst a cloud) and Mohamed, unable to bear the thought of all that good water going to waste as it rained and rained, commandeered the men guests to brave the thunder and lightning to take the lids off all our cisterns.

And I remember the times Ali tricked the ship captains of marine lines they handled with his dinner invitations. Hospitality, you must remember, is a prime current in the flow of Arab life, and invitations to dinner in Arabia, as in the rest of the world, are the usual manifestation of hospitality. But those captains were positive their invitations were special, because Ali always told them, "I'd like you to meet my wife," and they couldn't believe their ears. They were old hands in that part of the world, and they knew those Arabs never let their wives be seen by other men — why, even a veiled woman was rarely seen — so by the time they arrived at the house they were thoroughly convinced they were to be granted the rarest of privileges. And Ali gleefully gave them the full treatment. He greeted them alone, let the atmosphere build, waited until they were watching doors and listening for every sound, and then I came in. Pretending nothing was wrong, I'd walk in as blithely full of American bonhomie as you please — so hard for me to sustain after one look at their faces. Instead of a sloe-eyed Arabian lady upon whose beauty no westerner had ever gazed they got me, and their shock was almost always uncontrollable. I ignored their open mouths and questioning eyes until they could stand my inane chatter no longer and had to blurt, "But you're American!" "Well, *yes,* how nice of you to guess!" and their hopes were dashed to bits. Poor souls! We got away with it every time.

Once I boarded a ship of theirs by only pretending to be American, and once I drove a car in Jeddah's streets by pretending to be an Arab man. Doffing cloak and veil, I joined American secretary friends from Aramco* on a ship visit and wore their guise of cotton dress and scarf. Walking past Arabs standing on the dock, and proceeding up the gangplank, I was sure my bare face or my manner, or something, would give me away for the imposter I was, but I fooled them and even came home with a present from the captain — a piece of fresh yeast the size of a cantaloupe for the bread I was beginning to make in my idle hours. The captain wanted to make up for laughing so hard at the peppery ice cream I had served the night before. I hadn't known when I made it that Rogaiya had pounded my sugar in the same mortar she pounded peppercorns.

The time I drove was simply, I suspect, to shut me up about missing driving. Ali thought that if we went late at night and if I wore his headdress and followed his directions through the walled city, I could satisfy my longing and that would be the end of that. So one night he pinched one of his headcloths into little folds over my forehead, the way men wore them, put the black rope over my clothes, and off we went with me in the driver's seat. What happened then was purely a case of my being given an inch and taking a few miles, as I drove off and took us

* Arabian American Oil Company.

far afield of the planned course, landing us almost inextricably
in a dead end with precious little space in which to turn around.
What must have been the only person abroad at that hour suddenly had to appear behind us and Ali wanted to shrivel up and
die. I got to laughing uncontrollably, unbecoming of a "man"
in Arab headdress, while Ali muttered under his teeth, "Get us
out of here, you idiot!" And I *was* trying. It was just that it was
so hard to back up with my chin in my chest to avoid exposing
my beardless mien. Ali could at least have been grateful that the
stripped gears hid my laughter. He got behind the wheel as soon
as the coast was clear, and with a subdued me by his side drove
home past a stone edifice he said was Eve's Tomb. If he was trying to tell me something, I missed it; and I lost the opportunity
to express doubt that our fair city had ever been the Garden of
Eden. In any case, he never let me drive again.

Besides the pleasure of most pleasant and distinguished company, I got an eggbeater out of one party honoring the departing United States Minister to Saudi Arabia, Colonel Eddy, and
his wife. After dinner the colonel, one of his staff, and I were
discussing methods of cooking in Arabia and the lack of kitchen
equipment as we knew it, when I jokingly turned to the colonel
and said: "Speaking of such things, would you by any chance
have an eggbeater?"

"I'll look, by golly," he said, and next afternoon Ali got a shoe
box tied with string with an eggbeater inside wrapped in old
newspaper (which, incidentally, I read from first page to last, I
was that starved for reading material). With the box was the
following note on the card of William Alfred Eddy, Envoy Extraordinary and Minister Plenipotentiary of the United States
of America:

DEAR ALI,
Your good lady mentioned that she would like an eggbeater.
Here is a used one, the only one I have, with my compliments.
But remember the fatal proverb, "you can't make an omelet
without *breaking* eggs" . . .

I was the only lady in the house privileged to attend mixed gatherings, but the others probably would not have wanted to anyway. But all of us were always there to help prepare any party, be it mixed, all-male, or all-female, and in the latter instance, of course, it was the men's turn to seek seclusion. I would be interested to know if any of the Arabian men ever climbed at such times to vantage points on roofs or balconies to watch the goings-on of a women's party in, say, the garden below, as I know for a fact Arabian women and children often did to watch the men's gatherings; but I can only guess, and your guess is as good as mine. Peek or not, I do know they minded where and when they walked at such times and that our older houseboys also were careful not to intrude. *Older* means into the teen years, and I witnessed once a group of very upset women when one of these young men came unexpectedly among them. It was in Taif when a teen-age houseboy answered Mother's frantic call for someone — anyone — to catch a mouse in the room. More pandemonium was caused by his appearance than by the mouse's. Each lady grabbed whatever she could to cover her face — a pillow, a cigarette box, her hair tie or, much to my surprise, the hem of her long skirt, apparently preferring to let her pantaloons be seen rather than her face.

When we visited in other homes, especially one of the many houses of relatives, servants of long-standing greeted men and women whom they had known for a long time, coming to touch or kiss their hands, but when guests were not known to them they kept a shy and respectful distance unless called forth to perform a task. With the men who drove our cars for us the relationship was similar — informal with those who knew us and with whom we did not have to be as careful about the veil; but when others' drivers came to call for us or return us to our home, little was said in their presence and we were careful to stay covered.

Each family had its regular drivers (who usually doubled as shoppers for the ladies of the house), but for special trips or special outings a more skilled driver-mechanic would be assigned. Hayat and I were privileged females on one of those trips — a gazelle hunt in the desert northeast of us — and I wonder what our jeep drivers thought about our informality on that special occasion.

Ali and Ahmed had planned the hunt, and I'll never know how they came to permit us to go, but we were wild and young in those days and sometimes we had to do wild and young things to keep our sanity. They put us girls next to the drivers and Hayat and I had no idea what was in store for us until *vroom, vroom,* off we roared in a wild chase after the first gazelle we spotted in the area where we were cruising. Our vehicle seemed to match the gazelle's leaps and bounds as it fled and we pursued, but we had none of the animal's grace. Wind and sand whipped around us in the open car, threatening to blow us out if the careening jeep did not jolt or bounce us out first, and when we got close enough for a shot, the men shifted to higher points in the rear and I experienced stark fear. A shotgun blast directly behind my bobbing head scared the daylights out of me, as I bounced around in front and I thought, well, at least there's a choice of possible deaths: either our driver is going to lose control if I don't stop bumping into him (I was sure at times that he already had); or the two jeeps are going to collide head-on in the involvement of the chase and we'll all go; or, thirdly, I will simply lose my head. The floorboards chose that moment to come loose under my feet but it would have been death to straighten up. The desert poured in on me but I stayed bent, you bet, and as if that weren't enough, my taut legs started to cramp with the effort of bracing the rest of me. I must have looked awfully funny trying to beat out a cramp under those conditions, but I wasn't laughing.

I never asked when we stopped how fast we had gone, but the gazelle is a very fleet animal and, personally, I think we were airborne a couple of times. The animal was downed, though, and I remember how Ahmed ran to it to complete the slaughter by slitting the throat, as Moslems are required to do if they eat the flesh, and it made me sick. It wasn't the sight of the blood so much as the destruction of the animal's living beauty. But no time to mourn, we were soon off again in hot pursuit of another. I managed in subsequent chases that day to keep my head and its flying headdress on and to control the floorboards so as not to get pelted from below as I could so easily have been from above, and all in all we bagged three gazelles I think.

We stopped then, grimy, disheveled, sweaty, sore of bone, and body all kinked, to break open our knapsacks and eat and drink. True hunger and true thirst brought true enjoyment of the simplest of meals — fist-size cuts of coarse brown bread, crumbles of goat cheese, a container of olives in oil we sopped up with our bread, and plain, cold, delicious water — not the most elegant meal I ever had but one of the most enjoyable.

In more ways than one we had strayed from our norm that day, gone out of bounds, done something different. It was a great feeling to toot our way out of the compound and head for wide open spaces on such a companionable adventure, but it was always back to the confines — back again to the shifting layers of our connected lives where all day every day we were many things. Ali, for instance, was husband, son, brother, uncle, brother-in-law, father, and we in other instances each played our own variety of roles.

If we had privacy it was a changing state with different definitions at different times — qualified as single or conjugal privacy, a privacy among various combinations of souls inhabiting the house; or it could be called privacy when we all came at one time in a gathering of all men, women, children within the compound, sitting together, eating together, talking together, playing together. Sometimes, of course, we seemed at such times more like a club that meets once a month with nothing better to do than read the minutes of the last meeting, but that was no doubt because of the way we rotated in different circles most of the day and only came together to share the oneness of family when other activities let us.

A saving grace, for me at least, was the way we did manage to get away from it all from time to time — to another country. Some of these getaways were for special government missions, others for the purpose of doing business for the family firm, and some when Ali had to seek medical treatment for a back ailment which had plagued him since university days. The latter trips were not fun for anyone. His back attacks had defied diagnosis for a long time but almost always required hospitalization under the care of a specialist, and Ali had to go abroad for that. For whatever reason, we usually all left together on these trips and Ali was sometimes teased for the reputation he acquired of accepting travel duty for the government only if his family could go. The top echelons were quite aware of this, we knew, because Ali received a cable from the king once requesting that he leave on a particular mission and His Majesty ended his message with the terse sentence: "Yes, your family may go."

I loved to go, but there were times when I would have liked more advance notice to pack up and leave. Sometimes I received this order only hours before departure, but occasionally I would have all of overnight to prepare. On at least one proposed quick trip I was ready and willing to go in record time, and then Ali forgot for the rest of the day to let me know that our plans had changed.

So that no one will think me stupid for sitting with packed bags the better part of a day waiting unquestioningly for the signal to leave, I must explain our special procedure for departure. Flights were not only few and far between, they seldom arrived on schedule, so it only follows they did not leave on schedule, either. We *never* went to the airport at a prearranged flight time. We depended on the local telephone operator to keep a line open to the airport and notify us when our plane was in, refueled and ready to go, and *then* we'd start serious leave-taking. Luggage would go first, then the men, then the women, the latter driven practically to the door of the plane at the last possible moment so that: (1) they would undergo the least possible scrutiny on airport grounds; (2) they had a comparatively short wait as they sat veiled in hot cars; and (3) they had little time to sit veiled in a hot plane before takeoff. The airport situation, therefore, was my excuse for being so bovine in waiting for our trip to happen, although that did not excuse Ali for forgetting me. And he never did excuse himself. He just laughed and laughed when he came in and saw me ready at the drop of a veil to respond to the cry of "the plane's here, let's go!"

One lunchtime Ali announced we were going to Egypt the next day to buy 2 boats and 140 trucks and I said, "Whee! What kind of boats?" He explained the conditions of his successful negotiations for two Landing Ship Tanks (LST's from U.S. government surplus, I suppose) of World War II fame and said we had to deliver the money ourselves. My picture was one of briefcase stuffed with letters of credit, bank drafts and the like, but he meant just what he said: we were actually taking the money.

Awad, our major-domo, came in the late afternoon with eleven heavy-cloth sacks of heavy, heavy gold that he lined up like floppy soldiers on our bedroom floor and which I was instructed to pack in and around our belongings in our travel bags. I felt from the first that Awad should have said "Open Sesame" every time he struggled in the door with more, and when he left I sank onto the bed with my head at the foot, the better to gaze at the gold, and then I couldn't shake the refrain "Midas has donkey ears, Midas has donkey ears" from my giddy head. Eleven sacks of gold! In my bedroom! Ye Gods! I got up and hoisted a couple — boy, were the guys who picked up our little suitcases going to be surprised! And then came the giggles. The thought of putting all that gold among my hair curlers and nightgowns and Ali's shorts and socks gave me the mushrooming hysterical kind of laughter that wouldn't quit, and I was mighty glad for the kind of privacy I had right then.

Understandably, our luggage went with us instead of ahead of us the next morning, so I was able to watch the airport fellows come to get the bags Awad set out for them on the ground. The surprise of one was monumental when he went blithely up to my little overnighter which anyone could have lifted with one finger and had to use both hands just to get it off the ground.

It must be made quite clear at this point that the gold thus transported was properly declared at customs in Cairo, although I do seem to remember something about an upsetting effect on the local gold market the next day. But the purchase was completed, arrangements were made for getting the LST's to Jeddah, and we returned there ourselves with lightened hearts and lightened luggage to settle in until we were unsettled again.

In Arabia the LST's were rechristened *Yousuf*, in honor of our Uncle Yousuf, and *Zainal*, in honor of Ali's father's oldest brother, then deceased. The two vessels were put into service up and down the Red Sea transporting cargoes of wood, coal, and the like. Steta Oma, the old lady "Big-sister-aunt" who had visited me each day in Taif, got wind of it, except that she took it to mean that the men themselves were reduced to such menial tasks. In her senility she had forgotten that Zainal was dead and I suppose she thought Yousuf, whom she saw every week, was purposely hiding the bitter facts from her, and it made her angry. She couldn't imagine how the family had been brought to such a downfall that Zainal had to carry coal and Yousuf had to carry wood, and she demanded to have a full account made to her of such dreadful happenings. When Mohamed tried as gently and as clearly as he could to explain and to reassure her that all was well with the family business, she became so incensed in the belief that he was humoring her that she raised her hand and slapped him — she knew what she had heard! We women depended on the men to keep us informed of all such little stories. I look back on how much a husband and wife (perhaps Ali and I more than other couples because we could have been more aware of the separation of the sexes) learned about events in the other's circles. Ali told me things that happened in that part of his life where I had no entree, and I would tell him of events in mine and thus we shared what was not experienced together. It was almost ritual to go over each day's happenings and talk about people, activities, excitement in the city, and local gossip, if you will. Men I never knew became quite familiar through such talks, and Ali's recountings of meetings and dealings in business and government and the intertwined social obligations among the men helped me to keep abreast of actualities.

Ali couldn't have been all that interested in my offering for the day on what the Turkish ambassador's wife had served for tea, as an example of what was current and good, but sometimes I had news that was news. He couldn't sneeze at the interesting tale describing a large complement of local ladies at a "let's-get-acquainted" gathering sponsored by the new British minister's wife, who made the guests spend the afternoon participating in various parlor games, door drawings, guessing games, and simple games of skill — activities completely foreign to them. The funny thing was that they didn't have a chance of backing out, short of leaving. The hostess was the kind of chipper Englishwoman who forges ahead with indomitable will and won't take no for an answer. To help her, there were sufficient adventurous souls among the Arab ladies to give her party plans a try and since the people there are the same as anywhere else, once someone started and broke the way, the others followed. The language barrier was of no import that day because everyone's good sense of humor came to the fore and some of the party's success lay in the ladies' great facility for laughing at themselves, with credit of course to the hostess and to her guests' ability to respond.

Some stories of mine I was anxious to tell Ali before anyone else did, like the time I was driven to utter "Ga-a-aw-w-wd" during a dinner with Steta Oma and other elderly ladies who lived with her in the big old house in town, when one of their number let out a granddaddy of a belch. Hayat, sitting next to me, promptly choked on whatever she had in her mouth, proof again that we should always have separated on such occasions. We both had trigger-happy senses of humor and some thing was always happening to set us off, but I never saw her react to anything like she did that time. My utterance, like the lady's belch, came from the toes, as it were, and struck Hayat so funny that first she had to be led from the table, and then I had to support her to the door as we both had to leave. I assured Ali — for days and days — that no one else, especially "Sitti Baaahh," as we forever after called her in spite of ourselves, ever knew the real reason for our behavior and I was glad about that myself. Sitti Baaahh was normally one of the most soft-spoken and gentle souls among the *grandes dames*.

Besides the chit-chat concerning local happenings there was an enormous amount of information, anecdotes, and history that I gleaned about Ali's own family to recount to him later. He hated to admit it, but he learned a lot from me that he had never known before, and what surprised him most was the fact that I learned all these things from Arabic spoken to me. That wasn't saying very much for me and my intellect after I had been there several years, but I'd done it from almost the very first and it was an oft-mentioned source of amazement to him.

One day his mother and I joined together to make a pictorial history display of our good Ali that spanned many years. Mother always had a good sense of humor and the stack of old photographs of Ali that she chose to give me one morning proved it. We laughed ourselves silly over some of them and one of us — I can't remember which — got the idea to string the entire batch of pictures across our bedroom for Ali to see in all their glory the minute he walked in. There were the usual naked baby pictures, snaps from his boyhood and school days, some sporting the latest in the clothing styles of the day, and in general, the usual assortment of good and bad photographs that any family collects; and we included all of them in our makeshift gallery. Mother rarely climbed our many stairs after she moved to the ground floor, but that day she made the trip twice, the first time to bring me the pictures and the second because she wouldn't have missed Ali's first reaction for anything in the world. He made the trip more than worthwhile for her but swore that some of those pictures could not possibly be he. We could only say, for there's no denying it, "Mother knows best."

There were so many people in our family hierarchy that it was no easy task through the years to get and keep them straight. The ladies visited back and forth from family house to family house and on occasion I'd see their men, but I sometimes was at a loss to know who belonged to whom, whether their relationship was paternal or maternal, or how, exactly, they had sprouted on the family tree. Outside of the fact that it was an interesting game, it was also sometimes important that I know their identifying connection before I called them a name. *Aunt,* for instance, is a different word for aunts paternal and maternal, and *cousin* is "son-of-my-aunt" or "daughter-of-my-aunt," so one could make three mistakes right there without even trying. Thus it was of some importance while attending a family get-together that the tribe's lineage chart be more or less clearly embedded in one's mind. It was a long process learning it, and I was not overly successful in overcoming recurring confusion on the subject, plus I had to refrain, above all, from assuming that someone's importance tended to decrease in direct proportion to how far away he or she was from the family center. Family affiliation is a matter of great pride, and if any assessment of importance is evidenced it is only in the honor and respect always given to elders.

Ali had two outstanding half sisters who were anything but halfway in their love for and adherence to family ties. Kind women, charitable, generous, thoughtful, both strong-willed each in her own way, but ever fair and champions of right. As is common in people who are always doing so much for others, they had that trait of being uncommonly grateful for anything, however small, that was done for them.

Their mothers had been different, and physically they were opposites. Steta Khadija was short and round until illness wasted her, and Steta Fatma was slight and wiry. Their dissimilarity showed itself too in the way they did things. The unhurried calm of Steta Khadija was deceptive because she accomplished much in the hours of a day, and it also hid a temper, I was told, that could flare if pushed. She was elderly, older than Ali's mother, in fact, and was alone all the time I knew her. Alone as opposed to married — because no one in our family was ever really *alone* — but she had once had a marriage, the details of which I knew nothing. She became quite deaf in her later years, and in her constant concern for others was overly cautious about getting her voice too high or too loud, so her speech was practically soundless and we had to listen carefully for her soft words or read her lips as she no doubt had to read ours. "Inti bint taiyibah,"* she used to tell me, sometimes for a reason and sometimes just because she felt like it, but in my opinion she and sister Zainab are the only two people I have ever known who could be called perfect. My mother once remarked that Zainab had "the soul of a prophet and the kindness of God" and the saying fit them both. My fondest memory of Steta Khadija is the day she legitimately won the

* You are a good girl."

prize for pinning-the-tail-on-the-donkey at Hamida's birthday party, and I thought then that I was going to give a speech praising her marvelous spirit, but the time was not right. Illness felled her soon after and so my chances ran out to tell her how much I thought of her. She was one of the earth's truly good people.

Steta Fatma, the other half of this very special pair, was the nervous type, one not to be budged from any course of action or non-action once she set her mind to it. Stubborn, in a word, or having the courage of her convictions, if you prefer. Her childless marriage ended early in divorce and one of her joys then in life was to take orphans into her home and raise them as her own, giving them every possible advantage and setting them up in future life, be it marriage for a girl or business for a boy, and then starting all over again with another. Steta Fatma had definite ideas about people and places she liked and people and places she didn't, and her food habits (she never ate when other people did) and rest habits and travel idiosyncrasies caused through the years great concern to others but continued to give her, as her children did, many of her own true pleasures.

She was, besides, able to tell a good story on herself and the Good Lord has made things happen to her that have given her ample story material. I used to watch her sitting in front of her listeners, pushing her usually long straggly black hair out of her eyes or away from her thin, bony face, letting a click slip from her teeth now and then, her black eyes alive with humor behind glasses that slipped too, and telling the most outlandish but true stories that only she could have experienced.

My favorite of these was her mouse story, and it goes like this. Steta Fatma had donned her long nightgown preparatory to retiring, smoothing the cloth down over her, when she saw at her feet a tiny mouse who scampered away immediately, she knew not where. Thinking it might conceivably have gone hickory, dickory, dock up her gown, she ripped it off and continued searching the room. With her slipper at the ready, she went around and around carefully, quietly, stealthily, pushing her long hair away when it fell over her eyes as she stooped and peered. Then when she stood up to confront herself in a long mirror she saw the mouse — sitting right on top of her head, his tail probably the most persistent piece of "hair" she had been brushing aside. One good whack knocked him off his heretofore safe perch and she called off the hunt and let him go free. She knew when she had been capped!

The only other person I knew who could maybe match Steta Fatma in the same kind of story-telling was Sitt Nura, the Number One wife of Finance Minister Shaikh Abdullah as-Sulaiman. I met her and her two fellow wives (there's a special name for them in Arabic, but none to my knowledge in English) at someone's house early in my Jeddah days, and through the years she was a good friend. She was a flashy, bright-eyed, gold-toothed extrovert with a massive head of hair who didn't mind whom she shocked when she spoke. But she could also sit quietly, on the rare occasions when she wanted to, and fix her sharp eyes on anyone present and mentally size her up with an equally sharp mind. She was usually holding the floor, though, and the verve with which she told the most personal and often embarrassing stories on herself was extraordinary. She was always bursting with sheer energy or joie de vivre or something that propelled her on talk waves, and her voluble and volatile presence took any conversation away from the desultory.

She and her two co-wives formed the permanent part of Shaikh Abdullah's marital bliss, and the allowable fourth-wife position was kept in a state of rotation for many years. A Moslem is, as you know, allowed as many as four at a time provided he treats them equally and provides for them equally (although the Koran goes on to say that the heart cannot be divided) and Shaikh Abdullah apparently did a fantastic job in keeping his three "permanent" wives happy and congenial with each other and himself. Over the years the woman temporarily occupying the number-four position was tolerated by the permanent three probably because they thought she would soon be on her way like the others before her, but Shaikh Abdullah fooled them one year, to their great consternation, by liking the current Number Four so well that he kept her, too, making her just as permanent, if not more so, than they were. Nura's stories about the continuing episodes in that situation were priceless.

I knew the first three women best and was ever at a loss to comprehend in my own mind their togetherness, given the fact that they did, after all, share one husband. Either they were very special women as human beings go or Shaikh Abdullah was a very special man as husbands go. The women visited together, received guests together, rejoiced in each other's children, were solicitous and kind to each other, and even dressed alike. At least they were alike when I knew them, appearing at parties in solid-sequined floor-length gowns of high color and brilliance, literally outshining the rest of us. And one day I even saw them in matching shoes. My eyes were feasting on the glitter of their gowns when I spotted three pairs of gaily decorated Mickey Mouse shoes peeking out from under the sequins where they were all sitting on the divan. And why not? They were the latest thing from America to arrive in Jeddah's unpredictable *suk*.

Women's parties, men's parties, family parties — of these we had many, but one thing stood out on the social scene (for those who thought about such things) and that was the absence of cocktail parties (for men or for women). Liquor is forbidden entry into Saudi Arabia and has been for some time.* King Ibn Saud ('Abd al'Aziz' more properly) had at one time allowed the diplomatic corps to import liquor for their own use, but that privilege was rescinded by the king when one of his

---

* Those desirous of drinking have found their own ways of circumventing this law. A delicate subject.

subjects, already drunk, burst in on the British Consul demand-
ing liquor from the consulate's private stock. He was refused,
and became so incensed in his intoxicated state that he shot and
killed the Englishman. After that tragic incident those who
wanted alcoholic beverage had either to smuggle it into the
country, or make it themselves, which I have no doubt is exactly
what some of the more enterprising did. I asked Mother once if
any of the local people were ever that enterprising and learned
that in the old days at least there was talk of a raisin brew that
had a reputation for potency second to none. Mother also told
me of the one time she (unintentionally) became intoxicated
while trying to cure a severe headache. The usual palliatives
had given no relief, so she took the advice of an old crone who
recommended that she rub alcohol into the crown of her head
and that, according to Mother, really worked. It put the pain,
and her, out like a light for several hours at least, and although
I believed the story I've always meant to look into what the
medical annals have to say about it.

For my part, I've always been sorry that I never took some of
that good pomegranate juice we were always drinking to see
what could be done to make it more "interesting." The time
came when it was almost completely superseded by carbonated
soft drinks which had their advent first from Egypt (the Egyptian *gazeuse*) and later from the United States and Europe. Our
other main beverages, Turkish coffee and tea, were never
budged from their positions of great favor as part of the Arab
tradition of hospitality, and neither was another kind of coffee we had, Arabian coffee. That had its beginnings among the
Bedou of Nejd, and was always served by the Royal Family of
Saud.

Gawaha Arabi doesn't look or taste like other coffee because
it is made from the green bean, spiced with cardamom, and
produces a pale brew that tastes, to the unaccustomed palate,
like bitter medicine. But once a person develops a taste for it,
he may come to prefer it to other kinds. Special people make

the coffee and other special people serve it from big brass pots whose spouts are stuffed with a fiber of sorts to strain the spices from the coffee as it is poured into handleless cups not much larger than a thimble. The most important thing to know about this coffee is not how to drink it but how to stop drinking it. When it is being served to you there are only two ways to keep your cup from being refilled when you have finished: put your index finger over the top of the cup or wiggle the cup gently back and forth as you return it to the one serving it. A simple "no, thank you" won't do it — the cup will be returned to you time and time again if neither of the two rules are observed. Since the server usually waits until one guest is finished before moving on to the next, lack of this necessary knowledge could lead one to considerable embarrassment.

A supposedly true Arabian tale tells of a just-arrived British diplomat, in the old days, who was rushed from the boat to the palace to present his credentials before the king's annual visit to Jeddah ended and the court returned to the capital of Riyadh, which would necessitate the diplomat's taking the arduous overland desert route or waiting unaccredited until the king's next visit. His aides tried to include in their briefing everything he would need to know of palace protocol and procedure, but neglected to tell him about the coffee. The poor fellow was essentially a tea drinker to begin with, but in the normal course of his audience with the king he drank a most abnormal amount of the bitter native brew when he wouldn't even have enjoyed one cup of regular coffee. He finally ended his predicament by folding his arms militantly across his chest and looking away, but the king had certainly taken note of the fellow's extraordinary enjoyment and whispered something to his aide. When the audience was over, the man returned to his lodgings hoping never to see a cup of coffee again as long as he lived and found waiting for him several large sacks of the special coffee beans from the royal stores.

Chapter 12

WHAT WAS to have been my first full summer in Arabia turned into Ali's conducting us family women and children to Lebanon to escape Jeddah's heat, followed by a solitary flight of mine to Cairo to rejoin Ali when I least expected, followed by an equally unexpected trip to the United States, during which I was the only female member of a Saudi Arabian Finance Mission group. The first part happened according to plan, Ali taking us to Aley, a mountain village above Beirut, and getting us into a rented house before he left; but a few short days after his departure for Arabia he called me from Cairo and on a bad telephone connection managed to convey the message, "You have to be in Cairo by tomorrow afternoon if you want to go with me to the United States," before the phone went dead. My first reaction was "Ye Gods, I've just finished unpacking." Then I said, "I'll never make it." And finally, "I couldn't go anyway because Hamida is so sick."

But I had not reckoned with my in-laws. Mother and Hayat sped down the winding mountain road to Beirut to find the doctor whose permission for Hamida to travel had to be granted before all else, then Zainab assumed my packing chore by dumping all of my belongings in the middle of the floor and saying, "You separate out of that what you want and I'll do the rest"; and none of them for a moment let me hold the thought that the trip to the United States was not to be. "You'll make it all right if you are meant to," and then they went ahead to make sure I was.

After the doctor's O.K. for Hamida on certain conditions of diet and medication, Mother hastened the following morning to the Egyptian Consulate to get a visa on my passport, she stopped at the moneychanger's for some piasters and pounds, and went to the airport to see what she could do about getting a plane. We had been told on the phone that there were no scheduled flights to Cairo that day, but she wouldn't accept that until she saw for herself. There were for a fact no regular flights that day, but while Mother was at the airport a little Egyptian Airlines seven-seater plane chartered by a friend of hers, Madame Ibrahim Shak'er, came flying in from Cairo and Mother snapped it up for me for the return flight that afternoon. So, it seems, difficulties do fade when they are meant to.

It was hot and humid in Beirut that day and we were sagging in body and spirit, sad at taking leave of each other after the flurry of getting ready, and went to sip a good-bye drink together (cool lemonade) in a downtown coffeehouse. Thinking about how much we were going to miss each other, it made me even sadder to think of all they had done to get me off. Then Zainab excused herself to go up the street and when she came back we got the laugh we all needed to restore our waning spirits as she handed me a large wooden box of baklava from the pastry shop ahead, plus a heavy tin of pistachio nuts. It was funny because I could barely manage as it was with my traveling load — one child, a purse, a kit of medicines and another of special foods ordered by the doctor, a shoulder bag of extra clothing, and now the string-tied heavy goodies from

Zainab. It was a big joke when I thanked her for her thought-fulness, and the joke grew to general gaiety by the time we reached the airport.

I could see them still waving even after we took off in the tiny plane (that I likened to a kite at the time), and then I had to turn quickly to something else to keep my composure in front of the pilot and radioman who were with me in the tiny cabin. I started talking to them in Saudi Arabian Arabic and they talked back in Egyptian Arabic, mutually understandable, to be sure, but there are differences in pronunciation that were still very fine points for me then. But the men were pleasant and friendly and listened and answered politely as I tried to be knowledgeable about the plane, wondered how long the trip would be, what the local time would be in Cairo when we got there, and things like that and then found out that we had a fueling stop at the airport of Lydda in Palestine. In my very best Arabic I tried to get them to give me permission to stay in the plane when we landed but they assured me I couldn't pos-sibly do that, airport rules forbade it, and I resigned myself to struggling out and struggling in again, and then we were down. Both officers helped me out the door and then told me, in per-fect English, how nice (grin, grin) it had been talking to me, that they would see me shortly after I proceeded to the air-port commissary where, if I wished, I could enjoy a compli-mentary coffee or a *gazeuse,* if I preferred. One of them then handed me a rather dog-eared coupon on which was printed, in English also, GOOD FOR ONE CUP OF COFFEE. After their beau-tiful speech, delivered so flawlessly, I felt good for one com-plete fool, but it *was* a good joke on me.

Surprises never end! The one I got next was that Ali wasn't there to meet us when we landed in Cairo, and I didn't have an inkling what to do about immigration and customs, plus the fact that my hands weren't exactly free to do a lot of filling out of papers. I looked rather like a wandering peddler with the

assorted boxes and packages hanging from me (baklava anyone?) and at least the first part of the description fit as I wandered around getting lost a lot. A further surprise was that we
had landed *not* at the airport most accustomed and most
equipped to handle international travelers (*sic*), we had landed
at Almaza airport, which concentrated on military, domestic,
and charter flights. Consequently, there were no well-marked
passenger directions, and no other passengers to follow. I finally
stumbled into the right place and the Egyptian official behind
the steel-meshed cage did a double take at the obviously non-
Arab woman in front of him who presented, after much fumb-
ling and shifting of gear and child, a Saudi Arabian passport with no picture yet. I think the only thing that saved me
from investigation was his finding Hamida noted under "dependents," and she obviously was that so he stamped us out
through the only exit, to customs baggage check.

Hamida started to cry then, and that had me well on the way
to collapsing under the pressure of the past two days, when a
baggageman who had been watching from the far side decided
to come to my aid. He took the unfilled declaration forms
from my sweaty hand, asked if I had anything to declare, and
started to fill them out for me when I said, most piteously, "I
don't think so." He completed the forms for me, getting my
name and all from my passport, and then said something to
the lone customs inspector who had me cleared in minutes. I
can say in all honesty that only later did I remember that my
bags were stuffed with cuts of brocade, silver and brass objects,
wooden cigarette boxes and game sets in beautiful inlay for
which Ali and I had haggled in the old bazaars of Damascus
on a quick trip there before he left Beirut.

The end of this story is that an army officer gave me a taxi
he had called for himself, and I guessed that I wanted to go to
Shepheard's Hotel. We drove away from the buildings past a
few military checkpoints and then as we were passing through

the last one of the outer gate, guess who came zooming up the road in a big black chauffeured limousine? Yes, Ali and a former school chum I recognized as they whizzed by. Somehow the sight of their merry laughing faces after my travail restored my spunk and I deliberately let them go on in and look for me while I continued on my way. They caught up with me at the hotel just after I had established with the desk clerk that Ali was indeed registered there, and then told me the reason they were late was because they had first gone to the other airport. I told them my tale of woe. Ali thought it was so funny that he made me recount it for months after as a kind of "parlor trick" to anyone who would listen.

Our trip to America was delayed a few days so there had really been no need after all for the hectic race to get there. We were to go as part of Shaikh Abdullah as-Sulaiman's finance mission to Washington but there had to be preliminary meetings in Cairo first and they had taken longer than expected.

Meetings en route were also set up to meet Arab officials in various North African cities, but that was fine with me. I had nothing to do with that part of the trip and I had been the only woman before among Arab men, so I knew how to stay in the background. Shaikh Abdullah had been briefed, however, by an aide privy to western ways who had so impressed the good Shaikh with the importance of letting ladies go first (it was Shaikh Abdullah's first trip abroad) that I didn't have a chance to remain inconspicuous. At the first stop, Mersa Matruh I think it was, Shaikh Abdullah would not leave the plane until I did and not only that, he made me proceed across the tarmac a full ten feet in front of him and his companions, including Ali, in all their Arab finery. The sight of the strange woman leading the men they had come to meet must have looked very peculiar to the welcoming delegations. Shaikh Abdullah did the same thing to me at each stop on our hops across North Africa, and wouldn't even order a meal or eat until Hamida and I had at least started. Ali and I tried to convince His Excellency to remedy this state of affairs, but we gave it up when we realized he was not going to be budged. "Al usool kidda," * he'd say, and all that Ali could do was join the others behind me as I gave the impression of saying, as I forged ahead, "Okay, fellows, fall in, here we go!"

Hamida captured Shaikh Abdullah as she had other dignitaries on our trips, but after we arrived in Washington it was increasingly evident that she and I had to leave, especially after Shaikh Abdullah delayed two important committee meals awaiting my august appearance; so Hamida and I quietly bowed out and went to California to let the state of affairs make the proper transition to affairs of state.

We were not to get back to Arabia after that trip as quickly or as easily as before. I stayed in California long enough to have our son Faisal, and he was five months old before a succession of diplomatic jobs for Ali ended in New York with H.R.H. Prince Faisal and five of his brothers. We left the country in his company once more and each step of that journey home to Arabia involved some kind of trouble. One of the engines in our Constellation aircraft had to be shut down halfway across the Atlantic on our way to London, causing us to limp into Herne Airport three hours late; on the London-Cairo leg, young Faisal had to have oxygen most of the way because the unpressurized York aircraft had to rise above bad weather; Egypt was still in the throes of a cholera epidemic when we got there and anyone wanting to leave Egypt for Arabia, as we did, had to undergo a three-day quarantine at the Arabian end. It was not the easiest of times, but as Prince Faisal so aptly put it when awakened about the faulty engine, "We're still flying, aren't we?"

One nice thing for us, Ali's mother was in Cairo undergoing dental work when we got there, and we stayed together in the

* "This is the way it's done."

newly decorated, newly painted, everything but newly heated Shepheard's. We did a lot of catching up on each other's news as we ate our scaredy-cat meals of boiled eggs, Chester cheese and toast in rooms 249 and 150 while Ali was at his meetings. Daily notices were issued assuring all patrons that the hotel kitchen was daily inspected and that food emanating from same was eminently safe, but with the epidemic uppermost in our minds our appetites were not what they could have been.

When the Arab League meetings that the men had been attending adjourned, Prince Faisal decided to submit to quarantine and go home, but before Ali left with him we decided to have one evening out on the town, cholera or no cholera, and Mother agreed to baby-sit for us. We didn't think Faisal would be any problem and Hamida and Mother were great pals, Mother at the moment scoring more points with Hamida than her own parents in Hamida's self-devised system of grading her love. Sometimes, on a scale of 10, she loved us as much as 7 or 8, then she'd jump us down erratically to 3 maybe, but Mother was riding then on the crest of solid 8's, so when we left them together we anticipated no trouble. It was true, however, that Hamida had forgotten most of her Arabic during our long stay in America and we had not taken that into account. We returned to find Hamida in tears and a frustrated grandmother in near-tears, the one wanting something and the other not knowing what; and Mother hit her chest with her fist and said "Allah ikta'any, ya binti," * when we translated Hamida's heartbroken "*Why* won't Teta† give me some milk?" Late as it was, Mother made us sit down then and there and make an English vocabulary with the word for milk heading the list.

We waited in Cairo for the quarantine to lift, appalled by the very thought of spending three days on a hot, fly-infested Red Sea island, but eventually after Mother's work was done we

---

* "May I be punished, my daughter."
† Affectionate name for grandmother.

found inactivity in Cairo's bone-chilling winter not very appealing either and decided we had better go home. This was easier said than done, as getting safely lifted off from Cairo turned into a three-day ordeal.

Our agent, Shaikh Hamed Rowehy, made reservations all right, and the day to leave came, but Shaikh Hamed, bless his heart, is one of those people who have to get to airports and trains hours ahead of time, so for our scheduled eight o'clock takeoff he checked us out of our hotel at five on a cold, foggy morning. We hadn't eaten out of fear that the night staff were maybe not as careful about food as the "inspected" daytime crew, and with all the time at the airport we could surely get something for our hollow stomachs. Not so, and we didn't even take the plane that day. After waiting four hours we were told there was something mechanically wrong and to come back the next day. Our rooms were gone by then and we had to stay elsewhere in a miserable set of cold and bare rooms until Uncle Hamed came for us at the same ungodly hour the next morning. Both children had colds by then, nice juicy ones, and they sneezed and sniffled all the way to the again-foggy airport while Uncle Hamed regaled us with the story of how he had scared off a knife-wielding madman in a crowded restaurant once by being a knife-wielding madman right back at him.

Luck appeared to be with us when the fog cleared long enough for our plane to leave, but after we climbed and leveled off the NO SMOKING   FASTEN SEAT BELTS sign was still on and I wondered mightily why. Mother was watching it, too, just because she wanted to smoke, and I decided to ask. I almost wasn't surprised when a passing crew member answered my query with a hush-hush explanation that one of our engines was misfiring and we were trying to get back to Cairo if the fog would lift. That time I didn't even think of what Prince Faisal had said — I was scared and heart-weary and bone-weary. I did not want to go on to be quarantined, I did not want to go back to a lousy cold hotel room, but neither did I want to crash somewhere in an African desert. Then my ears heard, "Mommy, I have to go to the toilet," from Hamida, and what can one do? Nothing but march her to the buffeted tail of the DC-3 where there was barely room in the tiny toilet to support her, and then as if one kind of performance wasn't enough the child wanted to sing. I can think of no time in my life when I felt less like singing, but I said, "Okay, honey, what'll we sing?" and so help me she said, "Um-m-m, 'London Bridge Is Falling Down'!" Our rendition had to be lusty to be heard over the whistle of the airstream back there, and lusty it was! We gave it all we had, and I had a big prayer harmonizing silently with my part.

The pilot of that crippled plane of the budding Saudi Arabian Airlines poked the plane's nose around the skies until he found an opening and landed us safely on a runway lined with fire trucks, ambulances, and other emergency vehicles. Uncle Hamed was in a terrible state because twenty minutes earlier the word had gone around the airport that we had crashed and he still was not able to control himself even in relief over our safety. "Nushkoor Allah, nushkoor Allah" * was all he could say as he got us into another hotel while the plane was being repaired, and then he picked us up the next morning to catch it once more.

The quarantine island was something else again. We got there by plane, bus, harbor launch, and a lot of guts on the part of the people involved — those who took us and those who went. Maybe, and I say maybe, it would not have been so bad if the children hadn't been sick but . . . There were no proper buildings, just great spaces with walls around them and unsashed openings for windows, no proper facilities, no doctor, no nurses, no food, no telephone. Passengers found their own quarters within the area assigned to their flight, men of course in different sections from women, and did what they could to

* "We thank God, we thank God."

make them livable. Each of us made our own arrangements about food and I am not sure what others did. We had ours sent by launch from our house in Jeddah, thrown to us from the boat to the dock because the authorities of course would not allow them to land. If we had more than we needed, which we usually did, we sent it around to others, but it was unbelievable that it was necessary for us to provide for ourselves that way. What in the world would a foreigner have done had he been on the flight?

Then we learned that Lady Assia, Prince Faisal's mother-in-law, was there, having come in on an earlier flight. Her quarantine was up the following morning so she very kindly offered us her "rooms," which she had made as comfortable as possible with her own belongings from the mainland. But even with that bit of luck I didn't see how we could possibly stay. Both youngsters' colds had become worse and one child had fever that first night and everything combined seemed so hard that I almost went mad. The next day was worse — the flies were worse, the frustration was worse, the dull press of our difficulties was worse, and the children were worse. I had one good cry that lasted all afternoon, and then I decided to do something about it. I didn't care about the quarantine, I didn't care about government orders, I didn't care how I did it, but I was going to get those children back home and under the care of a doctor if I did nothing else the rest of my life. When our food launch came at the end of the day I threw the men aboard a note addressed to Ali telling him exactly what I said above, and I don't know how he did it, what strings he had to pull, but our planeload of passengers was officially released the following morning from the necessity of waiting out our quarantine.

It was good that we did. Faisal soon needed around-the-clock care for the punctured eardrum he suffered shortly thereafter and which drained for a week, and delirious little Hamida

caused us and good Bushir, the doctor we had to bring from
Mecca, considerable concern for days before her bad throat
cleared.

It seems incredible now that the children in particular managed to live through such things. I can't imagine myself now
going to live where health was so endangered, where we sometimes had to go to another city for the kind of help we needed.
There were so many things to worry about — malaria, typhoid,
smallpox, all children's diseases, eye diseases, skin diseases,
parasites external (lice) and internal (a circus of intestinal
ones), stomach disorders and dysenteries, insect bites, strange
fevers like dengue that depressed one to distraction. These
were dreadful things, but the people knew little about them except that they got them; they tended to accept it as their lot to
fall prey to them, uninformed as they were about the cause or
prevention of disease in general, and ignorant of the causes behind the high infant mortality rate. Most mothers had never
heard of prenatal care, nutrition, or modern child-care methods, and didn't know about available immunization programs.

Many children grew up without ever seeing a dentist; eye
troubles and skin eruptions often just ran their course while
victims were allowed to play with other children and no one
thought anything about it. Regular sleep and meal habits were
not generally practiced, subjecting growing bodies to strains
they could have done without in the light of their general health
picture. What continually amazed me was how few people
realized the role flies played in the high incidence of disease,
and believe me, flies were a factor then in Arabia. How
mothers and children alike could be so non-caring about flies
on their food, in their eyes, clustered on skin sores, was beyond
me. And when an obviously sick child was taken visiting or
a child with a communicable disease was allowed to mingle
with others, I thought how much had to be learned and done
before the overall situation could improve.

Luckily for us in Jeddah, a clinic opened by an American Public Health Service officer, Dr. Schötner, and his Lebanese colleague, Dr. Khalid Idriss, gave us the start we needed toward better care and better facilities. They were just the right kind of capable, dedicated men for the job and they did much to instruct the people as they treated them, educating them to better methods and not only showing them how but telling them why.

Other things were beginning to happen, too. Stirred by the development of vast oil resources, Arabia was just then pushing itself off to make the transition from old to new, to get the country and the people into the modern world. And people's ideas began to change as they came to the realization that they must start doing what had to be done: start challenging time instead of rocking in its cradle. The people had to have more than the rudiments of an education, and the poor had to be raised from their subsistence level; and for all there must be access to social and economic opportunities that others elsewhere take for granted. They had to be shown how to better their lot and educated to develop their potential, as the government learned to develop the country's potential. I watched these beginnings of change, and if to me and others the pace seemed maddeningly slow it was only because there was so much to do; and there was little many of us could do except wait. I could wish for a sudden jump into a more advanced Arabia, but all my energies were consumed in plugging along learning about things as they were.

That learning time for me was in Beit ar-Rawais,* and in terms of houses it represented that transition Arabia was starting to make, being better than the old houses in town but not as modern as those to come. And what a lot of bridging we did there as people, learning to merge our personal lives into a life that was shared.

Leaving at times the great halls where we welcomed others,

* "The House of the Rawais" (the desert region just north of Jeddah).

the tearoom where the samovar bubbled and flies buzzed, we of the *harem* left to be received in other homes, to call on the sick, go to weddings, drop gold into the cribs of newborn, and mourn when death came to relative or friend. The others always led and I always followed and no one knew if I would ever catch up. Each day I learned something, and finally I could stand where I was and think of success. I had taken on a new life and it had taken on me and we had made a peace, while I and those other beings with me had proved we were human but had not let it stop us.

Ali had to succeed in his own efforts to make a way in his country and it was sometimes my turn to encourage him. He had fiery ambitions at first to change in his work some of the old ways in the name of efficiency and order — too much time was wasted serving coffee, reorganization was needed, time clocks were a good idea, bills should be collected on time, favors and political backscratching should be done away with — but he mellowed as he had to without compromising his goals.

And he and the men in his family did much. They opened the first modern garage, brought foreign experts to find water, fought for electrification of the city, built and managed the first pier, set up the first soft-drink bottling plant, supported plans for both personal and national progress, and on top of all that did the best job they could to keep their *harem* happy.

Our requests for cars and drivers were always filled, lists of things we gave them to do were always given attention — get a plumber, a new houseboy, money, a prescription — and they kept eagle eyes and ears out for what was new, interesting, luxurious, or useful for us in the local *suk*, flea market, or auction, and if it pleased them to do so they bought it for us. They would have profited more at times if they had gotten together on their purchases; a local rug merchant kept Ali and his cousin Ahmed Yousuf bidding for weeks against each other on a choice carpet.

Their all-time prize purchase to my mind was the two bolts

of material they snapped up for us womenfolk. Ready-to-wear in the *suk* was for a long while limited to children's and men's undershirts, utility nightwear, socks, and very young children's clothing; and fabric was a now-you-see-it-now-you-don't item the minute it hit the shops. Getting two whole bolts, then, was a true coup and it didn't matter that they were the same pattern, one pink, one blue. Dress lengths, one of each, were cut for each female in the combined households, and sewing machines hummed for days. I felt like a ninny not knowing how to sew, but Zainab kindly made my blue dress and Hayat made the pink.

Shortly thereafter Steta Fatma's mother fell ill and we were called to town to join the family at her bedside. Well, you know what happened. We walked into a houseful of women all dressed alike and that was one time I was loathe to remove my cloak. The reason for the gathering was after all a sad one, so I had to choke back my laughter, but when one of the *jarias* entered with coffee wearing *her* new pink dress, Zainab and Hayat and I just had to laugh and Mother was torn between her own mirth and the motherly need to flash us girls glances of approval. I never saw women more amenable to looking alike, but it is a fact that they sometimes borrowed each other's dresses to copy, and at least one I knew did it so meticulously she copied in a mistake. Dress got more distinctive as the years went by, as women started to travel and as imports filled the country, but that fashion show *à l'Arabe* circa late 1940 was an unforgettable study of pink and blue on black and white.

The lady who had lain ill slipped quietly into death a few days later, and we went immediately to her house when we heard. I was reminded that mourning dress is white, and Mother had to give me a blouse for my white skirt and a white scarf for my head. My family were visibly shaken and I was at a loss to know what to say as we drove in silence to the house of the deceased. Walking up to the rooms, I noticed Mother and Zainab starting to tremble and their breathing becoming erratic. Never could I have dreamed what happened next. We opened the door through which strange noises were already coming, and there were women in convulsions everywhere, everywhere, their sounds nightmarish, contortions unbelievable, and I could not, for what seemed like eternity, move from the spot where I stood. In reality it was only seconds, because my companions soon collapsed like the others and I had to carry them out of the doorway. Dr. Idriss was making his way through with a trayful of syringes and saw that I was still on my feet and recruited my help. I held jerking arms as he injected relaxants and taught me how to put spoons in their mouths to prevent their tongues from being swallowed.

The scene unnerved me so it's a wonder I could do anything. It was the first time I had seen anything like that, although it was not the last. Convulsion is a common manifestation of grief in the Hejaz, where the mourning period is long and rigorous, contrary to the Nejd region, where women do not prolong their weeping at the death of a loved one and mourning is not allowed. For forty days they mourn in the Hejaz and the custom is strictly observed. The dead are washed, shrouded, and buried as soon as possible, and there is no group service over the body, but the bereaved family must every other day for forty days open their homes to receive people offering condolences and serve them coffee or tea, provide sumptuous luncheon and dinner meals for them, and endure fresh waves of weeping and sadness with each new arrival. The room where they sit is cleared of everything except carpets, so that even their surroundings are bleak and bare, little given to comfort mental or physical. A professional "reader" — one who recites from the Koran — intones special verses and the women too devote time to prayer. Family members somehow bear the emotional and physical drain thus imposed on them at a time when they most need quiet and solitude. I for one consider it an antiquated form of torture.

Chapter 13

AFTER FAISAL'S BIRTH the Arabs who had been calling me Oom Hamida ("mother of Hamida") called me Oom Faisal instead, according to their custom of naming parents after the oldest child or oldest son, but I felt like everybody's mother with all the children in the house, and I loved each as my own. Raising children is never easy, but in the Arabia of those days it was downright hard. Keeping them healthy was our prime concern and heat and humidity were factors in that. Hot and sweaty most of the time, it was hard for a child to gain weight properly or get a glow in his cheeks — the usual Jeddah complexion being a certain sallowness — and prickly heat was always a problem. Because of it the youngsters were often whiny and miserable, and didn't know what to do with themselves. We were luckier than most in having a yard, but the weather limited outdoor play, and any play on a hot, sticky day was hard to enjoy — just as sleep on a hot, sticky night was well nigh impossible. We sometimes slept on the roof to get whatever breeze there might be, but it was usually so humid that the cotton cloths placed over our mosquito nets were wet enough in the morning to be wrung out.

The matter remained of providing outlets for the children's energies besides letting them pursue too long their own brands of devilment or hie themselves too often to the servants' quarters. Arabic lessons kept some of them occupied a few hours a day, but in general, children's day at our house consisted very simply of these lessons, play as they concocted it, and rather elastic meal and sleeping hours.

Arab children traditionally have great respect for elders and any voice of authority in the home, and ours had four women and many maidservants directly or indirectly involved in their daily care (a formidable circumstance in itself). It must have been hard to be responsive to so many in a place where there was little to do outside the home, where recreational facilities were sadly lacking, and where being left to their own devices too often led to those voices being raised against them.

It seemed a pity to me that we had the beautiful Red Sea in front of us and couldn't go bathing. I had a wild fantasy at times of a Red Sea Riviera, getting carried away with the idea while out driving with Ali. With a flick of my wrist I would point out the best spots for a fine coast road, a boardwalk, beach cabins, colored parasols, and sunning bodies. But the only sunning bodies we ever saw were local fishermen standing knee-deep in the water getting bait maybe, or perhaps washing nets or even catching fish, I never knew. The time was to come for us and many others in Jeddah when we would have private beach houses and shores on the coastline some distance from the city where we could swim, scuba dive, and go motorboating, but for a long time I would have settled for just getting my feet wet and for letting the children wade and feel the squish of the sand between their toes.

Then we got permission to do just that, so I and Zainab and Hayat* scheduled almost daily trips to the beach with our

---

* Although seniority is ever important in Arabian life, Arabs commonly will say "I and So-and-So" instead of "So-and-So and I," as in English.

offspring, whose bathing attire wouldn't have won any fashion contests certainly, but it was functional. Saleh Bajanein, our driver from Hadhramaut, took us to a shore where reefs kept the water shallow for hundreds of yards seaward, where the children could wade and splash to their hearts' content in relative safety. We mothers waded, too, and got splashed in spite of having our veils tied back and our cloaks raised well above the water line. (We had the only sea-soaked cloaks and veils in town.) I must admit that at times in the heat of play and the heat of the day we came mighty close to saying "the heck with it" and diving in with the children.

Water games were the usual — chasing and splashing each other, playing catch with a rubber ball, skipping shells out on the water as far as we could, pulling up to examine the things we stepped on — but we had never counted on playing tag with a seasnake. One wriggled past to split our frolic in two one afternoon, passing directly between the children and me, and I screamed to one and all: "Don't move whatever you do!" Whereupon the snake ignored us and spared us the panic of having to thrash our way out of the water. We grownups had to thrash our way out of the water sometimes, however, when a strange car approached too close to our recreation area and its occupants might have wondered too strongly who the cavorting black-robed figures were that were acting more like children than children.

Shells (those that didn't walk away after the children gathered them), bits of coral, much flotsam and jetsam were carted home with pride to show Teta and Baba*, and I remembered my paleontology field trips in days past and sought and found many fossils. In a spot that was more muddy than sandy we found one day a strange-looking blob of animate matter not identifiable by us or similar to anything we had ever seen before. It looked like half a wet cigar and didn't like being out in

* "Papa."

the open — I was convinced it was a leftover from the mud primeval.

Saleh kept a close watch on passing cars, and on us too. He was always amused at our enthusiasm and loved taking us; he was always ready to take over the care of any of the children, who loved being with him anyway because he told them such good stories while they ate with him the treats that became part of our outings; and he was above all patient with the junk we took home and the way we filled "his" car with sand and wet spots. Our treks to the beach did us all a lot of good and we became so fond of them that it was utter woe when some of Hayat's brood came down with whooping cough and we had to separate all the children for almost three months.

Hard times for us and for the children were when we had to leave them in the big house under servants' care for long periods at a time. Their *DaDas** loved them with all their hearts but their methods of dealing with them sometimes clashed with ours and it was usually I who did the most clucking to change some of their ways. I couldn't stand it the first time I saw Hayat's children seated around a metal food tray on the floor while Saada pinched food in her fingers and popped it into their open mouths — they looked for all the world at such times like a nestful of hungry birds — and I created a stir that finally got the children seated regularly at a table in front of their own plates. Hayat and I began to "attend" their mealtimes. Good table manners were *de rigueur* under our watchful eyes, and with two of us standing over them there was no leeway for nonsense.

Each of us disciplined no matter whose child. When I played with mine the other children gravitated to where the action was and automatically fell under my field of jurisdiction. I was glad they wanted to join us because their aimlessness had concerned me, and it was obvious their being around also helped

* "Nannies," governesses.

me learn. My Arabic really grew by do's and don't's and it was amazing how much more I knew when I was angry than when I was not. They deserved credit, too, for maintaining such equanimity in the face of this threatening auntie when I called them to task in no uncertain terms. They are still wont to recall certain of those times, albeit lovingly, and I am glad they remember. We were growing together is my way of looking at it and I would not have missed the trouble or the fun of it for anything.

And fun we did have. They taught me their games and I tried to remember my old favorites. *Harami** was their card game similar to Old Maid, and they had shells called *kum-kum* that we rolled between our hands and threw like dice, points scored by the way they landed, open or smooth side up; there was a kind of Arabian jacks played with pebbles thrown from the palm to the back of the hand, a turn lasting until some fell off. Marbles, too, we played but their game consisted simply of knocking each other's lines out across the living room rug, so I dredged memories from my tomboy days and taught them a few more. A fancy card shuffle they mastered caused a run on decks in the *suk,* and when my string tricks tied them up for days I was sorry I hadn't thought of them sooner.

The children were so responsive to any activity that I determined to do more, remembering my early years in a day nursery and the fun of handicrafts, simple carpentry, and playing together. From the United States I got what I wanted in the way of supplies. We had coloring books, paints, crayons, modeling clay, colored construction paper, reed and raffia, paper scissors, tracing paper, construction sets, coping saws, a rope toss game, and songbooks. Ali had a playground set of swings, slide, rings, bars, and seesaw shipped in for us, and then indoors and out we really had activity. The best was still to come when Ali surprised us with a piano — a real, live piano — and I just couldn't

* "Thief."

believe it. I knew pianos (and musical instruments in general) were not allowed in Arabia because too many powerful people still believed music was evil, but all the dear boy would say was it had come into the country "normally" with a shipment of "house furniture" and I pressed no further. I played and we all sang, and there was truly a special quality in "Mary, Mary, Quite Contrary," "Baa, Baa, Black Sheep," "Froggie Went A-Courting," "Under the Spreading Chestnut Tree," and "I've Been Working on the Railroad" when trilled by my Arabian nieces and nephews.

There was no stopping once our Activity Hours started. Trudging upstairs sometimes before anyone else (including me) was up, the children hesitated only momentarily before gently rapping on our screen door, and then usually Huda's little piping voice said, "Oma Marianne, nigdar noorsoom daheen?" — "Aunt Marianne, can we draw now?" And who could say no? Not I, surely, so color we did, or cut, or paste, or model clay. Pictures of their choice were cut from coloring books, and if they were done well they could start another. They signed their works of art and hung them in their rooms and their pride of accomplishment was wondrous to behold.

One thing led to another. Oilcloth animals were cut, sewed and stuffed, plywood animals were created with coping saws, then sandpapered and painted — memorable projects all. For no reason that I can recall we made paper chains one morning and it was Cherine, I think, who got so carried away making hers that it was snaking its way downstairs before I got her attention shifted to weaving paper mats. The cook by then was wishing none of it had started. Our work did require a lot of paste, and he was getting short-tempered over the repeated forays into his kitchen to sneak flour.

Precious water soaked through bundles of reed as the more adept learned real weaving, and they all took prizes for the originality of their baskets. A happy clown face was our crown-

ing achievement, however, and one of the most fun. We num-
bered the holes where his eyes, nose and mouth were and made
sewing-scrap beanbags to throw at him. Everyone, from their
grandmother on down, enjoyed that, and one day it even delighted a group of aristocratic ladies from Mecca (descendants
of the Prophet no less) whose intended one-hour visit lasted all
day because they were having too much fun playing our silly
games to leave.

It was gratifying to look at the intent, bright-eyed group of
children around me engrossed in the same things I had enjoyed as a child; and since the boys were often wearing little-
boy shirts and short pants instead of Arab *tobes,* and the only
thing different in the girls' dresses was that their hems were
longer than most little girls', the scene (except for the language) could have duplicated one from my childhood. Chattering away as children will, they never seemed to notice that maybe
I was different in speech and manner from the other people
around them. It was rather wonderful to watch them "holding
their mouths right" while trying to cut a straight line or while
I guided their fingers through some craft.

One day something else was recalled from my childhood —
popcorn balls — called to mind by my Mother's surprising me
with a packet of half-popped corn from a local vendor, and I
decided then and there to make some. We were already constant nibblers. We'd been through mounds of roasted pumpkin
seeds, watermelon seeds (called *fiss-fiss* of all things), chick
peas, peanuts, almonds, and pistachios; but it was the first time
I had known corn was available, and being something of an expert corn popper in my day, I was sure I could get a higher yield
of exploded kernels than had the man downtown. So Mother
got me an *oka** of the unpopped kind, and I made my treats,
although as it turned out, the children were the only ones who
considered them as such. The molasses hadn't been right, the

* Measure of weight equaling 2¾ pounds.

vinegar had mother floating around in it, I had no cream of
tartar, the sugar did funny things, and the only thing that
turned out as it was supposed to was the shape, which stayed
that way for days and days. The crackly chewy mess never for
a moment daunted the youngsters, but poor Mother had to pry
hers off kernel by kernel and chew it *very* carefully. In truth,
those popcorn balls were the only things I ever saw the humidity
powerless to crumble.

Hamida, and certainly Faisal, were too young to engage in
the other children's activities, but Hamida kept busy in her self-
appointed supervisory capacity of keeping tabs on their work,
helping her cousins — whether they wanted her to or not —
choose pictures and the colors they used. The books we used
were made in the U.S.A., so American holiday pictures filled
their pages; and as the children colored turkeys and firecrackers,
Christmas stockings and Santa Claus, Valentines, Easter bunnies,
pilgrims and pumpkins, I came to realize how few holidays
they had to compare. Arabia's only national holidays are Eid
al-Adha, the Feast of the Sacrifice during the Pilgrimage; Eid
al-Fitr, the Feast of the Breaking of the Fast in the month following Ramadan; and the non-religious holiday, National Day,
on September 23. Eid al-Fitr most resembles our Christmas,
being family day slanted toward children's enjoyment and the
exchange of gifts. National Day commemorates the unifica-
tion of Nejd and Hejaz as a country under the name Saudi
Arabia and is the only holiday not determined by the Islamic
calendar. A Gregorian date was chosen to facilitate the sending of congratulatory messages by foreign governments on the
anniversary day and to provide a fixed date for the annual receptions held in Saudi embassies and legations abroad. All
other special days of observance are primarily religious, including the Prophet Mohamed's birthday, days of special prayers,
the observance of tithing and obligations to the poor and ful-
fillment of welfare deeds.

Our family had more holidays than other Arabians because its members always celebrated my Christian ones with me just as I celebrated their Moslem ones with them. At Ramadan I could feel just as righteous as they, breakfasting at sundown with them as if I hadn't had food and water all day, and allowing myself all that month to be awakened before dawn to eat yogurt, lentils and rice, and *fathat ras** with them. And I never complained when they all went off to Mecca and left me, although I did balk at staying home while my Moslem husband made the rounds of gay Christmas and New Year's parties given by the foreign colony in town. However, Uncle Yousuf always made the trip to my door each Christmas and Easter morn to pay his respects to me and engage me in a learned discussion of the comparative tenets of our two religions, never forgetting to remind me that the Moslems call Jesus The Blessed One. It was a beautiful regard for the other, this respect for one another's religion, and worthy of note that in all the years I was in Arabia no one ever tried to get me to change my belief, or even suggested that I might.

We *always* had a Christmas tree, if only a shrub from the desert, and we shared the joy of it with our immediate family and with family members from town. Mother never failed to get a turkey from somewhere, and it was her pleasure to involve the entire household in intrigue for days planning the special Christmas dinner to surprise me.

Somehow Mother also got the idea that the decorated tree symbolized all festivity in the western world, and she thoughtfully provided one in all its glory for Hamida's birthday one year. Under it we put a cake I had baked, the sad result of a rash promise I had made to my "kindergarten class" to make a real one after one of them had done a good job coloring a paper one. I baked many birthday cakes in my day, and did some

---

* Pieces of meat from the lamb's head mixed with bread soaked in meat broth, yogurt, and chick peas.

pretty good jobs decorating them, but nothing ever came out like that one. The effort has to go down, like the popcorn balls, as a labor of love, pure and simple. I didn't have the ingredients, I didn't have the utensils, I didn't even have an oven, but Zainab had some contraption that was supposed to bake cakes on top of a stove and when she finally found it among her belongings I alerted the household to the task at hand and set things in motion.

The portable burner was placed in my screened bedroom where flies were less numerous than elsewhere, Rogaiya took mortar and pestle and pounded sugar fine enough to cream with butter, cook sent his flour sifter (looking amazingly like the sand sifter with which my brother Boyd and I used to comb California's beaches), the houseboy was put aboard the donkey to fetch baking powder in the *suk,* someone else was sent to adjacent Bedouin camps for fresh eggs, a tin of butter was brought from the storeroom, and when the houseboy got back we turned him around again to get the vanilla I had forgotten. Milk had been boiled that morning so that was ready, but there were other problems. Liquid butter hot enough to *melt* the sugar spurted from the tin; the eggs were so tiny that six were needed to equal the recipe's three, but eleven actually had to be cracked in order to get six good ones. The colony of weevils I netted in the sifter almost terminated the project then and there, and when the houseboy came with the vanilla it was in the shape of a bean, and I *still* don't know what one does with that. Finally, either Zainab's three-piece oven thing was assembled incorrectly (a likelihood we didn't discount) or the engineering was wrong to begin with, because the "cake" burned on the bottom and never got done on top. Enough was salvaged to make a molded surface, but the frosting was sadder than the cake. A wire whip with one prong loose was all I had to beat seven minutes' worth of boiled frosting into shape and just try that for frustration!

It's a wonder I ever tried again, but the next celebration just sort of happened. I was reminiscing to Hayat one day about Mother's Day at home, about the flowers and cards, the roses we wear to church, the way we try to repay our mothers in some small way by taking them out of the kitchen for the day, when Hayat suddenly interrupted, "Let's give Mother a Mother's Day here!" So I checked my calendar (Gregorian) and discovered that Mother's Day that year was also Ali's birthday and we expanded our plans to a double surprise for mother and son. It was decided that Hayat would cook her famous Lebanese specialties, I would bake a birthday cake in my new oven and Zainab would get Mother out of the house on an all-day visit in town.

And it happened just that way. Zainab and Mother got off early to Uncle Yousuf's house, the houseboy brought the food ordered secretly the night before, and Hayat and I proceeded to the basement kitchen which, now that I was to work in it, looked less like a kitchen than it ever had before. A crude wooden table was in the middle of the room, a single shelf projected above the sink's single cold water faucet, one wall was partitioned for fire-building, a crock of coarse salt lay next to an old tin of tomato paste, and off in a corner lay a stack of gigantic kettles and a cluttered pile of smaller ones. And there was the new oven Ali had gotten me — a black tin box of sorts that sat over coals and could take one whole cake layer at a time.

Everything else we needed was somewhere else, so the maids busily fetched for us. By the time we got organized the morning and the heat were well along, and by the time we got started we were harried. All the bowls were too small for cake-mixing so I used a kettle instead, stopping my clattering to shoo flies occasionally from Hayat's work of carving raw legs of lamb to grind with onion and soaked cracked wheat until the mixture was the right consistency to mold into her most famous specialty, *kibbe*. She shaped pats of meat in her palm with her fingers until they were oval shells and then filled them lightly with sautéed pine nuts, meat, and onions, tapering the ends to sealed points before frying.

As we worked the weather seemed hotter than usual, but we attributed that to heating oil and glowing charcoal until we soon knew better. The wind gathered force, daylight seemed to be diminishing, flies buzzed and swarmed in such increased numbers that I thought God was sending a blight, and very soon the full storm broke, generating frightful noise and threatening to blow the whole desert in on us. Maids braved the fifty-foot stretch from their quarters to shut the slamming shutters from the outside but the wind tore them loose again, and as an eerie darkness descended upon us there was a new development. From every nook and cranny, and seemingly from the very walls, came hundreds of cockroaches, some three inches long, some no larger than a horsefly. They were suddenly everywhere and there was no escaping them. The fury of desert winds and whipping sands had driven them from daytime hiding places to seek shelter inside and now we had both flies and cockroaches to contend with. Wielding fans against the flies and moving our feet to evade the roach onslaught we must have looked like performers of some ritualistic dance, while the stomped-on roaches cracked out sound effects lost in the wind's orchestration.

To complicate matters, the stifling heat caused the meat to stick to Hayat's palms so she had to wet them constantly with the ice water I had to replenish from upstairs, letting the roaches gain on us. When the awful creatures reached tabletop we couldn't hear our own shrieks and giggles over the din of the rampaging elements, and in the confusion I almost forgot my cake. What really upset me was the way the layers came out of the tipsy oven. They were three eighths of an inch high on one side and more than two inches on the other, so it was just another case in life of matching thick to thin to come out even.

We looked a mess! Sand combined with sweat to form grimy

runny patterns on our skin, and it filled our nostrils, gritted on our teeth, powdered our lashes, and made our eyelids feel like sandpaper. The storm raged all day as we fulfilled our commitment in the kitchen, leaving only to see if the children were faring well and if they were complying with our order to keep kerchiefs around nose and mouth. We hardly looked at the rest of the house until the storm abated at nightfall and by then the others had arrived. Our sand-peppered surprise was as ready as it would ever be so we served it, dirty house or no, using candles for both effect and for lighting because the generator was storm-damaged. Mother's face glowed as she was made to understand the reason for the party and as she was moved to say, "God bless the Americans for having Mother's Day." Hayat's and my day appeared to have the full flavor of success after the trials we had undergone, but we couldn't help groaning when Mother impishly added, "When, pray tell, is Grandmother's Day?"

Chapter 14

A HOLIDAY of the excursion kind occurred when we accepted the invitation of Shaikh Abdullah with his three permanent wives to become part of his annual encampment at a favorite Red Sea fishing spot many kilometers south of Jeddah, down the road to Yemen. I somehow could not see us becoming part of this camp but it was obviously important that we accept because there we were late one afternoon rattling our way down the Red Sea coastline.

I hadn't a clue as to what we would find when we got there, and I am fairly certain I was not alone in wondering. Shaikh Abdullah was firmly entrenched in my memory as the attentive host on our trip to the United States, but now he would be host Arabian style, most accommodating still, but absent from our midst. He was the first Arabian I ever heard of who took a wife fishing, let alone three, and my curiosity was piqued. I had seen each of the Mesdames Sulaiman in her fine home, and I had seen them as a trio in matching sequinned finery at parties, but it was hard to imagine them bustling around a makeshift camp living in tents pitched on a barren windswept shore. But they were, and soon so were we.

Our arrival was hailed by one and all, but it is true that we saw only the women, mistresses and servants, the men in the camp staying discreetly out of sight. We were taken immediately to the women's quarters where there was some commotion involving the removal of a big spider from the tent assigned to us, not a good but at least an exciting start for our visit.

I have difficulty remembering much about that first night except the cries of "Gawaha!" * which started after dinner and went on far into the night. The call was relayed from the first man to take it up to others on through the camp, making the word a man-made echo until the coffeemaker at the end of the line got the message and hastened to comply. But the next morning is well remembered. Who could ever forget what Shaikh Abdullah had planned for us ladies that day? He was sending the lot of us fishing, and had so planned and ordered everything that all we had to do was go. I looked around the dock as we gathered at the appointed time, Mother apprehensive, Zainab already seasick at the thought of the sea, the cloaked House of Sulaiman beginning to get caught up in the thrill of something new, as indeed Hayat and I were, and then I disbelieved that anyone, even Shaikh Abdullah, could think seriously of sending such a gaggle of females out on the high seas in an open boat. If I were the men who manned the boats or who were otherwise charged with getting us out and back safely, I would have started worrying in earnest, because very gradually and then more openly we started to look on the whole thing as a huge lark. By the time we pushed off it was more a matter of toning down our enthusiasm rather than trying to instill some.

Our craft was a smelly, noisy, fumy, bouncy launch which rocked more when we anchored near a reef, but we normally sheltered and sequestered ladies dropped fishing lines, and in between occasional spells of *mal de mer* here and there, some

* Coffee!"

fish were actually caught. The men of course did all the dirty work, helping us all they could while trying to pretend they weren't seeing us, but the very fact that we returned with a catch would make Shaikh Abdullah so proud of us.

Then we had tea. Certain difficulties in maintaining equilibrium notwithstanding, it was brewed and served. While the men wound tangled lines and cleared the deck, we sat side by side in the lurching boat holding tiny tea glasses, tinkling their sides with dainty spoons as we stirred the sugar, and it was a sight to behold. It was the only part of the trip that brought a spark of life to Zainab, both from the tea she drank in her insides and from what someone spilled on her veil from the outside as she sat bent with head in hand. One of our group produced a box of chocolates to finish our refreshments, and we headed for shore then with the wind in our faces and the day behind us.

We stayed maybe two or three days in the camp — I forget — but long enough to realize what really great trouble and expense the good Shaikh had taken to have his ladies along when he could just as easily (and much more in line with the customs of the country) have left them at home. And his wives had to be admired for their part, refusing to stay in the niche made for them and having the courage and spirit to try something new. Happiness is as happiness does, they say, and it was refreshing and fun to be part of their *harem*.

In the months to come our *harem* did not fare so well. We had an upset when all of us except Hayat learned quite by chance that Mohamed had another wife, one he had married some time before in Egypt, a woman none of us knew. The shock was great to us but nothing compared to the distress it would cause Hayat when she got wind of it. We kept the secret, of course, hoping that Mohamed himself would tell her one day, and in the meantime we tried to keep our minds occupied with other things.

There was talk among the men of building a bigger and better house for us and of leasing the one we then occupied to the Banque de l'Indochine representative who had been our houseguest for months. There was talk too of going away for the summer but we didn't know where, the usual spots in Egypt and Lebanon somewhat risky because of the Arab-Israeli conflict.

All plans were held in abeyance when Faisal became seriously ill with malaria and dysentery and we had to get him well before we could think of anything else. He very nearly died one night of dehydration, but Dr. Idriss saved him and little by little he improved. He was a very thinned-down first-birthday child and it was mainly because of him that Mohamed finally made the decision to send the women and children out of Jeddah for the summer. The plans for the new house and the rental of the old had jelled, too, so all we had to do was decide when we had to leave and where.

One thing was sure, wherever we went. It would take practically an entire plane to transport us, and the factors involved in living after we got there were many. Housing would be a problem, and servants, too, whether we took our own or hired locally, transportation for so many of us was difficult, and we either had to take so much with us or buy so much when we got there that sometimes it hardly seemed worth it.

It was my good fortune that whenever we traveled thus *en famille* that Ali was the family man most often designated to take us, but that summer Mohamed wouldn't have gone anyway. He had by then told Hayat of his other wife and their son, and as a result his relationship with her was very tenuous at that point. Some weeks before, after she heard the news, she had managed to leave our house and him (she tried several times but at first no driver would take her and her clothes were confiscated) for her parents' house in Jeddah, but Mohamed had talked her into coming back with us. It was a period of mutual distress for everyone, living as we did together, and as the two

⚙

principals tried to regain what appeared to be lost, the rest of us trod on eggshells in the hope it would work out.

With the blueprints for the new house ready to be carried out and tenants ready to move into the old, we decided on our summer spot, and thank God it was not Taif. I don't think I could have stood another stay there with a sad Hayat; it was her lighthearted nuttiness that had helped me through my first Arabian months there. We were off instead to Asmara, the capital of Eritrea, situated on a cool, high (7600 ft.) plateau in Ethiopia where we could all enjoy ourselves and where the recuperating Faisal could become fat and sassy again. I had to look the place up on the map but my lack of knowledge didn't bother me — I hadn't known where Saudi Arabia was a few years back and look at all I had done since then!

A plane was chartered and the day of departure came and I not only felt sad at leaving Beit ar-Rawais I also felt like a fifth wheel among the departing family. It was my first experience with great bunches of us leaving Arabia together (sister Zakia and her children and servants added to our own considerable number) and therefore it was my first experience with the custom of passing the Koran over every departing head by someone staying behind. Every head but mine, that is; not because there were any manifest signs that because I was a Christian I wasn't eligible, but more my own desire not to bring such a point to the test. I saw what was happening. We were all exiting to board the cars for the airport and Mohamed, I guess it was, stood at the last door as each one passed the threshold and held the Koran up so he or she could pass under it. And I didn't know what to do with myself. I didn't know whether to stoop to avoid them the embarrassment of lowering the holy book or pretend I was straightening my stocking while it was moved to one side. I think the dilemma was solved by each pretending not to notice the other, something we all settled for.

The first thing of note that happened on our Asmara trip was that Mother, as she was fastening her seat belt, knocked over her black leather coffee-making kit, more important to her than anything else when she traveled, and broke the bottle of alcohol which fueled her little burner. The slant of the sitting plane caused the stuff to trickle back from under her seat, and when the engines started, the trickle changed to a flow of dancing droplets on the vibrating metal floor until they in turn dissipated to fumes which hovered around us the duration of the trip. No one lit a cigarette, I can tell you, and we all waited for the time when we could breathe easier, literally and figuratively.

We thought that time would come upon landing, which in itself was interesting because we made no obvious descent, gliding right out of the clouds onto the landing field, except that it didn't happen just that way. Waiting for the wheels to crunch, we heard instead a loud buzzing that frightened our breath away even before the pilot's up-and-away maneuvers did. An unlocked landing gear was the cause, I was told after we were safely down, but I spent a good deal of time wondering if other people were as susceptible to quirky happenings as we were.

It was Ramadan, so instead of trying immediately to find summer lodging we reserved the first part of our stay at the C.I.A.A.O. Hotel, where the personnel were very good about providing breakfasts at sundown and pre-dawn snacks for my fasting family. It took some of us a long time to acclimate ourselves to the rarefied air after sea-level Jeddah and we couldn't start house hunting anyway until after we were able to take more than two steps at a time without having our hearts race and our lungs gasp for air.

Every summer day it rains in Asmara, so predictably regularly that we could almost set our watches by it (a switch from Jeddah where the sun was our gauge) and we planned our sorties accordingly. We had much trouble in our house hunting, however, none of us, for one thing, being as proficient in Italian as we needed to be. Eritrea had been an Italian colony from 1890 until it was captured by British Commonwealth forces in 1941, and there were still 35,000 Italians there. There were real estate agents with us, to be sure, but since it was our money we were spending we wanted to be more aware of what was possible and what was not. The money was new to us, too, and often in a transaction of sorts we would convert wrongly and think mistakenly that we were getting either a terrific bargain or being cheated shamelessly.

Ali was the only man with us until a few more came from Jeddah to spend the feast with us and they were pressed into house-hunting service too. One relative who was very naive (he would have had to be) came in excitedly one evening with the "perfect house." There was room for everyone and to spare, he said. Each room had its own sitting room and bath, and a handy intercom (for such a big family) was already rigged through a switchboard downstairs. Wouldn't need a thing, in his opinion, except maybe clear a room for dining — for some strange reason the present dining area was a separate hall outside. What my dear cousin had found was a spacious brothel previously frequented by and indeed reserved for the officers of the Italian army during the Ethiopian campaign, and I have often wondered what the tongue-in-cheek agent who showed it to him thought of such innocent exuberance over the convenience of a floor plan.

The topper to this story is that the house in which we finally did spend the summer was formerly the YMCA building. It was called the Castello, the only structure we found, with the foregoing exception, that was big enough to hold us all. It was full of rooms and high halls, had a lovely garden with a small wooden teahouse covered with vines in one corner, and a large cemented area where we could cycle or skate.

We succeeded in our goal to be in for the feast, and outdid ourselves in shopping for presents. The shopkeepers hadn't had such a bonanza in sales in their history, I imagine, as the beauty of the local crafts in wood, leather, cloth prompted us to more and more buying — as well as the joy of giving and, for us, the freedom of being able to walk into a store and make our own purchases. We also spent many interesting hours tracking down grain houses where we could buy the requisite feast time measures of wheat to distribute to the poor according to religious custom.

It was also fun to food shop. The pompelmous were as big as soccer balls; the *gishta,* a segmented fruit of big black seeds covered with sweet, white flesh, were most interesting and I thought they looked like hand grenades; mango and cactus pears were of excellent quality; we followed our noses to the native hole-in-the-wall bakeries for crunchy bread more delicious than cake and came to know which Italian bakery had the most scrumptious pastry. Garden-fresh vegetables were like pictures to us and it was sheer pleasure to go into a store where dairy products were, by comparison to Jeddah, deliciously fresh and abundant, and eggs were three times as big as those we were accustomed to. Every day was a feast for us and the Feast of the Eid was downright spectacular.

The men left us for Jeddah in early August and we embarked on a summer program that took us out of the house as much as possible — with eleven children in the house it behooved us to do so. Asmara and environs afforded ample spots of interest for the whole family to enjoy. We first had mass tonsillectomies done before we started on our program but then there was no stopping us. We visited en masse the local waterworks, where of course some of the kids fell in the filter pools, to see how the area's water was purified and stored; we drove to Adi Ugri southward in beautiful wild country, where our picnic was rained out and the hotel there kindly let us move it indoors. Another day we accepted the invitation of C.I.A.A.O. Hotel manager Signore Gianfillipi to visit a local farm with a dairy, beautiful groves and gardens, fruits and flowers, and vegetables that astounded us by their size. In the dairy were the biggest cows any of us had seen, and the children stood in delight and awe before Generale, a magnificent monstrous bull housed near the barn, and their chorused "Oh-h-h-h" when shown two other young bulls, one only two days old, would alone have made the trip worthwhile.

We had a picnic that day, too — that was the most frequent and best thing we did — and the farm owners joined us. Tables were set in the mango groves and each group served the food it had, and for dessert we were invited to reach up and pluck what we wanted from the trees above us. The entire day was a rare, delightful experience for all of us, and especially for the children for whom so much was new.

Other days we drove through native districts with their quiet lanes and thatched huts that sat like high mounds of hay in a clearing, and the people who inhabited them impressed us with their quiet dignity, poise, and gentle manner. The women had the best posture I had ever seen as they walked straight and graceful down a street, and in our dealings with the men as small tradesmen in town, their enthusiastic pride in their city was always conveyed to us. Perfect strangers at first, they warmed to the fact that we were visiting them and gave us tips on points of interest which we followed to the letter.

We did not take it, but we looked down on the spectacular road which descends from Asmara forty miles to the port of Massawa, which has the none too envious reputation of being the hottest, most humid spot on the Red Sea. And we saw the cable rigged between the same two points which took a hooked-on passenger- or cargo-carrying cage on a wild, dizzying ride down to the coast in record time. No thanks for that, we said, but we had a pretty wild ride on the ground one day when we got tired of going to picnics the same old way. Although we had to canvass the entire local taxi fleet to find six carriage drivers to do it, we decided to drive out to one secluded spot in horse carriages rather than cars. They *clop-clopped* to our door at the appointed time and when we ourselves saw the sight of six horse carriages milling around in front of the Castello we thought it was lucky the townspeople had become somewhat inured to us and our comings and goings. The local photographer was there, too; he was going along to film the procession, and he didn't even blink an eye. But I think he was still in a daze from the problems he had incurred in making a series of family stills of us and our numerous progeny. He no doubt accepted to take movies of us with the thought that if we could come up with so many unexpected antics being "still" it would be interesting to see us in action.

The children vied for seats in the carriage of their choice with the adult of their choice, and I think it was this act of theirs that set the tone for what followed. Proceeding at first leisurely through town, a competitive spirit and team pride built up which, when we reached the open road, blossomed into true competition with exhortations to pass the carriage in front heard down the line. The drivers got caught up in the enthusiasm and responded so well to the hue and cry that very soon our orderly line of carriages was whipped into a hodgepodge of wildly dashing chariots jockeying for position in, around, and to the sides of the long country road. The photographer, in his desire to capture forever our zany madness on film, had the double task of keeping his carriage in good shooting position and staying out of our way, and somehow we all lived through the race. Mother was the only one of us who did not thoroughly relish the experience. She was in total terror the whole time, not for herself but for us, and we had to fan her into calmness for half an hour after we stopped. She could have killed the drivers while the race was on, but when it ended safely she gave each of them handsome tips before they trotted back to town.

The picnic lunch tasted particularly good that day and Mother, Zainab, and Hayat followed the meal with a rousing session of their favorite card game, belote, and I directed those children too old to sleep in a game of pussy-wants-a-corner among the trees. As if by magic before our startled eyes, there suddenly appeared coming through the woods a large group of native women carrying drums, of all things, which they then without invitation or explanation sat down and played. We wondered what kind of messages were reverberating back to the villages, but the women seemed pleasant enough, and their beat was excellent. Mother could play a mean drum, too, though, and not to be outdone, she asked one woman for her drum when the performance for the moment appeared over. It was given her and she started, the others picked it up, and at its wildest point, when the rhythm had us all clapping and swaying, Faisal broke loose into the middle of the drumming circle and performed a dance that could only be termed *native*. He had walked at nine months so at fourteen months he was agile and quick and just let the rhythm guide his feet. His dance and the utter abandon with which he performed it brought grins to our visitors' faces, and we were so glad the photographer kept his camera rolling. Many never believed our story until they saw the film.

The native women left as quietly as they came, but the echo of their drums seemed to stay with us for a long time after. That illusion was washed away, however, by a downpour that was not the usual afternoon shower but a full-blown storm that came out of the high mountains an hour or so before our driver was due to come for us. He had sense enough to come early, however, the storm was so unusual, and he scared us so with the report that the roads were fast becoming muddy and impassable that we decided to get as many of us soaked beings into the car as we could, thereby cutting down the number of shuttling trips he would have to make. Well, we started getting in, and in, and in, and laughed and laughed, and got more in, and more, and pretty soon everyone but Zakia's manservant, the faithful photographer, and Zainab's teen-ager Hussein, was somewhere in the jumbled mass of arms, legs, bodies, heads within the car. Slithering down the muddy ruts of the road we didn't even have room to bang into each other, we were that packed in, and when we reached home I thanked God it was near dark as we peeled off from each other and stepped out of the car. That trick circus car that disgorges clowns had nothing on us.

I was not to finish out the summer with the family. The United Nations meetings had been set for Paris and Prince Faisal had decided to go with the rest of the regular delegation. Ali cabled me to join them *en route* during the few days they would stay in Cairo so I could proceed with them to Paris. Mother usually resigned herself to departures in the family but she and I were both very moved at the airport the day I left. She went through all the restricting lines to accompany the children and me as far as the door of the brightly colored Ethiopian Airlines plane before she could finally say good-bye.

It had been a sad morning from start to finish for many of us. Days before, Hayat had made her decision to leave Mohamed and had reserved a seat on the same plane so she could go as far as Cairo with me and then on by herself to her family home in Lebanon — the desperate decision of a desperate woman — but she did not get to carry it out. She fell and wrenched her spine so severely the day before departure that travel was out of the question. I had left her inconsolable at the house and there was nothing anyone could say to comfort her.

Naturally, the flight was beset with problems. It did not surprise me one bit when we were told we were landing in Luxor in Upper Egypt rather than Cairo and would have to spend the night there. The problem was not mechanical; it was because of precautionary measures then in force at Cairo airport which prohibited giving landing clearance to flights arriving after sundown, to guard against raids in the continuing Arab-Israeli crisis. The American pilot told me, "It will be cutting it too fine if we try to make it," or words to that effect, and ten minutes later I wished he hadn't told me because we were rushed to the plane very suddenly and barely got ourselves strapped in before we were once more airborne and on our way to Cairo after all. I concentrated on watching the sunset, then, and that pilot or controller, or whoever, must have calculated the winds right down to the last whisper because that's by how much we made it.

Cairo, Cairo, Cairo — city of many things and not a one for me. The few days we spent there I either waited for the men to finish their meetings or helped them with paperwork afterward. Ali did call one afternoon to say he had tickets to the theater and instructed me to be all dolled up and ready to go when he came in, which I was. But we never got there. He came in late with Shaikh Hafiz Wahba and the two worked until 1:30 A.M. with me at their sides taking dictation, and all I got out of the evening was the comment that I was the best-dressed secretary they ever had and two horse-bean sandwiches when we finally went out to eat.

Paris, then, was something else, more alive than usual with the official and social activities of the United Nations. I missed out on many of them by almost dying from jaundice but got back when I was able to a place sometimes allowed me behind the SAUDI ARABIA plaque in committee meetings, to the never-ending reception lines, or to taking the children for a hot crispy *gauffre* — a kind of sugared waffle made sometimes at stands in the park — and for a ride on the hand-cranked merry-go-round in the Rond Point.

From the grand calendar of events, including the Gala held most elegantly at the opera house by the president of the French republic for U.N. delegates and wives, it is just like me to remember best another night at the opera. Our delegation had received the invitation to occupy the president's box for that performance and it was all very nice except that we were the

only ones in formal attire. We had dressed at the suggestion —
nay, *insistence* — of our very *comme il faut* secretary, a marvelous Englishwoman of a certain age (who after all was the
only one who actually saw the invitation). She not only sent
us off dressed to the teeth, she also made sure the proper boxes
of chocolates were tucked under our diamonds and we were
very grand when we entered. Throughout the performance,
however, except during applause, the men sat with one hand
covering their beards, and we women did no roaming at inter-
mission, no matter what. Princess Iffat had joined us in Paris
and was present that night, so at least I was not the only lady that
time.

I remember our New Year's party, too. All delegations had
dispersed for the holidays and we were in Nice when we ran
into Shaikh Hafiz, who invited us to be his guests for the big
New Year's party the Hotel Ruhl was sponsoring. For a reason
I'll never know, the management had engaged a string quartet
for the pre-midnight festivities instead of the usual band, and I
couldn't get over it. I like Brahms's "Lullaby" but I thought the
occasion called for a bit more gaiety. With my host's permission, I sent a note to the very fine classical violinist who led the
group requesting that they play as their next number "Flat-
Foot Floogie with the Floy-Floy." I thought that was good for a
laugh, and just might give them the hint that would stir them to
more lively entertainment, but I was rather chagrined when
the music stopped altogether while the group and a few others
huddled in the wings. We could see them discussing and gesturing, putting their heads together and calling in other people, and then, for heaven's sake, a drum set was brought in to
replace the cello and the quartet became a trio which actually
did play the requested number. I could have fallen off my chair,
I was so amazed. Then, after an acknowledging nod to our table
responded to handsomely by Shaikh Hafiz, they went back to
selections like "Yours Is My Heart Alone" until the coming of

the New Year finally broke the party open. Dr. Jamil Baroody was another friend with us and he helped get things going by bombarding two very sad lonely-looking elderly ladies with paper confetti balls, while others got the better idea of trying to land their confetti in the middle of the female contingent's décolletages. From then on, who needed music?

After the United Nations meetings adjourned at last and we were done until the next time with the grind of committee work, the listening to and delivering of speeches, the dickering, the lobbying, the voting, the failures, the successes that held up our hopes, we stayed only long enough to tie up the ends and prepare to leave. Before we left, however, we completed arrangements for Annette, a French girl we had engaged, to leave with us, and then took the boat from Marseilles to Alexandria, thence by car across the desert to Cairo, where the family group which had been in Asmara awaited us. Ali of course returned to Arabia while the rest of us stayed, all of us awaiting the completion of our new house in Jeddah. We moved to new addresses three times in the ever-difficult matter of housing our big family, to which a new member was born in the course of our Cairo stay, my son Tarik. I had said before that I wanted, if at all possible, to have all of my children elsewhere than Arabia — after watching sister Zakia have one of her babies with half the Jeddah townladies in the same room, chattering and chatting, smoking, drinking tea and coffee, commenting on and encouraging her every moan and groan. So far I had succeeded, but I had never said I wanted Ali to be elsewhere when I did it, which he was the last two times.

Hayat was still with us, having given up on her decision to leave, and Mohamed came to see her and us once in a while, but for a year it was only she, Mother, Zainab, Zakia and I, all our respective children, and the servants who made up our household. Ali came to visit when he could but seldom for more than a week and I sometimes felt throughout that year that I was married more to the family than to him. The new house would fix all that, we kept telling ourselves, maybe even for Hayat, so we got some encouragement.

Then came a letter: Saudi Arabian stamps, Ali's handwriting. With the news written all over the paper that we had given our famous house to the king, who had admired it. Unbelievable, but true, how true! I don't know how many times I read that letter, but when I finally got it into my head and started circulating again, that Friday became Black Friday. Ali did well to write me the news instead of deliver it in person, but I'm sure that entered his mind, too. Poor fellow, I didn't even think at the time of the hurt it must have caused him to give me/us the news in whatever form.

So it was back to waiting for another abode (which entailed making over for us the new structure originally intended as a guesthouse to the first one) and wondering still when we would be together under one roof again, while trying to keep the kids from raising the temporary one we did have. Thankfully I had Annette, who had turned out to be a jewel, marvelous with the children, fast and efficient, always neat and presentable, who also, glory be, liked Egypt and adjusted well to whatever each day brought. She was also attractive and very soon her days off turned to evenings out until one day she came to tell me she would be leaving us to marry the Egyptian army colonel she had been dating. Well, far be it from me to begrudge others what I had been rather wishing for myself lately — a married life — so I was happy for her and congratulated her and said I would release her from her contract when the time came.

Then came a strange phone call. A strange man's voice identified himself only as from the police, apologized for disturbing me, but did my husband have a secretary named Annette?

"No," I said, "but I have a *maid* named Annette . . ."

"Oh, then you are not aware that this girl has been saying that she is Shaikh Alireza's secretary and has told people that she accompanies him to parties and meetings when he is on business?"

"No, I certainly am not, and it's not true. She works as a maid and has one night off a week, and as for my husband, he is rarely in Egypt."

"Yes, we know, but tell me, please, if you knew when you hired Mademoiselle Annette that she had a police record?"

"Yes, we were told by the agent, but my husband and I talked it over and decided to give her the benefit of the doubt and another chance in life, as it were."

"Very commendable, but would you be willing to meet with us and answer a few questions?"

"Of course, will you come here?"

"No, and may I ask you not to tell anyone of this conversation or of our meeting?"

"All right."

"Now, madame, we know that you go with your children, almost daily to the Gezira Country Club. Would you be willing to meet us there alone today at, say, 3:00 P.M.?"

"That will be fine. How will I know you?" I said, feeling very cloak-and-daggerish by now. I was put properly back on my heels by the comment:

"Madame, *we* know *you*."

So to the wonderment of my family, who had never before seen me go off in mid-afternoon by myself, I went to the club and almost immediately was approached by two men, one in military uniform, one in civilian clothes, and the three of us went to sit at one of the tables on the grass near the pool. With no preliminaries, they proceeded to open a rather large dossier and asked me to identify a picture of Annette to begin with, then showed me picture after picture of other people whom I had never seen before. I had the feeling I was not being very helpful in whatever it was they were trying to ferret, but they continued methodically asking me questions.

Then I said, "You know, she has told me she is leaving to marry an Egyptian army colonel."

They said, "Yes, we know about that, but we can tell you, madame, there will be no wedding."

"Oh dear," I said. "What will I do about that if I cannot tell her?"

"We beg you, madame, do nothing and say nothing. We are most grateful that you have talked with us but, please, you may tell only your husband when he comes." Then they thanked me and left, and I suddenly felt that none of it had happened.

I returned home then as silently and as mysteriously, to the family, as I had gone. Annette continued to date her colonel, she did leave in a few months "to get married" and I wondered again if I had dreamed the encounter with military intelligence. But I hadn't, and they were right: there was no wedding. I don't know what happened to her after she left us, but many months later when Ali was in Cairo she read in the French daily that he was in town and went to him for financial help, which he gave, and one other time he helped her solve her passport difficulties so she could return to France. Thus ended the saga of Annette as far as we were concerned.

Chapter 15

WHEN TARIK WAS a month old, my mother came from California to be with us at Christmas. She had always been afraid to fly, refusing once to take a thirty-minute flight, but when we sent her a round-trip ticket for Cairo she threw her fear to the winds and came. My Arabian family greeted her with such love and joy that she was literally overwhelmed the first day. A feast the likes of which she had never seen was a welcoming banquet for her, cables galore came from family in Jeddah thanking God for her safe arrival and welcoming her, and young and old in the house were anxious to please her in any way they could.

The two mothers, Ali's and mine, took to each other immediately, going around calling each other Sister and jaunting off to shop together when the two of them couldn't even converse. They had humor, though, and the bond of family loyalty. Once in the local bazaar Ali's mother got her dander up at a shopkeeper whom she overheard remarking that her companion was American (presumably to give her a tourist price) and gave him a tongue-lashing I bet he never forgot. "She is my sister, and you give her the same price you give me, or I'll never set foot in here again."

The two of them even went off on the train to Alexandria together, and furthermore took four-and-a-half-year-old Hamida along as interpreter for the sightseeing they were going to do. I don't think my mother learned much about Alexandria's history, but she did get plenty of pictures, and Hamida spent the day looking from one grandmother to the other and saying, "Teta, what did Nana say?" or vice versa.

The constant Arabic rattled my mother so that she was sometimes driven to say, "I no speak English," and although I made vocabulary lists for her she did not do much better in Arabic than her Arabian sister did in English. The hardest times for her came at the table, when everyone talked at once, dishes rattled, silver clacked, servants hovered over her asking strange questions, and racket was general. Once when she was upset about having to leave the table, she said to me, "You come sit in my chair and see what it's like," and I had to say, "Mother, I've sat in that chair."

My mother's contributions to the Arabian family was teaching them all how to play canasta, which she and they played well, for hours and hours. She also taught them to beware of April Fool's Day, because she was still with us by then and couldn't let the day go by without doing something. She forged a notice (with my help) from the post office telling Ali's mother that she had a perishable package to be picked up as soon as possible. Ali's mother, never one to let grass grow under her feet, immediately ordered the car and off she went in search of the package someone had kindly sent her. We were living then in a quarter of Cairo called Zomalik so off to the Zomalik branch she sped first, arriving just as the metal shield was being lowered over the front for the noon closing hours. Jumping from the car waving her notice, she made them open up again because her package was perishable. "Ma fresh hagga, ya hanam," * said the man, after checking delivery room for something in her name, but added that maybe her package was being held at the main

* "There's nothing here, lady,"

post office. That never closed during the day, so "Down to the main post office," she told the driver. There the clerk read the notice, checked what he had, and informed her as before that they had nothing for her.

"But I know there is, there must be, it says so right there, and I have already tried the other branch."

This time the clerk turned over the notice to see our words APRIL FOOL on the back and he started laughing. "Someone is playing a joke on you," he said, and Mother was vehement.

"The post office is playing a joke on *me?*"

"No, no, lady, someone you know is playing a joke on you," and suddenly she knew who.

There was nothing to do then but return home, where we were beginning to get worried about her, she had been gone so long. My mother was also beginning to worry that her joke had gone too far, and was somewhat apprehensive when Ali's mother appeared. But that good Arab lady, accepting that she had been fooled, walked in smiling broadly, albeit shaking her head and wagging her finger at the culprit, whom she then approached with outstretched arms, and they patted each other on the back as they embraced, calling each other, "Sister, Sister." What a pair!

We had hoped that our second new house would be ready in time for my mother to go to Arabia while she was in the area but it wasn't. She would have to wait a few more years and in the meantime we went instead to America with her, which just proved once again that we seldom knew what we would be doing next or where we would be doing it. The need for business meetings took us to America and the need for a vacation kept us there a while longer. Then, after the joys of carefree days, we had the sadness of leaving my family behind again. No matter which way we went, someone always had to be told good-bye.

August was the month of our return to Arabia, just in time for peak heat, just in time for peak pilgrim travel — making us glad we could get a non-pilgrim plane from Paris that took us seventeen hours to Jeddah — and just in time for peak disappointment on our house, not yet completed. The rest of the family had come from Cairo and were billeted here and there, at Zakia and Ahmed Zahid's house mainly, and my children and I stayed there for a short period too. That was a nightmare of too many people and too little space, crying, sick children, a nightmare of futility in our efforts to sort out and cope with our problems, with the sad scene each day of people who love each other getting on each other's nerves because of upset personal lives and too much big-family life.

At first we stayed in Mohamed's small private house in the Nuzla, an area just outside of town. Ali had to go to Riyadh to report on his trip to the United States and when he left us at his brother's house Mohamed was gone. I was glad for that, at least until we got settled. Mohamed knew where my loyalty lay in the matter between him and Hayat, and although we maintained generally good surface relations and kept our rapport on an even keel, the association was far from intimate and far from warm. Still, through the years, we each did things for the other when the occasion arose.

One of those times occurred when he returned then from Egypt sooner than expected and was promptly reminded by his staff that he had promised them the next week off to go to the Pilgrimage. There was no one left but me to cook for Mohamed and the six to twelve cronies of his who made the nightly meal with him almost a ritual. Any normally unengaged cooks always had work at Pilgrimage time so there was no chance of hiring one, and the town was almost empty by then of anyone, not just available cooks.

I know how to cook but I didn't know how to cook Arabian meals in an old-fashioned Arabian kitchen, but nonetheless I took on the job willingly and only hoped that whatever I turned out would be edible. I realized it was the first time that I had none of the other women around on whom to rely, that whether I succeeded or not depended entirely on me and on Saleh Bakhudlagy, a teen-aged trainee houseboy, the sole surviving servant in the house. I think it was his first time, too, for bearing the full brunt of shopping, and neither of us knew how much of anything was the proper amount for the number of people we had to serve. Add to that the fact that most shops and stores had shut down for the week and we had a full-blown predicament before we even started.

Saleh brought what he could find and I managed in the primitive kitchen. I got dubbed "Hajjia* Miriamanna" the first night by Abu Ali, that Lebanese cousin of Mother's of whom I was so fond, but I don't think it had anything to do with my cooking. It was presumably because it was Pilgrimage time (or maybe because the Hadj time was the specified period of my stint as cook), but I certainly never got to Mecca and I spent that Pilgrimage juggling kettles as big as laundry tubs over hot charcoal fires. I cooked the usual rice, meat, and a vegetable or two, and when Mohamed in appreciation came in one night with a two-oven range run on kerosene, which he gave me the job of assembling, I showed my appreciation by adding cookies and apple pies (from dehydrated fruit) to the menu.

When the Hadj was over Ali was still gone, Mohamed had left again, and my son Faisal needed a doctor badly. People were just beginning to drift back to Jeddah, but not the person I wanted — Dr. Idriss. Faisal had a grape-size purplish infection directly over his eye that needed professional attention, I knew, and it was frustratingly impossible at that time to get any. Word had been left at every doctor's office in town, but no one came and I was getting desperate. I got out some sterilized packages of penicillin — the kind that are used once and thrown away — that we had gotten in the United States, and wondered if I should try to use one, although I had never given an injec-

---

* *Haji* and *Hajjia* are titles of honor given to a man and a woman who have performed the Pilgrimage to Mecca.

tion in my life. Fear about Faisal's condition had almost over-come the fear of trying to give him the shot when I heard Faisal emit a sharp cry of pain and I saw that the ball Hamida had been bouncing had caromed off the wall and hit him directly on the eye, opening the infection slightly. Pressure on that particular spot was the worst thing that could have happened and it was hard for me to believe that it had.

And then at that very moment, so help me, while I was looking in shock at what had happened to Faisal and was still holding the unused syringe in my hand, in walked Dr. Idriss and the English doctor from the British Malaria Commission. They had re-turned from a trip together investigating breeding grounds of suspected malaria-carrying mosquitoes in certain areas in the desert, had both found the messages my driver had left waiting at each of their offices and decided to come together. They gave the injection and stayed for two hours, taking turns lightly touching salt compresses wrapped around a tongue depressor and, I have no doubt, saving the child's life. They told me after-ward how very serious it might have been had any of that matter been pressured to the brain, and we were all, each and every one of us, awed by the timeliness of their arrival.

Thus, I went from one thing to another, Ali went from one trip to another, we moved twice, and finally I put my foot down and got him to move us into the house, finished or no. I had had enough of separation and doing things on my own, and no I did not want to go to Taif with the rest of the family. But conjugal togetherness never lasted long and Ali insisted that I join them there when another trip was taking him to Europe.

Abu Ali, the adventurous cousin with a knack for making pastry, was to take me and the children to Taif, and although I loved Abu Ali, I was less than enchanted with the prospect of that place again, and ever so tired of saying what will be will be. But, what was to be was to be, as the men made all the arrange-ments.

On the day we left, our expert driver-mechanic Sambo (and

that was his real name) brought the car from town, cook packed a food basket, servants packed everything else, and by early afternoon we took off, a one-car safari that wasn't to make it even as far as the non-believer's turnoff, because a flat tire stopped us on the main road. Sambo and Abu Ali fixed it while the children and I scuffed our shoes and picked desert plants, and then we were on our way again, up past Wadi Fatma — the oasis where our bananas and fresh vegetables grew — wending our way over the bumps and ridges when, oh day of disaster, the clutch went out. This certainly was not auguring well for our trip, three hours out of Jeddah and only one hour closer to our destination, but after more repair, more delay, we resumed our route, only to have, unbelievably, a third mishap. And this time we were stopped for good, because a stone had caused a leak in the radiator and bent the cooling fan out of commission.

The sun was down by now and it was beginning to get dark. Nothing but desert and mountains surrounded us for as far as we could see. Not a house, not a tent, why, even the road was not a real road. Abu Ali and Sambo told us to stay in the locked car (adding, quite unnecessarily, I thought, that wolves and hyenas frequented the region) while they took turns scouting for signs of life or shelter. In twenty minutes we had the incredible news that over the crest of the hill to the left was a band of Bedou guarding stores and equipment of the experimental farm of His Highness Prince Abdullah Al-Faisal, and the Bedouin in charge had asked that we join them. They would be glad to see to our comfort, he had said, and dispatch a truck to Mecca to make our plight known to Prince Abdullah, who would doubtless inform our families.

We climbed the short way to the camp, and as I approached the men averted their eyes respectfully and made no attempt to get a better look at me. One walked us to the site they had chosen as best for our stay, the top of the small hill at whose base their camp was, spread a small carpet for us on the sand and

said it would not be long before his men would make our camp-
site; they were preparing to do so then. I sat with the children
and watched the bustle in the camp below, thankful, oh so thankful for our good fortune, when ten or twelve men started up
the hill and I suddenly wondered if we were as safe as we thought.
Abu Ali no doubt experienced the same doubts, for he placed
his great bulk squarely in front of me as the men proceeded up
the incline; the lamps some were carrying threw flickering shadows on their faces, but far from wishing us harm their only
concern was to see that we spent the night in real comfort.

They seemed to take pride in working toward that end, chanting, and making rise out of the sand as if by magic a huge, multicolored tent, and spreading beautiful carpets for flooring, thin
pads for beds, and bringing ample supplies of pillows, clean
linen, and blankets. They hung the lamps and brought water
jugs with clean glasses, soap, towels, and a wash basin. Then,
after all that, they had the marvelous kindness to inquire respectfully if we had need of anything else. It was too much!
Truly astounding to look around that luxurious tent on a barren
hilltop and have those men, desert men whom we had never seen
before and would never see again, catering to our every comfort. They had even brought our effects from the car and the
car itself, they said, would be sent for repair to Mecca and returned eventually to Jeddah. As for our trip to Taif, another
car would be sent us in the morning, and we need not worry
about a thing. Astounded by the extent of their kindness, we
thanked them as best we could and after we assured them once
more that our food was sufficient, they left us to enjoy our meal.

Human nature is indeed a strange and unpredictable thing!
As we prepared to eat, it had been but a bare hour since we had
broken down on the desert, our chances slim of finding people
or help on a route so seldom used, and the possibility of death
had even hung over us. But we had been fortunate and were
scarcely through shaking our heads over the miracle that had

saved us, when we had the gall to sit there by our food basket and shake our heads in disgust. The cook had forgotten our bread, and in pondering that disaster we had so soon forgotten our deliverance from the other. If it had been anything but bread, perhaps Abu Ali could have remained thankful for all our blessings, but bread is life to the Arab. Many will not sit at table until bread is on it, and Abu Ali was one of those. He stormed how impossible, absolutely, it was to eat anything without bread but he did amazingly well I noticed when he forced himself to try. His grumbling never stopped, and he never forgave the cook, but there were mighty sparse pickings in the food basket by the time he got through.

As if on a signal tea was brought as we finished and we were once again asked if we lacked for anything. I prepared the children for bed to Abu Ali's praise, "Upon God, you're a good one on a trip, yes you are, God knows it!" and it made me warm and happy. I was in fact feeling a peace such as I have rarely known as we sat for a while until the children settled. Voices of the men below reached us and we heard drums and barking dogs of other Bedou we knew not where. Every sound came so clearly on the desert air it seemed we were part of a settlement, but we knew that with the dawn the sounds would go and what we had heard could nowhere be seen. I went inside to sleep while Abu Ali prepared his pallet outside, and when all was quiet and I peeked it was just as I suspected. His great strong body was stretched to block the tent's entrance and I should not have liked to be anyone attempting to cross over it.

In the hour before dawn Abu Ali wakened me to say that Prince Abdullah's personal car and driver had arrived to take us the rest of our way and it would be wise if we started before the heat of the day. Ali and family had been informed of our safety, so our only worry now was to get to Taif, summarily done without incident, the only thing of note being that Abu Ali finished almost singly a two-pound tin of English crackers I thought I had brought for the children. It must have been his continued nervousness at our cook for forgetting the bread, and it must have been impressive for me to remember it all these years, for I can still see him in his white cotton skullcap relating to the driver, with his mouth full of crackers, the full account of the day before. Abu Ali was one of my favorite people in Arabia and I was sad to hear some years ago that his death had been a lonely one, far from sons and family. He had been such a good companion in life.

We did finally get settled together in our house at Kilo Five (so called because it was five kilometers out from Jeddah on the road to Mecca), just in time for Christmas 1950. The children and Ali drove out to Kilo Ten and got a "tree" with very long limp piny-like needles and fairly even branches which we decorated beautifully and all our stockings were hung with care, even those of the family. Christmas morning the excited discussion between Hamida and Faisal that awakened us had to do with her getting four walnuts in her stocking and Faisal only three in his (among other things), but Faisal made up for that when all the family gathered for the present-giving. He scooted around opening for himself any package he could and would come to me bubbling over with "Oh *thank* you, Mommy, for my present," said article being powder puffs for Hayat, or a pipe for his uncle. But then I got one from him that was like no other.

His father in the past week had bought presents by the dozens and spent night after night wrapping great Scotch-taped creations of paper and ribbon that were masterpieces of devotion if nothing else, and he put the children's names as donors on some, inscribing them "To Dear Mommy from So-and-So," beautiful things the children never saw. Faisal apparently had felt the spirit of giving as he watched and wanted to give on his own, for with the other presents under the tree for me was the little crooked package of his with a knotted ribbon top and a tiny cloth case inside containing three caramels and a pistachio nut. No jewel I ever had could ever compare.

The regular happenings, like meeting and greeting each morning, varied only in the way we did them. Sometimes the children and I caught Mother still splashing cologne and water on her hair, her glasses not on yet, and sometimes she would puff up to our place muttering, "Ajezzna," * on the way and then sit and visit a spell. Sometimes we'd walk in on Zainab while she was still praying, and then we'd sit on her floor while we shared her early morning tea and she let us finish shamelessly all her *shaboorat* and cheese. Or Zainab came after her tea to enjoy coffee with me and stayed to see us through a morning and participate in whatever we had going. Hayat, our only late-riser, usually made it up the stairs in late morning hours to get whatever choice thing my "bakery" had in store that day, or we burst through her shuttered room to unwind the *shershif* from her eyes and get her up.

Mohamed wasn't with us. He lived next door in a two-story mansion he had built on the same grounds as ours, and his second wife lived there with him. To greet him each morning Ali and children trotted across the yard, but I never went and I wrote Mohamed to tell him why I never would. Firstly, I had been brought up to think differently of marriage, and secondly, I could never accept his second wife as long as I was living with the first. It was Hayat who had been introduced to me as his wife when I arrived in Arabia, I told him, and it was she with whom I had lived as a sister. I could not and would not add to her unhappiness, which I was sure my greeting the other would do. I think he appreciated my frankness, if nothing else. We didn't talk to each other sometimes but I still baked bread for him and his guests, did decorator-type sewing and upholstery that I learned, and he remained most generous, understanding

* "We have gotten old."
† Salty, spiced Zweiback.

of my needs, appreciative of the things I did for him, and never let anyone criticize my action. He even told Ali once to leave me alone when Ali was trying to explain my action — I had a right to my beliefs and Ali was to mind his own business! It was nonetheless a basically bad situation and it never really got better.

Hayat's older children were by then in boarding schools in Egypt, English ones for the boys, French for the girls, so I was more than ever in sympathy with her. She was so lonely for them, living for vacation times and cursing departure times, and in the meanwhile had in her lonely personal life to look out each morning to the house where her husband lived with another.

When it reached the time for Hamida's schooling, we were at a loss to know what to do. *Eustaz* Aish gave her Arabic and instruction in the Koran each day except Friday (I had agreed before marriage that our children would be Moslem) but we wanted her also to have English. I had strong feelings about children needing to spend their formative years in the home, so I began to think of ways I could keep her there and still give her a good education. I asked my mother to help me and she found the perfect answer in the home correspondence courses offered by the Calvert School of Baltimore, Maryland. Specifically designed to enable parents with no previous teaching experience to instruct their children, Calvert gives comprehensive education from kindergarten through high school. All school supplies and beautiful and excellent books are supplied, plus a teacher's manual with each day's lesson outlined and instructions and suggestions on how to present it. It was just like Christmas again when the big box came.

We progressed through farm projects, community projects (model city with trees, airport, groceries with clay vegetables and fruits), scrapbooks, calisthenics, Indian crafts — tepees, canoes, paddles, a drum out of a coffee can, an Indian rug, a clay bowl — all this, and one day we were asked to pretend we were Indians on a hunt (to sharpen our imagination). Ali came in about the time it was really getting sharp. Hamida, Faisal, even Tarik, and I had just gotten our bows and arrows and gone to the river's edge. He was splitting his sides as we then got in our canoes, rowed to hunting grounds, got out, hunted and spotted deer, shot each one of us one, hefted them to our shoulders, and toted them back to our canoe by the river. He welcomed us home as we paddled in, happy with our day's luck. I guess it was pretty funny. Tarik always joined in on such things and even on Hamida's other projects. He had a passion for drawing and paper and colors and Hamida always let him. Besides, she thought he was a genius. She woke us up one morning sparkling with pride in her baby brother and the words he had just spoken. "Tarik just said 'diarrhoea' and 'Marie,' Mommy. I think he's going to speak French." I know where he picked up "diarrhoea" but it's a mystery where he got "Marie."

As it turned out, Tarik expanded that French vocabulary before he expanded his English, because the family went off that summer to Paris. This worked out just right for me, too, because I was expecting our fourth child in July and was afraid for a while that my record of having children outside Arabia was going to be broken.

Prince Faisal's wife, Princess Iffat, was in Paris too and expecting a child at approximately the same time I was. We were both still very much waiting, however, on Bastille Day, July 14, which is also our Faisal's birthday, and some of her children came to the party we had at our apartment on the Champs-Elysées. It was something for a four-year-old to start his birthday party with a parade of soldiers, sailors, desert troops from the Foreign Legion, guns, tanks, and bands right outside his window, and of course he thought it was all for him. It was Zainab and Hayat's first trip to Europe and they had never seen before, either, such a display of pride in country and military might.

The royal baby was born only a day before our daughter.

They named their princess Haifa and we named ours Nadia and she was another blue-eyed girl. Tarik showed his love for her the first week she was home from the hospital by lining her crib with his father's shoes as she lay sleeping and I thought he was napping. A wonder he didn't drop one on her before we discouraged this show of affection.

Other family had appeared from wherever they were to spend the summer with us: Hussein from the University of California at Berkeley, our old stomping grounds, Hayat's sons Essam and Abdullah from London, Zakia and her children from Arabia. It seemed we were always going either to the hospitals or to the airport. We had moved out of the apartment to a big rambling house in St. Cloud which was pretty awful but did have room for everyone. My very elegant French doctor had to visit me once at the house and by the time he reached the second landing he already wasn't believing it. Approaching my bed through cots of sleeping *enfants* as the last of many obstacles on the way up, he was shaking his head and I had to laugh. He saw that I understood and felt free to ask, "How many are you, madame?"

"Doucement, let's not tempt the evil eye, hein?" I replied with a twinkle in mine. "Entre nous, we are quite a few, but never let anyone hear you say it. One thing we Arabs never do is count heads — it will surely bring bad luck."

"Incroyable" was his only comment, as he got to the business at hand, and he could have meant anything.

Everyone but me and my children returned to Arabia in October. Ali took the family and left me because he was returning to Europe soon, but it was sooner than expected because his back problem flared and he was forthwith returned to Paris on a stretcher. He was seen by many specialists, and finally those in London operated for the removal of a disc in January of 1952. Ali's mother, the children, and I stayed at the Dorchester Hotel. She and I visited him daily at London Clinic during the three weeks he was recuperating; between times Hamida had her Calvert lessons regularly, we all went for walks in the park, and we shopped for nothing but fruit.

His Majesty King George VI died in February and we watched the three-mile long funeral procession from our hotel windows. It was a procession replete with pomp and ceremony as only the British have, and it was the most outstandingly impressive sight I have ever seen — sad, beautiful, grand, heartrending, touching, spectacular, tragic all at the same time. None of us who witnessed it will ever forget it.

Ali's recuperation was long and beset with complications; he was in and out of the hospital several times and had to wear a steel brace, but when he recovered enough to travel we returned to France for a while and then to the Middle East before we returned to Europe again so he could have further treatment.

Late in 1952 we accompanied Prince Faisal and Princess Iffat and entourage to the United States on a business and pleasure tour. Ali was going to fly with Prince Faisal while the rest of us, men, women, and children, went by boat (the *Queen Mary* again), but His Royal Highness decided that sitting for a long period on a plane was worse for Ali than getting sea legs on a boat. So Ali joined us: Dr. Bushir from Mecca; Said Ahmed Abd-el-Wahab, a young Saudi who grew up in Prince Faisal's home; the princess; her sister Muzaffar Hanam; Mme. Gemila Pharaon, wife of Dr. Rashad, once private physician to King Ibn Saud and then Minister to France; her sister Madame Ahmed Abd-el Jabbar; and myself.

Some of the princess's children and ours had corresponding ages so that made it nice for everyone concerned. Hamida kept up with her Calvert lessons nonetheless and so did Faisal, in kindergarten by then. All in all, we formed rather a spectacular group as we sailed into New York and then joined the other men and traveled together here and there in the United States. Some one of the children was always having a birthday party, the men had business and formal dinners, all of us together had many informal ones, we did a monumental amount of shopping.

Tarik quarantined the whole party at the Mark Hopkins Hotel in San Francisco by coming down with a severe case of measles and delaying plans of all the higher-ups. We went then to Los Angeles in a private railway car, then to Florida — where the hotel manager gave the run of his own house to us Arab ladies so we could wear bathing suits and swim in private, it being inadvisable to expose ourselves on the hotel grounds — and so forth until we reached New York again. There we kept up the schedule of meetings for the men, socializing of women during the day and socializing as a group at night, and the children meanwhile participated in outings, had their meals together wherever they happened to be, and engaged in frequent play in the hotel, seldom quietly. When Princess Iffat outfitted the entire gang in fancy western outfits from F. A. O. Schwartz, the children could then be found most any day cutting each other off at the passes in Central Park.

In March our business and pleasure, as far as the United States was concerned, was almost over and reservations were made to return — the men by air again, the rest of us by boat. The only boat available at the time we wanted to leave was — you guessed it — the *Queen Mary*. Departure date was on my birthday, March 28, so on the twenty-sixth Prince Faisal gave me an early surprise party at El Morocco, then Ali and the children gave me their presents while we were still all together on the twenty-seventh, and the princess had a party planned for shipboard on the twenty-eighth. Waiting for me at the ship was my family's gift of silver and a "private" present from my mother — a rock-hard doughnut (the way I like them) similar to the ones she had sent me always when I was a student and always had on hand when I returned home from anywhere. The doughnut sat for days on my dresser in the stateroom and I would not let the steward throw it away. No one but I, and certainly not the steward, understood my attachment to it.

Arrival at Cherbourg was typical of some of my experiences. It called for a five-thirty breakfast and the tide was so low we couldn't dock (shades of Liverpool) so all passengers had to be transferred from the *Mary* to a small ferry and then to pier, train, and Paris. As we all said, it would be good to sit and twiddle our toes at home in Jeddah, which did look finally to be in our future again.

Some of us parted ways in Paris and some went on to Cairo. From Cairo we were ten in all in the big DC-4 the king sent us, and when we circled for a landing in Jeddah we passed over our house at Kilo Five, where we could see the family out on the balcony looking and waving. I couldn't help remembering that other first time when we landed and it seemed the entire male population of Jeddah was there again to greet Emir Faisal, and Uncle Yousuf, family, and friends came into the plane as before to see me and the children until the commotion outside subsided. I told them all it was good to be home, and it was.

The children were delighted, too, to be home. The first few days we couldn't get young Faisal to remove his Arab cloak and headdress — "just like Daddy" — except to eat. Although Tarik constantly favored us with the song "Jambalaya" that he had learned in the States, and Nadia couldn't get out of the habit of singing "Happy Birthday" to all those whose parties she had attended on our trip, all of them fit solidly back into the Arab pattern of living and picked up where they had left off.

Our penthouse apartment was much improved. For the first time we had air conditioning in the bedrooms, and Ali had beautiful electric appliances installed for me (we ran one generator during the day and another at night), plus a kitchen counter-bar planned and shipped by Macy's in New York. He also screened in a portion of our balcony to give us a charming nook for family suppers or relaxation in the cool of an evening, and built us a "schoolroom" on top of our west wing. The latter was a marvelous air-conditioned room as long as the house was wide and we reached it by ship stairs from the kitchen;

it had big-view windows for which I made gorgeous red drapes, desks for each of the children, a built-in sewing corner for encouragement of my learning efforts, and a perfect spot for the 16-mm movie projector we bought to show films if and when we could beg, borrow, or rent them.

Arabic lessons were resumed as soon as we returned and the English lessons continued on a regular basis in morning sessions, patterned as closely as possible after those in real schools. We had the same lesson time each day, and insistence upon regular and serious application during the two to three hours required each day. Different grade levels were handled by starting one child on his day's work, and going to the next, until the time the last pupil was busy the first one was ready for something else. Best daily papers and monthly tests were always mailed to Calvert, where the professional teacher assigned to each pupil at the beginning of the semester studied the work and gave comments, criticisms, and suggestions by return mail, enabling us to proceed satisfactorily toward the certificate awarded at year's end. I always learned so much myself that I think I should have gotten one, too.

Eustaz Aish was unfortunate in having to settle the children into Arabic lessons immediately after their English ones, when the children were ripe for fun. Faisal habitually slipped into their lesson room (the middle-floor dining room) beforehand to load the ceiling fan's blades with homemade confetti (probably the English papers he botched), knowing that the first thing their *eustaz* did was turn on the fan, and all of my brood liked to sneak into the adjacent toilet and pull its chain which, for some odd reason, set off the most disconcerting vibrations, rumbles, gurgles, gasps, and clankings you ever heard, drowning out anything within a radius of two floors.

My contribution to delayed lesson time was the mid-morning treats I sent them. It was just as long to lunchtime for the *eustaz* as it was for the children, so he always got his portion, and although he complained loudly that the consumption of said treats delayed them considerably, he was the first to inquire of their whereabouts when they failed to arrive. Popsicles and ice cream sandwiches were his favorites and he was always very good about sending back the stick handles for future use.

It has always amused me that the only real rapport I had with the man who taught my children was a kind of culinary one. I was never consulted on their learning — that was their father's job — but I had the *eustaz* consulted once on his teaching. Faisal passed on to me the gem he had gleaned from one lesson on religion that anyone not Moslem would end up in Hell. Now that might not have been what the *eustaz* said at all, but that is the way it reached me, and I promptly saw that it reached Ali, who got a good laugh out of it. He did say he would speak to the *eustaz* about it, but it's riyals to doughnuts he never did.

No discussion of the children would be complete without mention of Saima, a woman who came to us each weekend (Thursday and Friday) because we loved to have her and because she loved to be with the children. She was a widow whose husband had been a freed slave who held an important position in the Alireza firm. When he died Saima's interests became the interests of the family, first because it is required by religion and custom, and second, because Saima is one of those individuals who becomes "family" to those who know her. She never had children of her own, but at the time I knew her she had more children she called her own than anyone I ever saw.

For our children, Saima's being there meant charming story hours and the present she always brought them from the *suk* — a paper cornucopia of hot and peppery fried bean cakes called *muglia*, a cone of roasted pumpkin or watermelon seeds, or a stringy mess of the local *halawa tahinia*, a delicious confection of sesame paste and honey or sugar — and it meant fun and laughter with an easy-going, easy-tempered person completely amenable to going along with us on all our spontaneous activities. It also meant fighting between the girls and the boys over who was going to get her to sleep on the floor between their beds (where she always did for the first night), and it meant vying for her attention and playing tricks on her. And now that I think of it, Saima's being there meant all that to us adults.

No one's walk was the same as Saima's in the old dress styles of Arabia. They were admirably suited to her ramrod-stiff posture above the waist and the healthy sway she gave to them below the waist, while the soft old-time headdress could have been made to complement her lovely wavy-soft black hair, in whose ornament and care she was meticulous. She had rather deep-set expressive eyes, cheekbones so high they dipped to hollows underneath, a protruding mouth, and skin that was medium dark and ever so smooth. It was perhaps part of her charm that she was beset by fears which we tried through the years to cure — her fear of being alone amounted to a phobia — but looking back on it now, maybe all we really did was make them worse. We never stopped because she was such a good sport when we made fun of her and that led us to do it all the more.

Our favorite tease was when she prayed in a roomful of people and in the middle of her prayer we'd start to leave one by one. She watched us frantically out of the corner of her eye while desperately trying to keep her mind on her prayer, and God knows how many we disturbed. We called it the rise and fall of Saima, as each time she sat back after touching her forehead to the floor to find a few more of us gone. If we all disappeared before she finished, she would break off her devotions by unwrapping her prayer sheet and dashing after us. Another of our tricks was to make her leave a room by asking her kindly to get something for us in another part of the house, something she willingly did knowing that we were close at hand in case the *djinn* came after her and not realizing that we were the only *djinn* around. We would then turn off all the lights and sit quietly until she returned to the dark room and dissolved in panic. Picking up her long skirts and removing her flappy sandals, she fled pell-mell down the stairs and kept going until she found somebody, anybody. It was mean of us, to be sure, but once Saima found us again her laughter was as loud as ours and so it continued.

During the week, Saima lived in town and taught little girls to embroider at the only school in Jeddah at that time where girls could go to learn anything, educational or otherwise. While I'm sure her habile fingers and her way with the young taught many what they were there to learn, the younger sisters and brothers sent along by the parents with her properly enrolled pupils were the recipients of the finest baby-sitting service in town. It was typical of Saima that she let the "bonus babies" stay — only rarely and only for a good reason did she ever send one home — and the true tales she could tell are classics of diplomacy, of tolerance, of the way some people lighten another's burden by adding to their own. How Saima ever taught French knots and daisy stitches while changing diapers and burping babies (yes, she fed them all, too) that weren't even in the bargain, I'll never know, but knowing Saima I believe every word of it.

Saima always went with us to our beach house on Fridays or on our boating trips, fishing or anchoring at one of the small islands near Jeddah (even the old quarantine island), after we acquired a seventy-three-foot pleasure boat. It wouldn't have been the same without her, but only we knew what it took for her to entrust herself to our cars which could have an accident "Allah mahafuzzna" ("May God protect us"), to our boat which could sink "burra wa baeed" (figuratively, "Heaven forbid"; literally, "outside and far away"), or to wading in the Red Sea where a shark could eat her up "Allah iktahom" ("God curse them"). She said her beads and mumbled prayers the entire route to and from but had a thoroughly good time in between.

Chapter 16

Life in the home and life outside the home got better. The government had started spraying the streets with insecticides and clearing them of refuse on a regular basis so the fly problem became minimal; the efforts of the malaria team greatly reduced the incidence of malaria and dengue fever; the first clinic was followed by many good hospitals; a big hotel went up (the first of its kind); and modern stores with every conceivable item and service opened their doors. Professional buildings replaced town eyesores, and a soap factory and one for shoes opened. Facilities to accommodate the thousands upon thousands of pilgrims each year between their arrival and depature times were vastly improved by the government; communications networks were expanded and modernized; we began to be able to get reading material for news and for pleasure more easily; a new airport was built on the site of the old one; and the young Saudi Arabian Airlines became bigger and better. Existing roads were improved and new ones built on main routes, and even before the old walls of Jeddah had come down the surrounding desert began to be dotted with new houses and new gardens. One could see the new order in things.

The winds of change that were gathering force got their real impetus from the oil, which more and more opened up the country and from whose revenues came the massive amounts the government was beginning to spend on improving the country, while pursuing at the same time its goal of setting up an administrative system that would not only carry Arabia into the modern age but would allow it to function there effectively. Much still had to be done, but ideas were moving and people were moving, beginning to get the incentive to move forward with the times. It was a mental tug-of-war for some who were not sure they wanted change, and it was enthusiastic anticipation for others who were sure they did. As for me, I felt by then like a theater-goer who had paid dearly for the best seat in the house but had to watch the show from backstage.

It was a real show sometimes, too, when people could get ecstatic over things like a vacuum cleaner as an example of progress. Ali brought a new one home one night from the first shipment of the Eureka agency they represented and we applauded him three quarters of the way through the first big carpet before he realized he had already exceeded a mere demonstration. Then he couldn't find the release to expose all the dirt he had gathered — embarrassing with all the servants watching — and finally in desperation he hoisted the machine into his lap for a closer look. Then, of course, the clasp released and dumped the dust of his labors full onto his *tobe*. Normally, that would have been the end of it, after everyone had a good laugh, but in Arabia we had had too many instances already where servants not acquainted with our methods followed too literally our instructions, so Ali sat there with a lapful of sand until all present understood that was not really the way to empty the bag. I think it took much restraint on his part not to cry "Eureka!" when it happened.

Ali's enthusiasm for doing things single-handedly when the outcome promised to be spectacular was beautifully demonstrated on a fishing jaunt one night on the flat, open launch of our friend Mohamed Salama, the Jeddah pilot most demanded by foreign shipping to take their vessels safely through Jeddah's reefs. Mohamed was one of the Arab men outside the family with whom I could associate and I was present as we rocked at anchor that night with our lines over the Musmariya reefs, sixteen miles or so from Jeddah, and Ali most unhappily was the only one who had not yet caught a fish.

To be honest, I had the great advantage of the help of Mohamed and his crew as they taught me the intricacies of their methods, methods at which one might scoff until their effectiveness was proved. The first requisite is rocks, lots of them; the tackle is a ball of heavy twine complete with hooks. The procedure is this: Take one rock about as big as a man's fist and lay on it the baited hooks and some loose bait for chum. Put another rock over that and with the twine encircle and bind the two together, finishing with a slipknot, and then toss the whole overboard. This will hold together until your rocks hit bottom but will release when yanked from above, spill out loose bait and line, and catch you a fish — guaranteed. I had done some deep sea fishing in California but this beat anything I had ever seen.

Sitting there wrapping rocks to the encouragement of my Arab friends and pulling in fish to their loudly announced tally of my score just to tease Ali (who was getting madder by the minute), I could really think this is the life! I don't know why Ali wasn't having any luck, but he finally got into the act. He felt a pull on his line so tremendous he had trouble hanging on — not exactly good for his back, but he wanted to do it alone. He tugged and grunted and inched it closer (no doubt thinking as he struggled that we might have more but his was bigger), and we peered into the deep for the first sight of it; finally, slowly, as someone held a pistol to shoot it if it gave us any trouble, up it came with a bump — the biggest, orneriest, thorniest, rough piece of Red Sea coral you ever saw.

We chugged home then and the only thing that restored Ali's pout to normal position was the *sayadiah** that the crew cooked over an open fire built over a bed of rocks on the deck. This is a dish invented by Jeddah fishermen of old, and is made by burning onions in oil until they are almost black, adding water to take on the dark color, replacing the onions with rice and hunks of fish and simmering until done, seasoned with lemon and salt. The rich brown of the rice makes the fish whiter by contrast, so it appeals to the eye as well as the palate. Side dishes of fried fish and fried bread, and raw onion if desired, are served with *sayadiah* and the very best way to eat it is with your fingers.

Another thing we always ate with our fingers on the special occasions when we had it was *saleeg*. This is a Bedouin dish consisting of a whole lamb (head and all) boiled in milk to which rice is added when the meat is tender. The resultant savory pottage is steaming, messy, and delicious.

There were so many good things to eat! I had a passion for *moottabug*, the crispy delight special chefs in town made of large sheets of crisp paper-thin dough filled with a choice of caramelized banana, soft white cheese, or chopped egg. They were masterpieces and I'd give my right arm to know how they're done. A cinnamon roll is nothing!

And the names they had for things. It was exotic just to say some of them, and one felt one should dance first. Some were misleading, though, as I was to discover. There was one syrup-soaked goody called *turroomba* that looked like a straight ridged doughnut and its name fascinated me. *Turroomba, turroomba* — why, it could almost mean the beating heart of the Bedou drums at night, and I loved to roll the word around on my tongue. That is, I loved to do it until I learned the word had two other meanings, which were "pump" or "enema," as the case might be.

When we received presents of five-gallon tins bulging with

* Literally, "of the hunt"; *fishing* in Arabic is "fish hunt."

dates from Medina I wondered how we would ever finish them, but somehow we managed. They were delicious as only good dates can be, and I was astounded at the variety. I always "sterilized" them before we ate them, however. They sometimes were not as clean, outside or in, as they should have been, so I spread them on large oven trays and gave them just enough heat to purify, but not enough to cook them. The only kind I didn't treat that way was an unripened date sent *en branche,* whose large red-colored fruit was naturally sweet, crisp, and juicy like an apple.

Of course, I introduced a few things myself, and I lived to see some American favorites become household words in Arabia. Why, Kool-Aid, an imported drink mix of imitation fruit flavors that I blended with fresh juices, came to be a favorite drink with which to break the Ramadan fast, and it was from the same mix that I made the popsicles. My Arab family liked my pots of baked beans on a picnic and southern fried chicken, while I preferred *foule medemas* — horse-beans mashed and seasoned with garlic, cumin, lemon, and sprinkled with oil — and their fried fish with spices stuffed in the gills.

For interest's sake, I once made a study of how many American things Mother liked but couldn't say, and there were quite a few: "bancake" with the accent on the last syllable, "abblebie," "bobcorn," "bobsicles," "marshymellow," "beanut-brittle," "wallf" for waffles, and tender "bobowers." But she always tried, that was the important thing, and she was a good sport in allowing us to call the beef frankfurters we imported by the literal translation of *hot dogs* in Arabic. Our household became so accustomed to calling them *kilab hara* that we sometimes forgot other Arabs had never heard of hot dogs, and we shocked guests dreadfully at times by yelling to a servant to add a platter or two of *kilab hara* to the supper fare. A dog is considered by the Moslem to be a very unclean animal, so the concern engendered by our request was enormous.

Every so often Ali had to leave for quick medical checkups

and it was understandable that I didn't go along with him for such short trips, but I certainly minded when I did not go to London with him when King 'Abd al-'Aziz appointed him one of the Saudi Arabian representatives to Queen Elizabeth's coronation. In due course he received the formal invitation taken from protocol lists and then many, many more came addressed to "Shaikh and Madame . . ." but only his Shaikh-ness went. I hopefully cried, "I'm not really an Arab you know," but Arabian protocol would have none of it and I stayed home. I drooled over the fancy scrapbook of memorabilia he brought home with all the invitations and such pasted in, and every time I saw my name on one I shed a little tear. What an occasion to miss!

In between such momentous events, however, Ali continued to require treatment for his back, and it was never too long before his mother, the children, and I found ourselves in London or Paris again, hovering over him in a hospital bed. He had other operations and other tests and treatments and the many related problems never made it easy for him or for us. His pain was always severe and he began to get very depressed about the slow and incomplete recovery he was making and about having to suffer so much both in and out of the hospital.

After one session in late 1953 Mohamed insisted that Ali take it easy for a while and we moved into our Paris apartment just as Nura Sulaiman (*sans* co-wives) and her ever-so-numerous party of servants, secretaries, and friends were moving out. Shaikh Abdullah had requested the use of our apartment for her, but he returned earlier than expected from a business trip to Germany and they settled at the Trianon Hotel, making everything work out for everybody.

Then one day the following happened: The children and I went to the park on the Champs-Elysées in the afternoon, stopped at the Lido on the walk home for tea and ice cream, then went back to the apartment, where they were washed and pajamaed and having dinner, when the telephone rang. Busybody Hamida answered and all of us sitting in the adjacent dining room heard her say, "Allo . . . all right . . . all right, Ammo* . . . good-bye." She bounded in to inform us, "Uncle says to pack our bags quickly and that the plane for Jeddah will take off at midnight." He hadn't told her why and she hadn't asked — or did not have a chance to — so we didn't know why we had to pick up and leave so suddenly. He must have realized it as soon as he hung up, for he called again almost immediately to say quickly that King 'Abd al-'Aziz had died and hung up again. We found out later that the haste was due to Shaikh Abdullah's insistence on leaving immediately, in the hope of reaching Arabia for the funeral, although everyone knew the chances were slim for making it in time because dead are quickly buried in Arabia and even the body of a king does not lie in state.

We had our orders, though. So we dashed like mad people to pack, undress, and redress the children, and were on the tag ends when another telephone call told us that plans had changed; we weren't leaving until nine o'clock the following morning. Breathe, breathe, that was a relief! But before the hour was up another telephone call came with the information that the plane that was to have come for us from Frankfurt could not leave on account of bad weather, and that we had to take the one at midnight after all. And that was that! We were in the air and on the outskirts of Paris by half past. We were being taken to Jeddah by a United States Air Force Special Services Unit aircraft, provided on a moment's notice by the United States ambassador in Paris. There had been no commercial flights which could take us all, the Saudi embassy had tried unsuccessfully all afternoon to find one, the French government had tried, and finally Ali went to the American ambassador and told him the situation. Without hesitation he said

* Affectionate term for *uncle.*

not to worry, that an airplane would be at our disposal and ready to leave sometime that evening.

The plane itself was ultra-comfortable and beautifully fitted, but our flight was a long one. Because of bad weather over the Alps we had to go the long way around, six lightning-filled hours from Paris to the U.S. Air Force base in Tripoli, Libya, our first stop. There we were taken into the sergeants' dining room for breakfast, I in a mink coat with a child hanging onto each mink, the men in *tobes* and headdresses preparatory to landing in Arabia, and what a picture we must have made. We waited a total of two hours in Tripoli breakfasting and anticipating a break in the rain (the base was already flooded about one and one-half feet in spots) and then we took nine hours to get to Jeddah. When we arrived I told the American crew I could certainly imagine how they felt after the trip, since we who had not been working or piloting were dead-tired, and the sergeant who had been so kind and waited on us the entire flight said, "Yes, and we had already had a full day's work when we were assigned to this emergency." Imagine!

Shaikh Abdullah and all of us were overwhelmed with the way the ambassador and the air force came through to help, and as an American I of course was proud. The ambassador had gone so far as to arrange for cars and a bus to meet us at the door of the plane on the Tripoli landing strip, and to get an American major who spoke Arabic to be with the party while we were there. It was a valiant effort on the part of all concerned, but of course the men were too late to be there when King 'Abd al-'Aziz was laid to rest. Prince Faisal was the only one of his many sons who was with him when he died, Crown Prince Saud arriving from Jeddah too late. When the two met, however, in Taif, Prince Faisal greeted his brother publicly at the door pledging his allegiance, and the king publicly acknowledged the other as crown prince. Thus they fulfilled the promise each had given to their father before his death and the transition was easy. Mourning among the Nejdis, you remember, is not permitted, so life took up where it left off: "The king is dead! Long live the king!"

Jeddah then was the busiest I had seen it. There was hardly a day when we did not have a dinner party to arrange, and our guest annex was full from the day we arrived. The biggest affair was the dinner party Uncle Yousuf gave for the king. It was truly like something out of *Arabian Nights* to us women and children watching from the balconies. The entire grounds were carpeted and tables for five hundred men were laden with the most sumptuous dishes in the most staggering amounts. Everyone who was someone was there to honor the king, including members of the Ulema, a college of learned religious men whose influence on the ruling house and on the country as a whole is great. They were easily identifiable by the huge turbans they wear in lieu of the *sumada* (or *ghutra*) and *igal,* gold or black, the other men wore; we played the game of spotting them or others we knew from sight or from pictures. The children for days after made their own pictures, drawing with crayons, of those scenes from the party that were most vivid in their memories.

When we had the big rainstorm — rainstorms tended to be milestones in Arabia — a few days later, I thought in the havoc it caused what a double disaster it would have been if it had happened the night of the king's party. It would have made a shambles of the actual event besides making conditions in the town so much worse. Jeddah was crowded with extra people and vehicles — goodness knows how many people behind the scenes, secretaries, aides, servants, drivers and the like, represented each person at the party —and activity was at a peak.

But the storm came after the party and destroyed some 2000 houses of the townspeople and the Bedou. At our house it practically washed us out of our top apartment. We had a running river from the French windows in the living room which opened to the balcony, out through the corridor, and down the stairs; and it ran for two days in a row. It was a new experience for me in Arabia — having more water than I could handle.

Poor Shaikh Hafiz was our houseguest at the time and he got rained out of his apartment in the guesthouse in the middle of the night; Ali did him out of a bath in Riyadh years before, but he got an unexpected one that night. He woke up to find knee-deep water sloshing around his bed and, elderly soul that he was, was unable to do anything about it but stand there and yell, "Ya walad, ya walad, elhagoony, elhagoony!" * until someone did.

The desert around us was a lake for days after the storm. To keep the walls around our yard from tumbling, the men broke holes through them (one way to water the garden) and for two and one-half days water rushed through and filled the enclosure. It soaked in quickly, however, and in a few more days the desert around us, inside and out our walls, had a green fuzz on it.

Our entertaining continued, sometimes with me present, sometimes not, but I and the other women in the house continued to be always involved in it one way or the other. We had a long succession of houseguests, illustrious and otherwise, and since the majority of them were *effrengi* the household looked to me as an expert in their care and attention. There were some, though, who saw to their own needs or requests. We had one, a Greek fellow, who arrived during Ramadan and announced after a few days of being waited on by fasting servants that he would fast, too, so to please bring him only cold orange juice all day long — probably the most tempting thing a dry-mouthed servant could possibly have carried to him.

Mohamed, although he lived in the house next to us, did most of his entertaining at ours, and I tried to plan it so that homemade bread piping hot from the oven was served as soon as he and his guests were seated. "Uncle" Ismail, a cousin visiting

* "Boy! Boy! Rescue me!"

from Bombay, joined Mohamed and his current guests every night for dinner. After a week or so of eating with the same group of businessmen, he came to me and said, "Look, even after their business is over neither these nor any other guests are *ever* going to leave as long as you continue to give them hot bread like that." As nice a compliment as I have ever received.

When we had guests whom we thought would appreciate our then crude beach house, we invited them to come along with us on Fridays, and those gatherings were a far cry from the generally formal ones at the house. We took the Duke of Hanover and his group there once and I had to laugh at just how informal we were. Children were running all over the place, tracking in sand and putting shells in the cigarette trays to keep them safe before taking them home, and the main meal was "served" where there was barely room to stand and where wind blew in sand from the south if we kept the tiny window open and suffocated us if we shut it. It was strictly a put-on-the-table-and-help-yourself affair as far as the food went, and come teatime we had everyone out digging up the tiny clams that inhabited our beach. Eyes popped then as one of the youngsters took the clams into the minuscule kitchen (it had a few cupboards quite overrun with cockroaches and a two-burner kerosene stove) and fried them in garlic butter until they split open, ready and delicious to eat.

Swimming there was always done with one eye on the lookout for sharks, and some of us used both eyes. Quite often we would see huge sea turtles paddling around and always there was the beautiful sight of the various coral beds, the sea plants, and the enormous variety of tropical fish among them. Every time I went swimming, of course, our male servants and drivers would have to stay confined to a small shack behind the beach house so they could not see me. This always amazed foreigners not used to our ways.

Through the years it has always tickled me that none of our

guests ever knew who did their shirts, because it was I. There was no local laundry service for *effrengi* shirts, the maids did not know how to iron them, and did not above all want to risk ruining them, so I was elected, and I relished the fact. It was part of my leading a life within a life within a life, sometimes able to join a downstairs group and play the big international hostess, sometimes left upstairs with the rest of the unseen *harem*, Arab but not Arab, American but not American, taking a step forward one way, a step back another. My smile couldn't help but be sweeter when, stepping into a room to greet the men who jumped to click their heels and kiss my hand, I could hug to myself the choice knowledge that I was not only their hostess but the one also responsible for their starched fronts and neatly pressed collars.

The party of parties in my book was one involving houseguest Aristotle Onassis, some of his associates, Alireza men, and me, in a rather unusual sequence of events involving field mice. One must first know that my brother-in-law Mohamed, husband Ali, and cousin Ahmed Yousuf had in adulthood never been able to shake a loathing (quasi-fear) of mice acquired in childhood. Ahmed Yousuf stalked a wee one with his rifle once, making his the best mouse story, but his crown went to Mohamed after the night in question. Mr. Onassis and friends and all of us were sitting in our living room waiting for dinner to be announced, when only I saw a tiny field mouse mother with a pink baby in her mouth scurry across the room and disappear. I let well enough alone, knowing how upset Ali and Mohamed in particular would be to know mice were skittering around, and I kept quiet the second time I saw Mrs. Mouse carry another pink baby under and around our feet at the dinner table on her way toward the same spot where she had first disappeared. But I had to tell when the old French saying *Jamais deux sans trois* held true; there, after dinner, was the mother carrying Baby No. 3 under the same armchair, against which

Mohamed was leaning, as he sat on the floor playing backgammon with Mr. Onassis. I quietly gave the word to Ali, who tried quietly to warn his brother in Arabic. The effect was to catapult Mohamed to a perch directly behind one of two huge Sèvres vases sitting on marble bases on either side of the arch separating living and dining rooms, and to cause Mr. Onassis to jump to his feet and wonder if he had to fight anybody. By this time Mohamed was yelling for the servants, who ran in and out and in again with sticks to comply with his order to kill the things, while Ali, I must say, stood his ground and even joined the search. But the sight of the one big man stepping gingerly across the room with his *tobe* hiked up and the other big man yelling frantically, "Don't ruin the carpets, don't ruin the carpets," from behind the rim of a big porcelain vase reduced our guests to flapping bits of humanity quite helpless with laughter.

This fear of mice was, I guess, exceedingly common, or maybe it was just dread. They got so plentiful one year that Mother offered the children a bounty of one quarter of a riyal for each dead mouse brought to her. Since she never let them get any closer than the downstairs landing if she was on the second and the children were dangling one by the tail, they were able to trick her. Faisal collected at least two full riyals in a couple of days until she caught on he was using the same mouse, and from then on made them hand their catch to a servant before she would pay the fee.

As far as I was concerned, there were far more serious worries than mice. Scorpions scared me to death when I saw their nipping claws and curved jointed tail, but luckily we were never stung by one. We'd see tarantulas from time to time and little Tarik almost put his hand on a big hairy one in his toy box once. Cockroaches scared me by the way they ran over our food, in the cupboard or out, because I knew that they also frequented dirty places, and of course I was always worried about flies and mosquitoes. Occasionally we'd get tiny red ants whose bites sometimes caused infections, and always there were lizards and grasshoppers in abundance.

The latter were not harmful but it wasn't exactly pleasant to see on one's ceiling upon awakening in the morning entire families of lizards lapping up the flies, or be sitting in a room and have one of the many jumping grasshoppers land suddenly in your hair or lap. And it was downright frightening to have the sky suddenly darken from the cloud of locusts coming our way, and sickening to watch our hard-won greenery devoured down to the last leaf as feeble humankind tried to prevent them. That happened once while I was in Arabia and it was unforgettable. It was the hottest day in my experience and came during the fasting month, so that all the men and women in the yard beating pots and pans in a vain effort to deter the locusts had to do so in the beating sun without being allowed one drop of water. And the moving carpet of voracious insects rolled over our land regardless, the oleander trees being the only thing their instinct told them not to touch.

And then there were centipedes. They could put the fear of God in us and upset a gathering quicker than anything I ever saw. The Arabs call them *oom arba wa arba'een* — "Mother forty-four," or "that which has forty-four [legs] — and believe they can pierce the skin and crawl through the body without the victim knowing it, and that they can get through ears and nose to drive a person mad. Once we were making preparations for an old-time Arabian wedding when one of the workers found a centipede in her stocking. It took her and the women who hadn't even seen it half an hour to stop shrieking, and I was glad it hadn't occurred during the wedding.

Weddings like that one are not common nowadays. It was "old-time," and traditional down to the fact that the bride and groom had not met. He was chosen by the age-old system of go-betweens, who visit the families and pass on descriptions and opinions and conduct preliminary negotiations between two families until a decision is reached. In other instances, wedding couples are related in some way, the tight bonds of kinship in some families still keeping their hold on the preference for marrying first cousins. It is a fact, also, that Arabia even today affords precious little opportunity for young people of different families to meet, but as the country progresses, as more young people travel and are educated abroad, and as more Arabian girls become educated in the schools now available to them, then perhaps criteria other than who a girl's father is will become increasingly important to a young man choosing a bride.

Those thoughts were not my concern the night I was a wedding guest. I was agog with the unusualness of it and fascinated by the old-world pageantry. *Zeffa* is the name given to the first part of the wedding, and although nowadays a bride may be wearing a white Paris wedding creation, *zeffa* is still very much a part of the ceremony. This is a literal drumming of the bride into her bridal chair to the accompaniment of shrill trilling by the women who escort her. The trilling is done by holding the open palm lightly over the mouth and moving the tongue very rapidly back and forth over the roof of the mouth to extremely shrill cries, strident and wild to the unaccustomed ear. The drum-heating ritual which precedes is fascinating, too, a picture of long-robed figures, some in black, some in gay sequined robes, turning and testing their instruments and thumping and sounding them as they begin to get the drums to take over the throb of their own excitement.

The bride wore heavy headgear and an assortment of undergarments under her already heavy gown, so that as she entered she had to be supported on either side. She came in veiled and was taken to one of two thronelike chairs set on a dais at the end of the room. It was forbidden that she look right or left: she was obliged to hold her head perfectly still, eyes straight forward, and one could easily see the strain caused by the tremendous weight of the headdress. The groom then entered, lifted the veil from her face, and looked at her for the first time. At that moment, I was told, he had the right to renounce her if he did not like what he saw, but I never heard of this happening. Usually each had a good idea of the other's looks, if the go-betweens had done their job well. The groom then shows his acceptance of his bride by throwing handfuls of gold coins out over the spectators, and since I didn't know it was coming I almost got trampled in the wild dash for them. The groom then takes his bride by the hand and they leave the room, but they do not leave the house together. The groom leaves to await her where he lives, and later that evening the bride's family men make great ceremony of conducting her to her new home.

The religious requirements of marriage are always performed separately and prior to the ceremonial part. Privately, in the presence of interested parties from both families, a religious *Shaikh* records the marriage contract and joins the couple according to Moslem law, and the actual wedding night ceremony may take place any time after that.

Because no wedding is complete without them, mention must be made of *mutfarrajeen* — literally, "onlookers" — heavily veiled and cloaked women who are present at all weddings and big receptions, permitted to attend without invitation on condition they remain disguised and unrevealed to the assemblage. (It was occasionally thought some men took advantage of this custom to get forbidden looks at women they were denied seeing in normal life, but this is highly unlikely — their lives wouldn't have been worth much if discovered!) The *mutfarrajeen* were not special individuals or a special group — they could have been from next door — they were just women wanting to satisfy their curiosity and be onlookers at events they normally would not attend. The thing I remember most about them was their undeniable talent for getting and keeping the best seats in the house, or garden, or wherever, at no matter whose expense.

At a wedding celebration at King Saud's Jeddah palace honoring seven brides and seven grooms, all from the royal family, I was pestered by three of these onlookers who spent a good deal of their time looking on at me. They followed me, peered at me from behind their veils, brushed close to me, and I did my best to appear not to notice them, assuming they were curious about me because I was the only obvious foreigner among hundreds of women. Women from the diplomatic corps, wives of American pilots of Saudi Arabian Airlines, and wives of foreign businessmen stationed in the country were almost always on the guest lists of women's parties, but this time invitations had been restricted to women in local Arabian families. The *mutfarrajeen* had not once asked me, as often happened at such affairs, "Inti min beit meen?" * But I soon found out who they were when they positioned their hooded faces directly in front of me and would not move until I could adjust my eyes to see through their disguises and identify them as Prince Faisal's daughter Princess Lulu (the word for *pearl* in Arabic), her aunt Muzaffar Hanam, and the Palestinian lady who had been a teacher and companion to the children in Prince Faisal's home for years. They had gone that night as *mutfarrajeen* for the fun of it, and decided to have their fun with me.

Come to think of it, that party had other firsts for me, at a time when I thought I'd seen everything. That was the night the king himself did the unprecedented act of appearing suddenly and without warning in the midst of all his lady guests, so dumbfounding the assemblage that no one could move to panic. The king had, apparently, just decided he wanted to meet them and it was as simple as that. He stood in the middle of the garden and told the ladies-in-waiting to spread the

---

* "From which house are you?"

word to all of us present that he was waiting to meet us. No one who has not lived in Arabia could ever imagine the predicament this posed for the good ladies: There we were, capes and veils left at the entrance, our arms and faces bare and our heads uncovered, and the king of the country which imposed veiling customs on us and which forbade us from mixing with men other than our own, was there in front of us waiting to meet and greet us, and had so commanded. As can be imagined, there was no great rush to comply — we had first to weigh what complying would mean when we got home and our husbands heard about it — but after the third trip or so around the bewildered assemblage, the ladies-in-waiting let it be known that His Majesty was getting impatient and some of the more adventurous of us threw caution to the desert winds and formed the first reception line of its kind in Saudi Arabia. Once somebody else started, the rest (or most of them, I believe) followed.

Well, it was the last party some of those women ever went to, poor things — their husbands just weren't ready for that sort of thing, king or no king — but I personally think it took a lot of courage on the part of His Majesty to do something that had never been done before (and has never been done since), and my heart went out to him for the effort. He wasn't through with us yet. He topped his way of showing unheard-of hospitality by showing bounteous generosity. After dinner a lady-in-waiting with a servant behind her carrying a large cardboard carton crisscrossed the palace grounds passing out to each and every guest a case containing a gold wrist watch with the royal insignia of palm tree and crossed swords on it and the king's name inscribed beneath. How do you say thank you for a party like that? It was by then hard to find anyone to whom to say it, so we clutched our party favors to our bosoms, put on our cloaks and veils (which seemed rather superfluous at that point), and went home to see what life had in store for us there.

Chapter 17

By the mid-fifties Jeddah was a city much-changed from the one to which I had gone some ten years before. We lacked for nothing (if we had the money to pay for it) and the city itself continued to improve in many aspects. It would be a long way ahead and a long time before it could be called a modern city in keeping with the times, but in relatively few years great strides had been made. The building boom continued and everywhere, in the city and out, were bare scars of scraped earth which were soon to be covered with a new house or a new business, new roads linked the old areas with the new, and trees for the first time made green lines over the heretofore strictly desert-hued city. We ladies still could not walk in the town (or anywhere else for that matter) but we could see how much improved it was as we drove through.

Christmas of 1955 saw Jeddah's *suk* full of Christmas spirit and Christmas goods to cater to the now considerable Christian element in the country, and of course to the combined Alireza families who celebrated Christmas, too. Ali drove me through the shopping section one night to show me what was available in the many modern stores and I never thought I'd live to see the day! To begin with, there were Christmas trees galore, and fresh flowers could be bought in a new shop just opened, and one new bookstore even had Christmas cards for sale. I was delighted beyond compare.

By special arrangement, Ali took me after closing hours to one shop co-owned by my friend Lois Scott, an American whose husband was a pilot with the Saudi Arabian Airlines, and I was even more astounded. There were toys made in U.S.A., cosmetics for the asking, small gift items, gift wrappings, lingerie, and ready-to-wear items, just like at home. Other stores' new plate-glass windows displayed beautiful luggage, and luxury wares in crystal, china, silver; and in other sports equipment, camping supplies, household goods, furniture, kitchenware were up for sale. There was anything our little hearts desired — all imports, of course, and very expensive, but at least they were there. I remembered when we had to bring in our own safety pins and toothpaste!

As another example of progress, Ali and I were beginning to step out on the town, not just take drives, able now to exchange visits with friends in mixed groups as long as we did not advertise or broadcast the fact. Evenings of note were those at the palace, where Prince Faisal and Princess Iffat received us and other guests in the palace garden. It was lovely to sit under the stars and exchange talk and ideas, partake of refreshments, feel the glow of friendship in the relaxing atmosphere of informality.

One night I had no reason to believe our visit was going to be any different from any other pleasant time we spent with them, but it was. Prince Faisal appeared carrying a magnificent falcon perched on his leather-gloved right hand. The bird had a hood over its head and a restraining leather strap and it remained quiet as Prince Faisal pretended, in his inimitable way, that he had nothing as outstanding as a falcon on his wrist and sat quietly and without comment.

It was the first time I had seen a falcon, although I had heard many tales of falconry among the Bedou and the Arabian royal family, and I was mightily impressed with the bird's beauty and the signs of its strength. I was soon lulled back to the conversation as Prince Faisal went on as if everything were normal, and my head was turned the other way when he suddenly uttered a blood-curdling cry. My startled eyes turned back in time to see the now unhooded falcon fly out like a bullet to a spot in front of us where the prince had thrown a piece of red, raw meat, which the bird clawed and ate with a frightening small-scale demonstration of what it could and would do when hunting live prey. Training the bird to associate the cry with fresh meat was what Prince Faisal was doing, but I think my reflexes got better conditioned than the falcon's. His Royal Highness emitted those cries throughout the evening when we least expected him to, and I practically fell off my chair each time. Relaxing it was not but it was most interesting to watch the fascinating falcon trainee taking her lessons.

Near the end of that year Hamida was asked to be a train-bearer and Nadia was asked to be one of the flower girls at the wedding of Princess Iffat's niece, Laila. A couturière from abroad was brought to measure the participants for gowns and shoes and one exciting afternoon their big boxes of beautiful new things were delivered to the house by special messenger from the palace.

The night of the big event hundreds and hundreds of guests were assembled outdoors waiting for the bridal procession to make its way down the palace stairs and out into the garden to the accompaniment of *zeffa,* and when the breathtaking *défilé* did appear, Princess Haifa and Nadia (the two little girls born within a day of each other in Paris) were leading the entire group, followed by the bride and her train-bearers — including Their Royal Highnesses Princesses Sara, Latifa, and Lulu (Prince Faisal's daughters), our daughter Hamida, and two other girls whose names escape me — holding one side of the bride's train and six young boys from the royal family holding the other. They proceeded then down the long long walk of the front driveway to the beautiful flower-bedecked bridal platform, where the bride seated herself, and her entourage arrayed themselves around her on the steps. The groom, accompanied on one side by Crown Prince Faisal and on the other by the father of the bride, and some of the groom's brothers behind them, then walked the same path until he faced his bride, lifted the veil, kissed her, and the two of them walked off arm in arm followed by the others. The scene was one of fairy-like beauty and thrilling to watch, and one of the first times I saw Arabian women apparently unconcerned over the possibility that their bare faces would be seen by strange men. Of course the men never really "looked" at such times — they had other things on their minds — but always before I had seen women try to cover or keep their faces hidden in some way, and it impressed me that night that no one did.

After the girls changed from their white gowns to pink ones, they joined me and a group of friends and some foreign lady newspaper correspondents with whom I was sitting, and after Nadia curtsied through the introductions she plopped down on the grass in front of us, pulled off her new pink pumps, which hurt her, and sat vigorously bending them from heel to toe to soften them as she had seen me do with new shoes. Everyone who saw her burst out laughing. It was so funny seeing the same child who had just impressed everyone with her poise in leading the truly fabulous wedding procession (during which she saw to it that she got a good look at the people lining the way but never once veered right or left), sit herself down so unceremoniously in front of honored guests, and knead her shoes.

Nadia then left with friends to watch some Bedouin women perform a dance, so she was not with me when the announcement of dinner caused, within minutes, the crowd of nice ladies to turn into a pushing mob crushing each other toward the fenced-off dining area in a far corner of the huge garden, making me frantic to find Nadia. She was only four and a half years old and if she fell before the crowds or was inadvertently knocked down, she would surely be trampled. Those with me joined in the search for her and after a desperate half-hour one of us finally spotted her. There she was sitting at the head royal table between Princess Iffat's mother, Sitt Assia, and the mother of the groom, just the two most important ladies present at the table reserved for the members of the royal family. All of them were dressed in the finery of the royal Nejdi dress, and I could hardly see the child from the overflow of sequined gowns surrounding her; but she was there, happily feeding her face with the slices of turkey the good ladies had served her and washing down her mouthfuls with orange juice. It was obvious that she couldn't have been happier. Other lost children cried for their mamas, but not Nadia. She ensconced herself I knew not how at the table of honor and never once asked, "Where's Mama?" Mama could take care of herself!

I was expecting our fifth child then, and in the spring the entire family went once more to Paris. I kept my childbearing record intact by having Ghassan there in late May, a blue-eyed boy this time. Ali kept his record, too, of not being around when any of his sons were born. He was off in Canada that time, and when he did come back it was to go almost directly to London for another operation. Poor Ali, he had had so much trouble the last time he had been hospitalized and became so depressed about it that he had sworn he would never enter another hospital as long as he lived, but of course he had to go and he knew it. He was changing, though. The fun-loving, active-in-sports, good-humored and loving companion I had married was secretive and detached. He was gradually being cut down in his desire to keep up with everything as he always had and he began to lose his patience along with his strength.

He was already a tortured man before Ghassan's birth but

after it he really began to cut us off from anything that concerned him. He entered the hospital in London and for weeks we heard nothing from him — how he was, whether dead or alive — and repeated attempts to reach him were blocked by his refusal of our calls to his hospital room. He had even managed to swear the doctors to secrecy and we could get nothing out of them, either. With a new baby to take care of and the many cares of the household in Paris (I was the only one who spoke French and everyone depended on me) it was the most trying of times, and even that is an understatement. In desperation I got our French doctor to attempt to get through and he was able to elicit only the information that Ali was still in the hospital and nothing else. Ali's mother and I were almost out of our minds with worry over him and concern over the situation he was causing. Something was dreadfully wrong but we did not know what, nor did we know how to cope with it in the light of our other binding duties. Eventually we lived out the fear and the frustration, Ali was released from the hospital and came back to us, but the detachment was still there. He had put up a wall and would not let us break through.

When Ghassan was four months old we returned to Cairo, and then Ali took his mother to Lebanon, Zainab and Hayat proceeded to Jeddah, and I stayed with the children in our apartment until Ali returned. In late October Ali had to return to London for a post-operative checkup, so he had Uncle Hamed get us tickets to return to Jeddah on October 30. We never got to take that flight. Israel attacked Egypt on the twenty-ninth and English and French airplanes attacked on the thirty-first, and we who were in Egypt were isolated from the outside. We could not get word out or word in to anyone anywhere; I did not know if Ali had made it to London or if the situation had caused him any trouble in England; and air raids were nearly constant, day and night, for ten days or more. We could hear each night the guns hidden in the hills of Cairo near the Mohamed Ali Mosque, and aircraft going over us. Blackouts were strictly enforced. If we ventured on the streets at all during the day I begged the children to speak only in Arabic. Feeling was high against the English as participants in the raids, and with every corner dug up into machine-gun nests manned by trigger-happy young Egyptians, I was taking no chances on being shot as an enemy.

Faisal and Nadia and I were caught downtown one day during an air raid and it was terrifying to run with other frightened people until we reached a place where we could be sheltered and where we could stay until the all-clear sounded. The children were marvelous in the way they reacted to the alarming situations which daily faced us, and I was most impressed with the manner in which the older ones always helped and comforted the younger ones when they themselves were full of fear. One thing we always got a laugh out of, however, was the way we always had to rush to get young Ghassan fed and settled for the night before we could no longer see to pin a diaper on him or find his mouth in the dark.

All schools closed and some of the young Saudis studying in Egypt were placed under my care for the duration of the war; neither their families nor mine — Arabian or American — knew if we were safe. I had no word whatsoever from Ali (I had thought he might get word through diplomatic channels) but there I sat with a houseful of children, half mine and half not, constant air raids, food a problem to get and a problem to cook (if we lit a gas fire after dark the guards downstairs yelled for the people on the third floor to turn off the lights), and as luck would have it, a boy who had come only for the day fell very ill during his visit. I waited for his family to come for him, but his poor grandmother was in such a mental state from fear of the raids that she had, quite simply, forgotten the boy until it was too dark to send a car for him. Then what to do? No doctors were available, all having been called to the front.

In desperation I called an Egyptian friend who listened to my plight and asked me to give her a half-hour to see what she could do. She pulled a few strings and got an Egyptian army doctor on leave to come. As I opened the door to his ring I was very impressed, for he was a very high officer according to the bars on his tunic; and he was impressed with me, too, since he obviously had not been told of the number of "my" children, who peered from every door and came from every room. He was trying to restrain his laughter when I said, "Go ahead, *laugh;* it *is* funny. Then please see what you can do for the poor lad who is sick. He has a fever of 40 degrees [centigrade] and is sometimes delirious."

Well, he examined the boy, diagnosed influenza, gave me a prescription to fill if and when I could, and added, "The boy must be isolated."

"Any suggestions?" I said.

He looked around at the still peering faces and laughed. "Well, that does pose a problem, I can see, but do what you can or you might have them all down with it." So the youngster was isolated, if you can call it that, in the parlor, where he had to stay until he was well enough to go home.

Dear Uncle Hamed managed somehow to get me and all my charges on one of the first planes out of Cairo. I still had had no word from Ali and was feeling very upset about it. I thought, if I can just do this one last thing — get all these kids, and the couple of friends' servants also placed in my care, and myself, safely back to Jeddah — I am going to retire from active travel. I'm going to stay home and vegetate and enjoy every minute of it. *No one* is going to get me out of Arabia for a long, long time. Sitting in the plane at departure time, however, it appeared that we weren't even going to make it to takeoff. The American captain of the old beat-up DC-4, I think it was, that was going to skip around the skies avoiding Israeli planes on the way home, stood for a good half-hour in the front of the cabin and told the Egyptian porters, "You've got to get all that stuff out of here before I'll even start warming up the engines!"

We were already two to a seat, and the panicked passengers had wanted to cart all their belongings home with them, so the airplane was filled to the struts not only with passengers but overflow of hand-carried parcels, baskets, food for the next year, and God knows what all. The captain watched them stack it as high as it would go in the back of the plane while he told them over and over it wouldn't do, it was too much weight in the tail, and finally convinced them it had to be removed. The porters were caught between his command, though, and the fact that they had already pocketed their tips for making sure the stuff got aboard, but they handily solved the problem. They moved everything forward behind the cockpit and the captain figured, "What the hell?"

I was sitting in front of where he stood and he had not taken me for an American in that planeful of Saudis because I already had the veil over my head. But when I asked him, "Do you think we'll make it, Captain?" he first looked at me as if to say, What the devil is *another* crazy American doing in a situation like this? and then shrugged and said, "Won't know until I try, so here goes nothing!" Barreling down the runway on that takeoff was the longest short time I ever went through, and eight hours later we did land in Jeddah, to the tears and prayers of thankfulness of all who met us.

Ali finally came home, too. He had been in Lebanon but had been unable, he said, to get word to us. Before his return, Mohamed and I had discussed at length in our apartment in Jeddah Ali's "disappearances" and his near obsession to keep us in the dark about his trips, checkups, condition, and whereabouts. Mohamed said that Ali had told him, too, what he had told me: that none of us were to inquire about him when he had to leave, that he would not let us know if and when he went to the hospital, and that we were better off just not thinking about him.

I told Mohamed of the dreadful time in Paris when Ali had followed through with such threats and we were both very concerned. With Ali, however, we tried not to show it — he got so incensed any time the subject was broached or even hinted at.

Mohamed had in the meantime given Ali and me a large piece of land directly north of the Kilo Five house. It was time we had our own home, he said, and I was thrilled. It gave us a much-needed feeling of common purpose, something positive instead of negative, and we put our heads together scribbling designs for the architect to convert to blueprints and trying to think of everything we wanted in the house for ourselves and our children.

By the end of March 1957 the new house was coming along and we had the great pleasure of watching it materialize. In the early years in Arabia I had often thought of having my own home but had long since given up the idea, and now there it was. Before it had been neither feasible nor correct — I could not have managed one until I knew the country and its ways more, and Mother would have been hurt if we had moved out — but everything changes and the old dream had been made a reality.

The cannon officially opened the month of fasting that year on the thirty-first of March sometime in the early evening, after someone in the Arab world sighted the new moon. In Arabic style it was then the eve of the first day of the month of Ramadan, which happened to coincide with April Fool's Day on my calendar. Thus we had our first *sahoor* about ten o'clock Arabic time (4 A.M.) the following morning. The men promptly go to bed until afternoon, but the women have children and households to supervise and special Ramadan cooking to do. Rest is snatched in bits and parcels throughout the day after the other demands on them are met; and the children, although they do not fast until they arbitrarily decide for themselves that they are desirous and capable of full observance of the fast, keep regular hours and regular lesson times. (Pity the poor teacher.)

The special foods that mistress and servant alike help prepare each day include the traditional soup thick with wheat and meat and vegetables; *sambusak;** *fatoosh,* a lemony salad of cress, cucumbers, tomato, and croutons; a peppery lentil dish; rice and meat (notably pieces of lamb's head mixed with broth-soaked bread); lots of yogurt and chick peas; eggs fried with ground meat and onion and tomato; and many many other dishes. Food was very much a part of the fasting month, when thoughts of what it means to go without it are strong.

In the actual breaking of the fast, however, food took second place. Going without liquid the long, hot, humid day was the hardest thing to do during Ramadan and so it was not food but a glass of something cool to drink that each person set before him while counting the minutes to the cannon's boom. The traditional drink is *Qamar-ad-din,* an apricot delight whose name means "moon of the religion," if you please; but at our house we also consumed gallons of passionate-pink-colored Kool-Aid mixtures, and there were some inveterate tea drinkers like Zainab who had to break the fast with hot tea to get rid of the headache fasting gave them. It is also traditional to have a plate of dates handy to eat during that first preliminary breakfast before prayer and the main meal which follows.

All of these things symbolize not only the goodness of God but the goodness of being together as individuals, and as humans in the universal sense, to share what God has given. I was tremendously impressed with the way these thoughts seemed always to be there even though they were not voiced. I could feel the import to their lives that these things had, and I partook of it with my own feelings of gratitude. They were to me also typified by the Bedou from our area and their habit of

* Fried pastries stuffed with meat and pine nuts, or cheese.

coming each afternoon to our gate to fill their skin bags with water from our supply. It was not by special arrangement that they did this; it was just that we had water, they did not, so it was known without question that we would share it with them. It was just as simple as that, or maybe even simpler, because to them it was really water that came from God, meant just as much for one man as it was for the other.

It is at nighttime in Ramadan when the town comes alive. Shops open, offices open, people do a lot of visiting and, whether one works or plays each night, it is a kind of celebration in its own way. Children at our house were allowed to stay up long past their usual bedtimes to participate in the fun and sometimes we all gathered upstairs and saw a movie together. Movies are forbidden so there were no public theaters, but authorities shut their eyes to the fact that many of us showed them in our homes. A few individuals in town had a permanent film library and others had a renting arrangement with companies, so those of us who had projectors took turns borrowing films for an evening's enjoyment, and sometimes we got some very good ones.

Probably because we often showed films for the children before the men got home, during Ramadan or at other times, I became chief projectionist, although I probably could not remember the first thing about it now. A "fillum" night (for some reason, *film* was hard for them to say) was one of great excitement in our compound. Servants hastened to complete their tasks, children spent the day wondering what the film would be and hoping against hope that it wouldn't be *Annie Get Your Gun* again, much as they had liked it the first ten times. By the time the "fillum" was finally showing and we reached rewind of the first reel, the lights would go up to reveal people in the room I swore I never saw at any other time. They were a good audience, however, patiently sitting through pauses while I Scotch-taped broken film or rewound an upside-down, backward-turning reel that someone else had left for us to correct. That seemed to make it all the more interesting for some — they couldn't understand the dialogue anyway.

Some of the people who shared such evenings with us belonged to the families of servants living on our grounds. They were given private quarters and facilities and lived their lives as we did, overlapping. One of my favorite families was that of Mohamed's driver and valet, Ali Bussfar. He had asked for the hand of a beautiful young girl, Sofia, whose family had somehow come to be connected with Alirezas, a poor family who depended on us for help. They married and Mohamed gave them one wing of the guesthouse, where they lived with her widowed mother and brothers and sisters, and raised a family of their own.

I happened to be the only one of our family on the premises when her first baby was being born and, because it showed signs of being a difficult first birth for one so young, Dr. Idriss was called and he asked that I be his assistant. Although my contribution consisted mainly of lending my hands and arms for her to hold on to and of encouraging her in her effort, I did help tie the umbilical knot and wrap her child in the simple swaddling clothes she had lovingly prepared, and in the lucid moments between pain she heaped blessings upon my head. Afterward she wanted me by her side for all her babies, and I did assist also at the birth of her next. I have always remembered how grateful she was for my doing something I considered a privilege — seeing a new life come into being is looking at a miracle — and it made me think how people who have what we call so "little" in their simple lives are often the ones who feel human closeness the most.

When the last cannon ended Ramadan and the Eid festivities were over, our hours returned to normal and we tried to do the same. With Ali I maintained a *laissez-faire* policy, as he continued to be preoccupied and distant, and lived each day as it came, which is all anyone can do. I was glad then that I had so many other people around to help me do it. Mother, Zainab,

Hayat, and I walked over each evening to the new house to examine the progress of the day, and there wasn't one of us who
didn't think about how we were soon to be living separately
after so many years together. I tried not to feel selfish about
having such a fine big new place in the near future, but they
made it easy for me by being typically enthusiastic about anything that made Ali and me happy. I told Mother we would
have to make her a lookout window in our new house like
the one she had in the old, and then she could have two favorite
places to sit.

Her Kilo Five spot was on her own little chair in front of the
second-floor entrance window, where she could work on her
sewing, answer the telephone, rummage in the big teak chest
which sat next to her, or just sit and gaze out at the yard, keep
an eye on servants' comings and goings, or watch the cars
speed to and from Mecca. She could be seen there almost any
time of day.

That open window of hers and the thought of her sitting
there now reminds me of the popcorn stand we always talked
about but never had. She used to sit and muse about all the
cars which traveled the road in front of us, and she'd say, "We
could make a million if we put a popcorn stand out there, or
perhaps at Bab Jadid* or maybe both places. Just think of the
money we would make at Pilgrimage time!" We had by then
consumed bushels of popcorn, buttered and candied, and since
it was one of her favorite snacks she was sure the venture would
succeed. A popcorn stand is the sort of thing she would have
liked to have had, I know. Pity we never did it!

I gave her a bubble-blowing lesson in front of that window
one day with some bubble gum she had acquired from somewhere. I never liked the Arabian gum, *luban Arabi,* that some
of the women in the country liked to chew. It was natural gum
as it came from the trees, I suppose, and it had a medicinal
taste to me, plus it took good jaws to chew it. I also did not like

* "New Gate," a busy portal to the city.

the way some women popped it; with just a few of them chewing away in the room it sounded like crossfire with machine guns and it nearly drove me out of my mind. I would leave a room before I would sit long with that, and Hayat deliberately taunted me at times just to see me cover my ears. None of us, Arabian or American, were really great gum chewers, but once in a while Mother would get us some *luban effrengi* and one day it was "bubble" *luban effrengi*. She wanted to know how it was done, the bubble making, so I showed her. She did all right until she reached the stage where the gum film is formed over the tongue and then has to be pushed out with the breath to form the bubble. Mother blew her wad so hard it popped out of her mouth and right on out through the open window, arcing itself gracefully down to the garden below.

April, May, June — time to talk of going away for the summer, but I remembered my promise to myself and said, Oh no, not I. Besides, I liked watching our house go up and I wanted very much to stay for a change with Ali while he worked there all summer. The heat was no problem, I said. We had put up with that even before we had air-conditioned bedrooms, and as for taking care of our needs I was quite capable by then of running the big house and counting out the riyals into the servants' hands each night. Thus every one of my daytime bunch took off except me — Mother to Cairo with Mohamed, Zainab and Hayat to our summer place in Lebanon with their children — and I and my children stayed home.

It was not as idyllic as I had imagined, however, because Ali was soon gone again, too — off to Europe for some reason or another. He had intended to be gone the usual "three or four days" that always turned out to be more like three or four weeks. The pattern held true this time, too, plus we seldom heard directly from him. Rumor then had it that he would be going to the United States with Prince Faisal before he returned home, something I couldn't believe until I did get direct word from him confirming the fact.

Many things happened in the next few weeks. Ali had another attack and was taken to the hospital in New York, Mohamed and Mother flew there from Cairo when Prince Faisal notified Mohamed, and when the crisis was over Mohamed cabled me that the children and I should go, too. I consented (after some hesitation, for I believed that Ali did not want me to go) and Ahmed Yousuf made the necessary arrangements.

In the days before departure I remembered that we, the women in the house, owed many visits in town. There were many rumblings getting increasingly louder that we did not return visits paid to us — a true breach of etiquette and custom in Arabia — so I thought that before I left I would take care of those social obligations and asked Saima if she would go with me. She consented willingly after her mother agreed to take over her school, so we made our appointments and ventured forth on our calls.

Never had I seen Saima so chic and never had I seen the town ladies so hospitable. Saima and I were given the royal treatment wherever we entered, and it was obvious they had done everything they could think of beforehand to make our visit a pleasant one. We were truly honored guests, as special pastries were served with the usual coffee and tea, every brand of cigarettes in town was on hand to make sure there would be one I liked (and I had never learned to smoke), and not just a token few of the ladies of the house were present, they all were. We held great conversations and they kept us long after the usual visiting hours, then thanked us effusively for the thoughtfulness of our visit. Saima and I made six or seven of those visits (we really were in arrears socially) and then the children and I left Arabia for New York. At Kilo Five on the morning of our departure, the Koran was passed over the children's heads and the servants crowded around our car and told us as we pulled away, "Allah Ma'akom." *

* "God be with you."

Chapter 18

MANY THINGS happened in New York after I got there. From his hospital bed shortly after we arrived, Ali divorced me by saying one sentence in front of an official from the Saudi Arabian Consulate in New York, and presumably signing a paper to that effect. That was all he had to do, as a Moslem, to free himself from me, although it did not free me from our California marriage. It was just as sudden as I have said it: no reasons were given and none, Ali told me, had to be given. A friend took on what he called a sad commission, telling me the news over the phone while I sat with the children in our room at the Waldorf Towers. The only thing that Ali could or would tell me in explanation was, "It won't work, I know myself"; to my mother who came and asked him why, he said, "It is God's will."

There was nothing I could do but let it happen, completely dependent on Ali as I was (never having thought to put anything aside for myself). On top of everything else, I was not even in my own country as an American. My U.S. passport had been locked in Ali's safe in Jeddah when I was called to New York, so I had taken the chance of entering the United States as a Saudi Arab.

I could not believe any of it was true, and certainly not that Ali would carry out his announced intention of sending, when he got out of the hospital, the children to Egypt to be placed in English boarding schools. But that was true, too, as he put all of them except Ghassan on the plane with his mother for Cairo while I stood helplessly by. I had been reminded that under Moslem law a divorced mother has no right to her children after they reach seven years of age. In my waking hours I sat, walked, talked, ate in a fog of disbelief and when I could sleep I woke up saying, "It's all a nightmare."

After the children left, my passport situation got straightened out with the help of understanding officials and I went to Rome, where Ali had promised to send the children for their Christmas and Easter holidays. But he never did. My first direct news of them came from Arabian friends who saw them in Egypt and came to visit me in Rome in late spring. They also told me that Ali had gotten married a few months after he divorced me. As the old saying goes, "You could have knocked me over with a feather," the one Ali had in his cap for having kept it from me so well. The woman he married had been in Jeddah on and off for years visiting her sister who was married to an American working there, and she herself was married at the time, if I remember correctly, to an American army sergeant.

Ali's wife and her sister are Lebanese nationals and they had been in my house on occasion. The first time I met them was when Ali invited them and their children to one of our youngsters' birthday parties. I saw them now and then after that at the American women's group coffee or tea parties, but never with Ali in the mixed group gatherings and parties held by the American element in Jeddah with their Arabian friends. Those were the times I had to play Arab. At any rate, the first I knew of it was in Rome from my friends, and with that news were found so many of the lost pieces in the mixed-up jigsaw puzzle of absences and actions in the previous two years or so of our life together. I could see so clearly the retrospective picture they formed, showing what I had never been able to see before.

I did not see the children all that year, not until Ali finally sent them to boarding schools in Switzerland, where three-year-old Ghassan and I high-tailed it as soon as we heard. Since New York I had been dispatching letters and cables to Ali and to the men in his family, urging them not only to send the children where I could at least see them but to get Ali to come and sit down with me to discuss a legal settlement of all our lives. None of the requests were answered. In Rome I initiated efforts to secure American passports for the children, proceeding with the utmost of caution. I was not sure as it was that I would ever see the children again, and I knew I never would if Ali got wind of my intention.

Reunited in Switzerland we had marvelous times together, but there was nothing secure, none of us had our roots down again. I continued my efforts to get Ali to work together with me, with no better luck than before. Thus, when after almost a year and a half of work I finally had the United States passports for the children in my hand, I decided to slip the children out of Switzerland secretly and take them to the United States. It was a real cloak-and-dagger affair and, as a matter of fact, it was the first of two such trips I had to make to keep my children.

On the first one I scooted out with them in 1959 after selling some of my jewels for our fare, and after the meshing of some rather delicate plans and timing of same. We took off safely bound for Los Angeles from Geneva airport with nothing but a jewel case and the clothes on our backs, and in New York put the inspecting agent of U.S. Customs into a state of shock that a mother and five children could arrive from abroad with nothing to wear but pearls, rubies, diamonds, and sapphires. We dashed over to the T.W.A. desk for information on our continuing flight, and in answer to my query about reservations supposedly waiting for us, the man said: "Sorry, you left Geneva before we could get word to you that we were unable to book you on through."

"But that's impossible," I said. "I *have* to get to Los Angeles today! Isn't there any flight you can get us on?"

"Hm-m-m, six people. Well, there's a flight that makes several stops, getting you into Los Angeles in fourteen hours."

"Fourteen hours," I groaned. "We've just *had* a fourteen-hour flight and I don't think our nerves will take another." And then I remembered reading about the new jet planes which had recently started domestic service, and I said to him, "What about those new planes I've seen advertised — any chance there?"

"Oh, lady, those jets are booked months in advance and besides, there's only one more today and it leaves in fifteen minutes." My look of desperation must have reached him because he said, "But I'll call just to make you happy," and he picked up the phone as I watched his face for any sign of hope. "Hey, Jerry," he said, "I've got a party of six out here who have to get to Los Angeles today. Anything on that seven-oh-seven just going out?" I watched his jaw drop, his eyes open in amazement, and heard him say two simple words — "Ticket it!" — before he hung up in bewilderment. "There are," he told me, "just six seats on that plane, no more, no less, and I'll never understand how. Go quickly now to that drugstore over there while I write up the tickets and get those kids the hamburgers they're asking for, and I'll see that the plane is held long enough for you to get on it."

Not talking about what my action did to Ali, my getting away with the children was a shocker in Arabia, but the general reaction was, "Marianne is not to be blamed for what she did — any mother would have done the same," knowing the while that most of the women could not have done the same. It was not approval for a woman — a mere woman — doing something that went against the powerful wishes of her man; it was more a kind of hurrah for my succeeding in something everyone knew meant so much to me, keeping my children against the odds. Besides, they had felt and returned my good faith in going there to Arabia to live with them and they were upset, as Arabs and Moslems, that it had ended thus.

What my trip forced Ali to do was to negotiate until we signed an agreement — after five months of uphill work on the part of my lawyers — and I then returned to Switzerland, where the children reentered their schools and I lived near them. The agreement did not set me free but it outlined both our responsibilities and obligations to each other and to the children. I was content, anyway, for the moment, to act as an anchor and give the children some semblance of security and lots of love.

No one of the family ever really wrote me about the breakup, but what was there to say? Various nephews came to visit me on their way to and from universities and business. Dear Hussein brought his bride to meet me on their honeymoon, and Mohamed came and, generous as always, gave me money enough for a down payment on a house, sending the check from France with a fine note wishing us happiness in our new home.

And one day Mother came to visit me. When the phone rang and she said she was across the lake in Evian and wanted to come to see me, I knew she remembered as I did. I had not seen her since that awful day at the New York airport when she had gone off through no fault of her own with the children, and we both needed to erase that memory. I went to meet her and Zainab when the boat from Evian docked at noon at the Swiss port of Ouchy the following day, but because I couldn't park my car I had to watch from afar for sight of them among the disembarking passengers. Mother saw me then, as I saw her, and she broke into a semi-run as she came across the quai that separated us, with tears streaming down her eyes that made mine start as I went toward her, and took me in her arms. It was sad, our embrace, and it was glad — saying things words couldn't, expressions of silent eloquence, expressions that needed no translation.

We spent then a wonderful day together — relaxed, fun, companionable, just like old times. Mother had kicked off her shoes and unrolled her stockings almost as soon as she was in the door, something I had seen her do a hundred times, and with that she set the mood for our day. She had a present for each of us — thoughtful, simple things, that were more touching because they were — and when mealtime came she was ever so pleased that I had thought to prepare her favorite foods. We got out the carom board I had brought from the United States, and that amused her, and with it we discovered that she couldn't play any better than she ever had, and that amused us as it had never failed to. As I said, it was just like old times, except that times were not as old as they seemed; it had not been all that long since we were apart. I was reminded of the story of the little boy who ran away from home but got so homesick and lonesome that he returned in a few hours. He walked in, and his father and mother waited for him to say something, whereupon he looked around with a grateful sigh and said, "Well, I see you still got the same old cat!"

Ali's mother came twice to see me in Switzerland, and it was not long after her second visit that I was forced to make, in July, of 1963, the second getaway. There were only four children, then, Hamida having been married to her first cousin Essam in January of 1962 while on a Christmas holiday with her father. I was "forced" to leave because of Ali's surprise court action against me, obliging me to turn in all of the children's passports, American and Saudi Arabian, and appear to face his petition to take the children out of Switzerland and into Arabia for the summer, a prospect that at that time chilled me. Plus I resented having to do or refrain from doing anything under threat of fine and imprisonment.

From the very first notice of this action I started making plans for leaving the country with the children if I had to, and when I found out (I'm not telling how) that the judge was deciding in Ali's favor, I immediately set those plans in motion. I had two and one-half days to succeed or fail in them. During the court sessions I had been ordered not to leave, but no such post-session injunction had been issued — yet — and I had to leave while I was still legally free to do so. With Ali in town we could not just pack up and leave for the airport, and besides I had strong suspicions that we were being watched, suspicions that were confirmed Monday morning after we got away.

I thanked God that my passport had not contained any mention of the children as dependents, because if it had I would have been obliged to hand it in, too. Now I could put them on mine, which is exactly what I did as the first step. My children were still half-American and, Moslem law and adverse court decision notwithstanding, I was determined to keep them. I thanked God for my friends, too — without them I never would have made it. A telephone call to the far end of Switzerland assured me that one friend would get down by train in time to get to the bank and give me money for air fare and other expenses; another call assured me of other friends' assistance in taking us on a "picnic" cruise on their boat, during which they would quietly deposit us on the French side of the lake where we could speed away in the car I would have left over there the night before; finally, a series of coded cables to and from a friend vacationing in Spain assured me that tickets would be reserved for our flight out of Barcelona and that she would meet us at a specified spot in Palamós, Spain, where she had arranged for us to stay until the day of our flight.

By Friday afternoon the boat "picnic" was canceled because it was considered too risky, so an alternate plan was concocted by an old friend living nearby whose wife was, coincidentally, vacationing in Spain with their children. His plan was that I was to take all of our luggage to his place under cover of night. Then on Sunday his houseboy would make us an early breakfast, the luggage would be loaded into my friend's car, and he would drive out with it through one border while I and the children went out through another border in our car with nothing but a picnic basket. After getting into France I would drive on for eight kilometers and then take a switchback side road to rejoin my friend at a prearranged spot in Annecy, France, where we would change over the luggage and we would head for Spain and he would return home.

While all this was being worked out our young friend Miss Juliet Colman, a former school chum of Hamida's, arrived on the scene and when we told her of our flight she promptly announced that we were to include her — she was going with us to participate in our escape and see us safely on an America-bound plane. She had been "family" to us for years but we thought being part of the family on that trip might pose difficulties for her, but she said no, she just *had* to go, so we let her. And actually, she became the perfect accomplice. She rode in the other car as the "girl" of my friend, a good forty years her senior! It would help explain all the luggage.

And come Sunday, that was exactly the way it happened, except for one thing. My friend the boat owner had not received the cancelation order directly, it had been relayed to him by his son, so he had called the house just to make sure he had the message right, and eleven-year-old Nadia, the *only* one in the house who did *not* know that the "picnic" he was talking about meant something other than a real picnic, told him it was still on. "Oh yes," she chirped, "we're still going on our picnic." So the poor man waited four hours for us Sunday morning at the dock, all gassed up and ready to go, with boxes and boxes of sandwiches he had ordered from the hotel for our trip.

We left our house Sunday morning at seven in picnic garb

and tennis shoes for our "Sunday picnic" on Plan 2, had breakfast at my friend's house, and left with him our dear dog Jerry
— a splendid German shepherd whose mother and grandmother were much awarded for their rescues of avalanche victims. We were eight cars away from France when a Swiss police
car came zooming up on the shoulder of the road to the check
station, and we thought for sure it was on account of us. Gradually our wheels inched over the border after one of the guards
looked in and asked only one question: "Whose guitar is that?"
Faisal, who was holding it on his lap, said, "It's mine." Before
we were waved on I made a point of asking if that was indeed
the way to Chamonix, and we rolled into France.

When we made our rendezvous with the others Coley said
her border experience was a bit different. Her mother, Benita
Hume, and her stepfather, actor George Sanders, were returning from the south of France by car that same day, and Coley
thought how funny it would be if they and she met at the border going opposite ways, and her parents looked up to see their
dear daughter sitting in a strange car full of luggage in the
company of a strange gentleman old enough to be her father.
Coley said she could just see her mother's face when her daughter gave her a twiddly wave of salute and gadded off to adventure.

Our first stop of importance was at Frontignan, France,
where we came out of the dusty inland route we were traveling
and saw before us the waters of the beautiful Mediterranean
at the Gulf of Lions and knew unanimously that we would have
to stop for a swim, so we did. I got banged on the head by a straw
hat when I punned that, pooped as we were, we could March in
like mice and surely come out like Lions. Because it was July
I had put bathing suits in the picnic basket, so we put them on
very casually and unabashedly in the ditch beside the road and
flung ourselves with delightful abandon into the glorious cool
wetness of the surf. That swim was delicious.

We sat on the sand then and ate, and stayed much longer than we should have. The swim, the sun, the feel of the sea breeze cool and relaxing on us had stripped us of the urge to move, and I don't think we could have left sooner if we had wanted to. Restored, we continued then, and with a car full of sleeping bodies I pulled into Palamós, Spain, at a quarter to midnight.

Some of us stayed at a friend's house and some of us stayed at a hotel. Although in the ensuing days we did not know what was happening in Switzerland, we found out later that those who had been involved in our departure were a good deal more active than we were in the sleepy Mediterranean fishing village. We also learned that the new order forbidding me from leaving came to my house by registered mail on Monday morning but was returned to the post office because I was gone. We had made it by a hair.

I am convinced that we would have been stopped if we had left any other way than we did — on a picnic with no luggage — because that Monday morning my friend who drove out with us went to my mailbox to retrieve a mailed copy of a telephoned cable that it was important no one else get ahold of. In the afternoon the police came to his house, having traced him through his car license, which had been noted while he was on my premises.

A very funny incident occurred in the confusion that existed at my house a few days later when *all* of my friends gathered there to clean it and pack things away. In the assembled group was a Britisher, an Australian, a Swiss, a Sudanese houseboy dressed in *galabeeya* and turban, two Spaniards, and an Italian, all running around the house doing various things — cleaning the refrigerator, vacuuming, sweeping — when two policemen walked in.

"What are you all doing here in Madame Alireza's house?" they inquired.

"Well," said a spokesman, "we are friends of hers and we just thought we'd come and clean her house for her while she is on vacation."

How any of them, including the police, kept a straight face at that I'll never know, but while the poor agents tried again to elicit some information that might help them locate me, the international housecleaning crew continued to busy themselves with the work at hand. As I understand it, the police only gave up and left when my darling Swiss friend kept reappearing from the kitchen and interrupting their efforts with questions posed to them about what they thought she should do with all the garbage.

I could have stayed in Palamós forever, I liked it so well, but perhaps my wanting to stay was more fear of going ahead. Whatever, the day came to leave and we drove to Barcelona airport, first leaving the car in a city garage so that at a later date still another friend could drive it back to Switzerland, where its owner, Ali, could pick it up. We all then kept stiff upper lips as we bade the best of friends good-bye and flew off to America to we knew not what.

I, for one, had come and gone many ways since the first time I had left for Arabia to begin a new life, and to my thinking then, I was taking the best way I could for the children's sake. With them I was to go back to where I had started, and as I did it I left with many marvelous memories tucked under the belt I was now going to have to tighten. I will never be sure that what I did was right; I am only sure that I had to do it in the hope that it was. We only put our small weights on the scale of life; we do not balance them. Sometimes we get full measure or more from what we put in and sometimes returns fall short. And the scale does not weigh our hope; we do, as we try to even things out the best we know how and make it count for right in the final assessment.